THE AMERICAN NATION
A HISTORY

FROM ORIGINAL SOURCES BY ASSOCIATED SCHOLARS

EDITED BY

ALBERT BUSHNELL HART, LL.D.
PROFESSOR OF HISTORY IN HARVARD UNIVERSITY

ADVISED BY
VARIOUS HISTORICAL SOCIETIES

IN 28 VOLUMES
VOL. 5

THE AMERICAN NATION
A HISTORY

LIST OF AUTHORS AND TITLES

Vol. 8 Preliminaries of the Revolution, by George Elliott Howard, Prof. Hist. Univ. of Chicago.

" 9 The American Revolution, by Claude Halstead Van Tyne, Ph.D., Asst. Prof. Hist. Univ. of Michigan.

" 10 The Federal Constitution, by Andrew Cunningham McLaughlin, A.M., Director Bureau Hist. Research Carnegie Institution.

GROUP III.

DEVELOPMENT OF THE NATION

Vol. 11 The Federalist System, by Andrew Cunningham McLaughlin, A.M., Director Bureau Hist. Research Carnegie Institution.

" 12 The Jeffersonian System, by Edward Channing, Ph.D., Prof. Hist. Harvard Univ.

" 13 Rise of American Nationality, by Kendric Charles Babcock, A.M., Ph.D., Pres. Univ. of Arizona.

" 14 Rise of the New West, by Frederick Jackson Turner, Ph.D., Prof. Hist. Univ. of Wisconsin.

" 15 Jacksonian Democracy, by William MacDonald, LL.D., Prof. Hist. Brown Univ.

GROUP IV.

TRIAL OF NATIONALITY

Vol. 16 Slavery and Abolition, by Albert Bushnell Hart, LL.D., Prof. Hist. Harvard Univ.

PORTRAIT OF WILLIAM PENN AT 22

By courtesy of the Historical Society of Pennsylvania

THE AMERICAN NATION: A HISTORY

VOLUME 5

COLONIAL
SELF-GOVERNMENT

1652–1689

BY

CHARLES McLEAN ANDREWS, Ph.D.

PROFESSOR OF HISTORY IN BRYN MAWR COLLEGE

WITH MAPS

NEW YORK AND LONDON
HARPER & BROTHERS PUBLISHERS
1904

CONTENTS

xii   CONTENTS

MAPS

EDITOR'S INTRODUCTION

IN the history of the English colonies there comes a natural break at the point where the original system of charter colonies directed from England was thrown into confusion by the disruption of the English monarchy. The year 1652 marks this change, for in that year the southern colonies yielded to a parliamentary fleet; and soon after began a hostile feeling towards the Dutch, which ended ten years later in the annexation of their American possessions. It is at 1652, therefore, that Tyler's *England in America* ends and this volume begins.

The period is further characterized by the development of a new colonial system, which for a century and a quarter was consistently followed by the English government; hence chapters i. and ii. are devoted to a study of the navigation acts and of the administrative councils to which eventually the name Lords of Trade was applied. Upon both subjects Professor Andrews has found new material and expounds new views. The neglected problem of the execution of the acts of trade has been fairly faced, and by delving in manuscript records Professor Andrews has, for the first time, been able to disen-

xiii

tangle the early council of trade and council of foreign plantations.

Chapters iii. and iv. describe the territorial and political readjustment in New England, and throw new light on the charters of Connecticut and Rhode Island and the first movement against the Massachusetts charter, subjects which heretofore have been involved in much confusion. Closely connected with the status of New England are the annexation and organization of the new colony of New York (chapters v. and vi.); and this volume solves some of the most perplexing problems as to the motives for the conquest and the status of the Duke's Laws.

Chapters vii. to x. deal with the foundation and development of the Jerseys and the Carolinas. Here the English archives have yielded rich material on the underlying motives for these simultaneous colonies, on the personal influences behind them, and on the perplexing questions of territorial claims and transfers. New Jersey has always been a specially difficult subject; but Professor Andrews disentangles the various threads of proprietary, Quaker, and Puritan settlements. In the Jerseys and the Carolinas appear the Concessions, which were a sort of popular constitution bestowed by the proprietor; and in the Carolinas there is opportunity for the discussion of John Locke's celebrated Grand Model, an example to succeeding generations of what a colonial constitution could not be.

On the beginnings of Pennsylvania, the same careful investigation of out-of-the-way sources, both printed and manuscript (chapters xi. and xii.), has given to Professor Andrews control over the difficult subject of the circumstances of Penn's grant and his efforts to establish a free government in a prosperous colony. The place of Pennsylvania is made clear, as the seat of German and other foreign immigration, the first on any considerable scale.

In chapters xiii. to xv. the author takes up the account of Virginia and Maryland where Tyler left it off in the preceding volume; but, besides his lucid account of the commercial and political development of the two colonies, he has a fine field for treating a dramatic episode in his account of Bacon's Rebellion.

This period of disturbance in the South was also a period of unrest and contentions in New England; and in chapters xvi. and xvii. Professor Andrews depicts Sir Edmund Andros, the representative of a purpose to make one colony out of the whole New England group, together with New York and New Jersey.

The volume is concluded by two chapters describing the social and economic conditions of the colonies about 1689, especially interesting as showing the wide commercial relations of New England and the middle colonies.

The most commanding figure of this period is William Penn, at the same time a great Englishman and a great American, whose portrait is pre-

fixed to this volume.   An unusual opportunity to use
unpublished records has been improved, so that the
foot-notes to this volume are very full and explicit;
and in the bibliographical essay the most significant of the secondary and primary materials on each
colony are selected.

The importance of the volume in the *American
Nation* series is that it includes colonies of the three
types which persisted down to the Revolution—the
crown colonies of Virginia and New York and New
Hampshire; the proprietary colonies in the Jerseys,
Pennsylvania and Delaware, Maryland, and the
Carolinas; and the three New England charter colonies, Massachusetts, Connecticut, and Rhode Island.
On one side the volume emphasizes the variety of
conditions and experiments in government.   On
the other side it brings out that characteristic which
gives the volume its name, the steady determination of the colonists in all three types of colony to
enjoy self-government in internal affairs.   This persistent and unquenchable determination made the
English colonies of that time different from all other
colonies in the world.   In vain did the English government set up a system of commercial restriction;
the colonies evaded or ignored it.   In vain did the
English government, through Andros and through
the courts, seek to annul the charters of New England; by passive resistance and by active protest
the colonists reasserted their privilege of discussion
and of legislation.

AUTHOR'S PREFACE

THE period of colonial history dealt with in this
volume presents certain well - defined characteristics. By 1650 each community had settled its
government along democratic lines — that is, had
put into practice the principles of manhood suffrage,
proportional representation, and the co - operation
of the people in legislation. The direction that
government was to take in America was already
definitely determined.

Yet during the period of this volume, 1652–1689,
conditions in England underwent a great change.
Constitutional monarchy was definitely established;
national life quickened; new interests, fostered by
men who had gained experience in trade and commerce under Cromwell, supplanted the old; and an
era essentially modern began. Enthusiasm spread
for whatever would strengthen commerce and extend the revenue; the plantations assumed a place
undreamed of before.

Such interest in the colonies took the form of the
navigation acts; the founding of new colonies; the
establishment of Privy Council committees, and of
separate but subordinate boards and councils for

trade and plantations; the regulation of the plantation revenue and the appointment of new revenue
officials both in England and in America; the despatch of special commissioners to New England in
1664, and of Randolph in 1675; the ordering of
troops to Virginia and New York; and, finally, the
attempt to unite the northern colonies more closely
to the crown, which centred in the mission and government of Andros.

In consequence of this attempt to formulate and
put in force a system of colonial management, trouble
inevitably arose between the people and the royal
and proprietary governors in New York and the
southern colonies; and between New England and
the crown. With a government in England endeavoring to shape a definite programme of control,
and a king on the throne who had no patience with
the colonial demand for English liberties, it is little wonder that the era culminated in a series of
exciting and dramatic episodes.

A part of the labor of investigation for this volume has been borne by two of my students, Miss G.
Albert, who has aided me both in England and
America, and Miss H. H. Hodge, who has helped me
with the history of the Massachusetts Bay colony.
I have also had the advantage of seeing Miss Kel-
logg's essay on *The American Colonial Charter*.

CHARLES M. ANDREWS.

COLONIAL
SELF-GOVERNMENT

COLONIAL
SELF-GOVERNMENT

CHAPTER I

NAVIGATION ACTS AND COLONIAL TRADE

(1651-1672)

BY the middle of the seventeenth century the first period of colonization had come to an end, and the English settlers were scattered in isolated communities all the way from the far-lying fishing villages of the Maine and New Hampshire coasts to western Long Island, where a few towns accepted the jurisdiction of the government of New Netherland. Separated by a wide space from their fellow-countrymen of the north were the colonists of Maryland and Virginia, who occupied a coast low-lying and deeply indented with wide river-mouths. In 1650 all these settlements contained something more than forty thousand people, of whom about twenty-five thousand were New-Englanders.

Between the settlements of the north and south lay a wide stretch of coast, practically uninhabited, except by the Dutch on the Hudson and the islands adjoining, and by the Swedes at Fort Christina (Wilmington), New Gottenburg, and New Elfsborg, who laid claim to the territory from the Schuylkill to Bombay Hook for a Swedish colony in America. Traders from New Haven also sought opportunities for business on the lower Delaware, but met with such opposition from both Dutch and Swedes that they were compelled to withdraw. With the approach of the mid-year of the century began the struggle for supremacy between the Dutch and the Swedes. Five years later (1655) the Swedish colony, unable to obtain support from the home government, surrendered; and henceforth the region from the Hudson to the Chesapeake was claimed by the Dutch, and, at a few points, occupied by Swedish and Dutch farmers and traders.

During the early years of colonization the machinery for controlling the colonies was little developed. In 1622, King James I. appointed a committee of the council to control navigation and trade; and later Charles I. did the same. After 1643 the Long Parliament took control and appointed a commission of prominent parliamentarians, headed by Robert, earl of Warwick, as governor-in-chief of all the colonies in America.

After the execution of Charles I. in 1649, Parliament directed the colonies to maintain their existing governments, and in 1651 despatched a fleet to Barbadoes, and a commission to Virginia and

Maryland, to reduce those provinces to their due obedience to the Commonwealth of England.[1]

About the same time the control of the colonies was placed in the hands of the Council of State, one of whose committees formed a council of trade, which met at Whitehall and for a few years transacted business. References to its meetings still exist. But in 1655 a separate board was established, consisting of six lords of the council, seven chief judges, ten gentlemen of distinction, and about twenty officials and merchants of leading seaport towns. This body, the precursor of the councils of the Restoration and the first Board of Trade properly so called, was authorized to consider "all ways and means for advancing, encouraging, and regulating the trade and navigation of the Commonwealth." It sat in the Star Chamber at Westminster, and was responsible for a number of the ordinances issued by the Protector and Council of State for the promotion of commerce.[2]

During the Commonwealth came the beginning also of that far-reaching system of control of colonial commerce to which the names "Navigation Acts," "Acts of Trade," and "Colonial System" have been applied indifferently. Although, from the point of view of English state policy, the English

---

[1] Schomburgk, *Hist. of Barbadoes*, 268–285; Thurloe, *State Papers*, I., 197.

[2] Thurloe, *State Papers*, IV., 177; British Museum, *Additional MSS.*, 12438, iii., f. 17.

colonies in America enjoyed a large degree of self-government, they were not legally independent, but formed a part of a colonial empire founded and maintained for the glory and interest of the mother-country. Like France, Spain, and Holland, England was confronted with a situation that was new in her history, and was called upon to perform a task for which she had no precedent. It is hardly to be wondered at that, during the great crises of revolution through which England passed in the seventeenth century, English statesmen should have failed to formulate any uniform or consistent plan of colonial management or to have grasped the significance of a colonial empire. It is, however, a fact of equal interest, that from the days of the Long Parliament to the reign of William III. the colonial and commercial policy, such as it was, suffered fewer changes than did any other department of national administration. Even Charles II. was obliged to carry out the commercial schemes of Cromwell, because they were in accord with the needs and interests of the English people.

Inasmuch as the discovery and development of the New World had been due to the rise of national states like Portugal, Spain, France, and England, it naturally followed that in governing the colonies of the newly discovered continent these states should adopt a policy national in character—that is, one having as its main object the strengthening of the state. This policy was based, not on any theory,

but on the needs of states which were outgrowing
their mediæval life and were raising the interests of
the king and central government—that is, of the
whole nation — above those of the towns and
boroughs. A larger life had come into being; and
as states began to compete with states in the field
of commerce and colonization, England became in a
new sense the rival of Spain, France, and Holland.
To meet the new situation, each state desired to
become the absolute mistress of all its resources, and
to prevent rivals from sharing in any of the advantages it possessed. Out of this international com-
petition a doctrine of national expediency took
shape during the seventeenth century, to which has
been given the name of "Mercantile System."

The underlying purpose of this doctrine was the
strengthening and preserving of the state, into
whose hands had now come the control of industry,
trade, and commerce. To the statesmen of the
seventeenth century the welfare of corporation and
individual was of secondary importance as compared with the welfare of the state. A strong state
demanded a full treasury, a large population, and
an efficient navy and merchant marine. To these
ends, each state sought to increase its available
wealth by monopolizing specie wherever found; by
fostering trade for the sake of increasing the customs
revenues; and by creating a favorable balance of
trade, so that exports, which brought coin into the
realm, might exceed imports, bought from other

countries with money, and hence draining coin out of the kingdom.

That it might have a large stock of available goods for export, each state imported, as far as possible, only raw materials, which it could work up at home; and England in particular encouraged the immigration of foreign workmen, not only on the ground of efficiency, but also of fashion; for French patterns and styles had such popularity at the court of Charles II. as to disconcert the advocates of the mercantile policy.[1] Furthermore, each state encouraged agriculture, that the supply of men might be sufficient for the army and navy; and each labored with exceptional zeal to extend shipping, by encouraging such subsidiary interests as fishing and ship-building, and by arranging treaties with countries that controlled the supply of "naval stores"— that is, raw materials, such as timber, tar, pitch, hemp, and flax, which were needed for the equipment of the navy and the commercial marine.

The colonial policy of all Europe was shaped by the principles thus laid down. Colonies were valued only so far as they contributed to the strength and wealth of the mother-state; and for more than a century their number was increased, not only for the purpose of extending the territory and prestige of the state, but of enlarging its resources also. The industry of the colonies was confined to raw materials, not from any desire to curtail the activities of the

[1] *Journal of the Lords of Trade*, I., 84–90.

colonies, but in order that the state might obtain from its own colonies, in return for manufactured goods, those supplies which must otherwise be bought from rival states. The trade of the colonies was restricted to the home market, for the double purpose of preventing other states from sharing in its advantages and of swelling the revenue from customs.

Thus the colonies were subordinated, as were individuals and municipalities at home, to the one great end of increasing the power and wealth of the state. To the statesmen of the seventeenth century, colonies were valuable only so far as they extended trade and offered a market for English manufactured goods, furnished naval supplies and other raw materials, opened up mines of precious metals, employed English ships in the fisheries and carrying-trade, and added to the king's revenue for the expenses of the kingdom by paying duties on the commodities which they sent to England. Colonial self government and colonial administration were considered of importance only so far as they affected the efficiency and productiveness of the colonies, and made them more useful to the home government.

Nor were Englishmen of this period without a precedent for this policy of protection. In the reign of Richard II., long before the era of colonization, a law was passed restricting imports and exports to ships owing allegiance to the crown of

England; a statute of Henry VIII. established a
second principle, that such a vessel must be English-
built and a majority of the sailors must be Eng-
lish-born; legislation of Elizabeth's reign also dealt
with this question, and, according to contemporary opinion, caused a large increase of merchant
shipping. Soon after actual settlements had been
made in America a distinct colonial policy began
to develop. In 1624 a proclamation was issued,
followed at a later date by orders in council, prohibit-
ing the use of foreign bottoms for the carriage of
Virginia tobacco; and in 1641 a number of English
merchants urged that these rules be embodied in
an act of Parliament. The Long Parliament, in
1644, with the double purpose of conciliating the
colonies and encouraging English shipping, forbade
the shipment of whale-oil, fins, and gills, except in
English-built ships; prohibited the importation of
wine, wool, and silk from France; and enacted that
no export duty be levied on goods intended for the
colonies, provided they were forwarded in English
vessels.

It was necessary that England should be on the
alert in these matters, for the Dutch had for forty
years been gaining control of the carrying-trade of
the world. These rivals were not only a maritime
people; they built vessels more rapidly and more
cheaply than their neighbors, because they knew
how to gather their materials at the point where
they were to be used; or because, as an English critic

said, "they knew how to congregate at one point
all the subservient trades that concur towards the
fabrick of a ship."[1] The low customs duties in
Holland also cheapened ship-building, facilitated
business, and enabled the Dutch to have more ships
than the English, and to charge lower freight rates
than any other maritime state in Europe could
afford to do. To break this monopoly was England's object; and to raise his country to a position
of leadership in the commercial world was one of
the greatest ambitions of Cromwell.

The first so-called "Navigation Act" was an
ordinance of 1651. Contemporaries ascribed the
act to the influence of the lord chief-justice, Oliver
St. John, who had been sent as an ambassador to
negotiate a treaty with the Dutch. According to
Ludlow, St. John, angry because of the failure of
the negotiations, prevailed with the council to move
Parliament to pass the act.[2] Clarendon, while
acknowledging the influence of St. John, believed
that the passage of the measure was in the main
due to Cromwell, who wished to provoke war with
the Dutch in order to avoid disbanding the army.[3]
From the tone employed by Parliament towards
the Dutch ambassadors who were sent to expostulate
against this act, there can be little doubt but that

---

[1] Downing, in *Journal of the Lords of Trade*, I., 91.
[2] Ludlow, *Memoirs* (ed. 1698), 345, 346; Cobbett, *Hist. of Parliament*, III., 1362; Clarendon, *Hist. of the Rebellion* (ed. 1888),
V., 251, 252.
[3] Clarendon, *Hist. of the Rebellion*, V., 260.

both the Parliament and the people of England were in sympathy with the measure.

The act of 1651 declared that only those ships of which the owner, the captain, and the majority of sailors were Englishmen or colonials had the right to carry on: (1) the trade between England and her colonies; (2) the coasting trade, whether between English or between colonial ports; and (3) the foreign trade of England so far as it concerned the plantations. The only exception to this act was the permission given to other nations to bring the products and commodities of their own country in their own ships, an exception which did not lessen the severity of the blow to Holland, inasmuch as that country had relatively few manufactures of her own, except woollens. But the exception made the operation of the act less injurious to such countries as France and Spain, with whom England had important trade relations. In forbidding the Dutch to carry any goods from the English colonies to England or her dominions, England indirectly deprived them of the lucrative privilege of storing such goods in their own warehouses before shipping them to England, and so destroyed an important source of their wealth.

Had the enforcing of the act been as skilful as the draughting, it would have ruined the United Provinces; but the Dutch colony on the Hudson River enabled them to evade the act in America with little difficulty. When war broke out in 1652 be-

tween England and Holland, Cromwell sent an expedition commanded by Major Robert Sedgwick to
New England to demand aid of the colonies and
to overthrow New Netherland. Sedgwick obeyed
his orders, and with a force of nine hundred men
and a troop of horse prepared to advance from
Boston upon New Amsterdam; but before the
expedition could start, peace was made between
England and Holland (1654) and the attempt was
given up.[1]

Though for the moment Massachusetts, Connecticut, and Rhode Island prohibited the export of
provisions to the Dutch or French in America;
and though Virginia, ostensibly possessing the
right of free-trade by the terms of her surrender
to Parliament in 1652, was compelled to see, in
some cases at least, the act of 1651 enforced, little
more was done; and after 1654 the old conditions
were in the main re-established. Rhode Island resumed her trade with the Dutch; New England
traders, as well as the Virginians themselves, carried Virginia tobacco to New Amsterdam and there
reshipped it to Holland;[2] and free-trade was in full
operation in Massachusetts.[3]

The restoration of the Stuarts in 1660 marks an
epoch in the history of the colonies and of colonial

---

[1] *Cal. of State Pap., Col.*, 1574–1660, pp. 386, 387; Thurloe,
State Papers, I., 722; II., 418, 419, 425, 583.

[2] *N. Y. Docs. Rel. to Col. Hist.*, III., 48; Thurloe, *State Papers*,
V., 80, 81.

[3] Hutchinson, *Hist. of Massachusetts Bay*, I., 189.

administration. Royalists in exile, like Prince Charles and the duke of York, Clarendon, Carteret, Berkeley, Craven, and others, who were watching the course of events, appreciated the importance of the navigation act, and were prepared to re-enact the greater part of it. Parliamentarians like Ashley Cooper, Monck, Colleton, Noell, Povey, Digges, and others, some of whom had been resident in the colonies or had sat on special colonial boards and commissions at home, were ready to serve the new government and to uphold a vigorous colonial policy.

Immediately after the Restoration the ordinance of 1651 was renewed in what is known as the "Navigation Act of 1660." The passage of this statute has been ascribed to Sir George Downing, graduate of Harvard College, English resident at The Hague for many years, and one of the most influential, though not one of the most trustworthy, advisers in matters of trading policy. Downing, an enemy of the Dutch and an ardent mercantilist, threw all his weight in favor of the measure; but many other forces were at work also. The encouragement of trade was a cardinal tenet of the king and his ministers throughout the entire reign; and Clarendon fully appreciated the importance of the plantations, as well as of the fisheries and of the great trading companies, as a means of increasing the revenue. He urged upon the king, both in exile and after his return, "a great esteem for his plantations and the improvement of them by all the ways that could reasonably be proposed to him."[1] He urged upon Parliament in 1660 the "infinite importance of the improvement of trade," and whenever possible sought to demonstrate to king and Parliament the desirability of extending the navy in order to check the "immoderate desire" of England's neighbors and rivals "to engross the whole traffic of the universe."[2]

The merchants, too, who had gained their experience under the protectorate, "lamented the obstructions and discouragements which they had long found in their commerce by sea with other nations," due, they said, to "the pride and insolence of the Hollanders," and were eager to destroy the supremacy of Holland.[3] When the speaker of the House of Commons presented the bill to the king to sign, he said: "The act will enable your Majesty to give the law to foreign princes abroad, and is the only way to enlarge your Majesty's dominions all over the world; for as long as your Majesty is master at sea, your merchants will be welcome wherever they come, and that is the easiest way of making whatever is theirs ours, and where it is ours, your Majesty cannot want it."[4]

The king was "upon all occasions very zealous to

[1] *Life of Clarendon, written by himself* (ed. 1798), V., 171.

[2] Cobbett, *Hist. of Parliament*, IV., 128, 250.

[3] *Life of Clarendon, written by himself* (ed. 1798), III., 201.

[4] Cobbett, *Hist. of Parliament*, III., 121, 122; cf. *Journal of the House of Commons*, VIII., 548.

increase the trade of the nation,"[1] and was taught
by Clarendon that the receipts from the plantation
trade could repair some of the deficiencies of his income. It is significant that in 1661 a new royal
officer was created—the receiver-general of the revenues of foreign plantations—with Thomas Povey
as the first appointee.[2] Parliament, while making
grants for the expenses of the government, assumed no responsibility for the actual collecting of
the money, and the emptiness of the treasury in
1672, known as the "Stop of the Exchequer,"
showed that an increase of the revenue was a royal
necessity.

For this purpose Charles II. encouraged the
plantations and added to their number; he labored
to improve the Newfoundland trade and fisheries;[3]
he made treaties with Portugal, yielding to certain
unsatisfactory conditions "for trade's sake";[4] and
in negotiating with Savoy, Denmark, Spain, France,
and Holland, he kept trade advantages always first
in mind.[5] He turned into the treasury the dowry
received from Catherine of Braganza (£500,000),
and the money received from the sale of Dunkirk
(£225,000), and he borrowed from private individuals as well as from the farmers of the customs and
the goldsmiths in order to meet current expenses,

---

[1] Historical MSS. Commission, *Report*, XII., pt. vii., 72.
[2] *Cal. of State Pap.*, *Dom.*, 1663–1664, § 408.
[3] Historical MSS. Commission, *Report*, XII., pt. vii., 117.
[4] Cobbett, *Hist. of Parliament*, IV., 189.
[5] *Ibid.*, IV., 457, 458.

particularly after the disasters of the Dutch war of 1664–1666.[1] The king's interest in his revenues, as well as the demands of commerce and trade, the nation's jealousy of Holland, and the influence of men like Clarendon and Downing, must be taken into account if we would understand the navigation acts, the founding of new colonies, the establishment of new boards and committees, and the *quo warranto* proceedings to annul colonial charters between 1660 and 1688. The colonies were the king's colonies, and his also was the burden of providing money for the expenses of the kingdom.

Since the attempt to cripple the Dutch by the navigation act of 1651 proved a failure, the act of 1660, in repeating the shipping clause of the earlier act, made it more rigorous. Thenceforth ships must not only be owned and manned by Englishmen (including colonists), but they must also be built by Englishmen, and two-thirds of the seamen must be English subjects. In later acts of 1662 and 1663, provision was made whereby real or pretended misunderstandings of this clause might be prevented; and one of the most important functions of the later committees of trade and plantations was, by means of rules as to passes, denization and naturalization, and foreign-built ships, to prevent trade from getting into the hands of foreigners.

[1] *Cal. of State Pap., Dom.*, 1661–1662, § 613; 1663–1664, §§ 251, 252; *Life of Clarendon, written by himself* (ed. 1761), III., 919.

More famous than the shipping clause of the act of 1660 is that dealing with the "enumerated" commodities. This clause, though not added, curiously enough, till the third reading of the bill, and seemingly as an afterthought, marks a new step in the development of the mercantilist idea. It declared that sugar, tobacco, cotton - wool, fustic, and other dye - woods — the most important raw materials exported by the colonies—should all be carried directly to England. This provision gave legal force to a principle of colonial management that Cromwell never grasped, whereby the colonies were to become a source of raw materials for the manufactures of the mother-country. Cotton-wool and dye-woods were needed in England for the growing textile industries there; tobacco, a product of Maryland and Virginia, was enumerated because the government, believing it to be of mutual advantage to limit the colonial market to England and her dominions, had forbidden the culture of tobacco at home; and sugar, a product of the West Indian colonies in great demand at home, and also cocoa (added in 1672, when the drinking of chocolate became a prevailing fashion) were enumerated to prevent their direct shipment to continental countries, notably to Spain.[1] Cotton-wool and dye-woods were listed for the sake of the manufacturers; sugar, tobacco, and cocoa were listed for the sake of the customs revenue. In each case England be-

---

[1] *Cal. of State Pap., Col.*, 1669–1674, § 375.

lieved that the monopoly which she offered was a
sufficient compensation for the loss of free-trade,
for the increase in freights, and for the higher rate of
customs duties charged in England, in comparison
with other countries.

In a revision of 1663 another new and far-reaching
clause was added: all European commodities destined for the colonies must first be carried to England and there be unloaded and put on shore before
they could be transported to America; or, in other
words, all the foreign import trade of the colonies
had to pass through England's hands, and all ships
had to touch at England on their way to the colonies.
The object of the law was to make England a staple
for all European commodities sent to the colonies,
and to prevent the colonies from building up an
independent import trade of their own. If their
market for the sale of raw materials was to be
limited, so also must be their market for the purchase of manufactured goods. Should the colonies
be free to purchase their woollens where they wished,
without any restriction, they would defeat England's mercantile policy, which demanded that
colonial raw materials be paid for in England's
manufactured articles and not in coin; and they
would take advantage of the low price of French
and Dutch woollens to buy their goods in France
and Holland, to the serious injury of England's trade.
England alone must be the staple, the vent, and the
market, so far as her colonies were concerned.

The Cromwellian act carried with it no provision for the execution of the law, except the promise that half of the value of the forfeited cargo and ships should go to the informer: but in the act of 1660 a bond and security were required of all ships leaving England for the colonies, and of all ships clearing from colonial ports with a cargo of enumerated commodities; and an effort was made to interest the colonial governors in the enforcement of the acts by granting them a third of all goods confiscated for illegal trading   The act of 1663 demanded that the colonial governors take oath, before assuming office, to do all in their power to enforce the laws, under penalty of £1000, loss of office, and ineligibility for another governorship. Collectors of customs who disobeyed the law were to lose their positions and to pay a fine equal to the value of the ship's cargo.

A noteworthy advance in the systematic execution of the laws was made in 1672. Aroused by the reports of illegal trade in tobacco, Parliament enacted that in case the usual bond or promise to carry the enumerated commodities directly to England were not given, a duty should be paid to the collector at the port of clearance, as, for example, of a penny a pound on tobacco, which was to form part of the royal revenue. The object of this regulation was to put a stop to the carriage of goods to other plantations and their shipment thence to a foreign country on the ground that the requirements had been fulfilled. Though the machinery for the execution of this act was imperfect and its provisions were never fully carried out, yet the king by farming out the plantation duty during the Restoration was able to add to his revenue £700 a year.

CHAPTER II

ENGLISH ADMINISTRATION OF THE COLONIES
(1660–1689)

IN England, after 1660, the management of trade
and plantations was placed in the hands, first
of special boards, and afterwards of committees of
the Privy Council. A plan for such a body was
drawn up, some time during the later years of the
Protectorate, by Martin Noell, one of the commissioners for Jamaica, and Thomas Povey, a merchant
prominently interested in all matters relating to the
West Indian colonies, afterwards member and clerk
of the councils of trade and plantations and re-
ceiver - general of the revenues. This "Overtures
touching a Council to be erected for Foreign Plantations,"[1] contains recommendations for a select
council for the inspection, care, and regulation of
all foreign plantations, that the colonies might "understand that they are to be looked upon as united
and embodied and that their Head and Centre is
here." It provided, further, that a more certain
government should be set up for the colonies, and
information of every kind should be obtained from

---

[1] *Egerton MSS.*, in British Museum, 2395, ff. 270–286.

the governors and elsewhere, that "each place within
itself and all of them being as it were made up into
one Commonwealth, may by his Majesty be here
governed and regulated accordingly upon common
and equal principles." This comprehensive scheme,
based on the actual experiences of a group of English merchants trading with the West Indies during
the Cromwellian era, was placed before the king's
advisers after the Restoration, and doubtless helped
to shape their plans for the management of the
colonies.

July 4, 1660, a Council Committee for Foreign
Plantations was designated and continued to act till
1675.[1] Side by side with it was a second, advisory
council for trade proposed by Clarendon, to consist
of "several principal merchants of the several companies," to which he would add some gentlemen of
quality and experience, and for their greater honor
and encouragement some of the lords of his own
Privy Council.[2] It was duly organized in December, 1660. Clarendon was appointed president of
the board, among the members of which were Ashley, Colleton, Noell, Povey, and two members from
each of the great trading companies,[3] men already familiar with the trade of the plantations.

---

[1] *Privy Council Register* (MS.), Charles II., III., 125, etc.

[2] Cobbett, *Hist. of Parliament*, IV., 128; *Life of Clarendon,
written by himself* (ed. 1798), III., 201.

[3] Bannister, *Writings of W. Patterson*, III., 251, 252, quoted
by Egerton, *British Colonial Policy*, 75, *n.*

The board, of which five members constituted a quorum, at once perfected its organization and appointed sub-committees for the several colonies. The members were expected to inform themselves of the state of the plantations, and procure copies of the grants under which they were settled; to correspond with the governors and require accounts of the laws and governments from them; to use means for bringing the colonies "into a more certain, civil, and uniform way of government"; to investigate the colonial policies of the other European states; to secure transportation of noxious and unprofitable persons to the plantations; to propagate the Gospel, and to have a general oversight of all matters relating to the plantations.[1]

Of the activities of this council we know but little. Some of their minutes and reports are preserved, and Pepys and Evelyn occasionally refer to their proceedings. The merchants seem to have been largely in control, and till 1663 displayed considerable efficiency. They performed their work largely through committees, and busied themselves with the affairs of Jamaica, Barbadoes, New England, and Virginia. The membership was changed in 1668, 1670, and again in 1672, when the councils of trade and foreign plantations were united under the presidency of Ashley, with John Locke as secretary and treasurer and many of the former members as colleagues.

[1] *N. Y. Docs. Rel. to Col. Hist.*, III., 34-36.

This joint committee was to form a "standing council in and for all the affayrs which doe concerne the navigation, commerce, or trade, as well domestic as forraigne, of these our kingdoms and our forraigne colonyes and plantations."[1]

These frequent changes in the select council were due to the belief among those in authority that such a separate board possessing no plenary powers was inefficient and "without any considerable advantage to his Majesty or the plantations." A contemporary expresses a very general opinion when he says: "The council is obliged to have a continual recourse to superior ministers and councils, which oftentimes gives great and prejudicial delays and usually begets new or slower deliberations and results than the matter in hand may stand in need of." It was therefore felt necessary to appoint commissioners "out of the Privy Council, under the great seal, to consider the plantations, to give directions in ordinary cases, and in extraordinary to report to the king and council . . . [commissioners] empowered to act and order with as ample an authority as the commissioners of the admiralty now do." When in 1668 Charles II. reorganized the administrative methods of the Privy Council and adopted a system of "fix't and established committees," he set up a standing committee of the

---

[1] *Shaftesbury Papers*, MSS. in Public Record Office, X., Nos. 8 (vi.–ix.), 9, 10 (commissions, instructions, members added in 1670, 1672).

council, to act in conjunction with the separate board and to consider whatever concerned "his Majesty's forraigne plantations." This dual arrangement lasted fifteen years, but cannot have been successful; for in 1674 the select council of which Shaftesbury was president was abolished, and its duties were entrusted to a new standing committee of the council composed of twenty-four members, henceforth known as the Lords of Trade.[1]

This committee held its first meeting on February 9, 1675, though the commission is dated a month later. At first, five constituted a quorum, afterwards three, but the number present rarely fell below six or seven, while frequently ten, fifteen, and twenty attended the meetings. The committee generally sat in the council chamber at Whitehall, and it was attended by many of the most important men of the kingdom, including many men trained under the Protectorate. The king, the duke of York, Prince Rupert, the archbishop of Canterbury, the bishop of London, the chancellor of the exchequer, the lord privy seal, the lord high chancellor, the vice chamberlain, and others attended, some of them frequently. Occasionally the discussion in the council chamber was only ended by the entrance of the king to hold a meeting of his council. As compared with the inefficiency and inactivity of the permanent board of trade after 1720, a body too often made

---

[1] *Egerton MSS.*, in British Museum, 2395, f. 276, 2543, f. 205; *Journal of the Lords of Trade*, I., 1, 8.

up of needy politicians and placemen, the committees from 1674 to 1688 display dignity and devotion to business.

The committee was a hard-working body that
met frequently and sat long. It considered carefully every matter that came before it; sought to
settle every difficulty as expeditiously as possible;
obtained information from every available source,
summoning and closely questioning merchants, seamen, factors, colonial agents, and even colonial
proprietaries like Penn and Baltimore. It purchased books,[1] maps, charts, and globes, bade Locke
bring in all records and documents of the old commission, and even talked of continuing Purchas's
Pilgrimage from accounts to be sent in by merchants
and sea-captains. In its wide range of interests it
discussed treaties with foreign countries, watched
carefully the workings of the great companies, listened to their quarrels and complaints, called on the
commissioners of customs to suggest new methods
of encouraging trade, and asked for reports from
these officials and the clerk of Parliament, on the
trade of England. It demanded lists of English
ships with the burden of each, and endeavored to
lay down rules for the more efficient interpretation
of the navigation acts. It prepared instructions
and despatches, wrote the king's proclamations, and
even dealt with the granting of patents for inventions.

[1] See catalogue of committee's library in *N. E. Historical and
Genealogical Register*, XXXVIII., 261.

Towards the colonies the committee's attitude was one of eminent fairness. Large questions, such as the settling of a new colony, or the appointment of a new colonial governor, or the approval of a new series of colonial laws, often came before it. Other matters were called to its attention by petition or complaint, and naturally only those colonies in which disputes and difficulties arose were discussed at its meetings. Massachusetts and Virginia, Jamaica, Barbadoes, and other West Indian colonies were well known to its members; Rhode Island, the Carolinas, and Maryland were occasionally brought to its notice; while New York, New Jersey, Connecticut, and Pennsylvania are rarely mentioned in the minutes of its meetings.

In difficult cases, such as those touching the charters of the Bermuda and the Massachusetts Bay companies, the members of the board showed fairness and gave abundant opportunity for the colonies to state their respective cases. They never acted arbitrarily, and were always ready to discount the statements of prejudiced persons, and to compel complainants to prove their charges. In doubtful points of law they would order the charters to be scrutinized, or would submit the question to the legal advisers of the crown. Sometimes they would transfer the question to the king in council to decide. Naturally, they were ignorant of a great deal that was going on in the colonies, and were out of sympathy with the political ideas and practices

that had taken root in many of them.   Hence, they
sent over men like Edward Randolph, who were in
sympathy with their own point of view, and depended, unfortunately, too much on the evidence
submitted by such representatives.

Nevertheless, the Lords of Trade tried to remedy
these deficiencies and to obtain satisfactory and
adequate information.   They sent out written
queries to the colonies, asking for full answers regarding their affairs, and the answers they received
are among our best sources of information regarding
the colonies.   They called for lists of governors and
copies of the charters and grants, and tried to
accumulate among their records the details of the
history of each colony.   They recommended, in
1675, the sending of a commission of five men "of
sobriety and discretion" to Massachusetts in order
to obtain "a full information of things which at
this distance (and where no person appears on the
other side) seeme very dark."[1]   They allowed any
individual to send in a petition or address, on what
appear to be often trivial subjects, and they claimed
the right to act on these in the first instance.   Even
appeals from the plantations to the king in council
seem to have come to the attention of the Lords of
Trade before passing on to the Privy Council itself.

They draughted all the governors' commissions
and instructions, debating every clause with care,
even going so far at times as to call on the governor

[1] *Journal of the Lords of Trade*, I., 22.

himself to suggest modifications and additions. The development of the governor's functions at the hands of the Lords of Trade forms an instructive phase of the history of the royal administration. It is evident that these men had little appreciation of the democratic forces at work in the colonies, and they must have wondered at times at the ill-success of some of their appointees.

The committee was constantly called upon to interpret the navigation acts; and many important features of the administrative act of 1696 can be found already worked out in the minutes of its meetings. The Lords soon discovered that many violations of the acts were taking place in the colonies; and the complaints of merchants and others seem to indicate that New England was especially guilty. They therefore made inquiry as to how far the navigation acts took "cognizance of New England, what violations had been observed in the matter of that trade, and of what ill-consequence in point of profit to his Majesty and the kingdom such abuse of those people may be estimated at." [1] They not only insisted that all governors be required to take oath and give bond according to law, but made a special recommendation that the New England governors should be required to swear that they would put the acts into force.

The Lords of Trade inquired further whether a ship that laded enumerated commodities and paid

[1] *Journal of the Lords of Trade*, I., 23.

the duty in the plantation (if declaration should
be made that it was bound for another English plantation) was not exempt from any other
bonds and was not then at liberty to carry such
commodities to what part of the world it pleased.[1]
As early as 1678 the question came up whether a
royal governor could erect courts of admiralty, and
whether vice-admiralty powers came from the king
or the lord high admiral.   A decision was reached
that the king had full power to create a vice-admiral,
but that the commission and instructions were to
come from the lord high admiral.[2]   These queries
show that the committee was often very uncertain
how to act, and that the interpretation of the
navigation acts was a matter of time and experience.

The machinery for carrying out the navigation
acts in the colonies during the period under discussion was very imperfect and incomplete.   An
official resident in England was appointed in 1661
to farm the revenues of the foreign plantations.[3]
In the colonies no royal customs officers existed
except the governors, before the passage of the
navigation act of 1672; although the farmers of the
customs proposed such officers as early as 1663.[4]
This proposition does not appear to have been acted

---

[1] *Journal of the Lords of Trade*, I., 67, 68.
[2] *Ibid.*, II., 197, 198.
[3] *Cal. of State Pap., Col.*, 1661–1668, § 435.
[4] *N. Y. Docs. Rel. to Col. Hist.*, III., 48–50.

upon, and the governors, who were very lax in the performance of their duties, were left to administer the acts very much as they pleased.

The first revenue official appointed by the crown to go to America seems to have been Edward Digges, who was sent to Virginia in 1669, in pursuance of an order of council concerning the redress of some neglects or abuses in the plantations. The duties of this office were amalgamated with those of the auditor of the revenue, first created by act of assembly in Virginia and afterwards controlled apparently by the crown.[1] The auditor examined the public accounts, dealt with the redress of abuses, and returned bonds. On May 19, 1680, the system of auditing the colonial revenues was still further improved by the appointment of a surveyor and auditor-general in England, the first appointee being William Blathwayt, secretary of the Privy Council.[2] To him were referred all petitions sent to the Lords of the Treasury that in any way concerned the finances of the royal colonies. The office demanded judgment and experience, and it is noteworthy that Blathwayt and his successor, Horatio Walpole (appointed in 1718), held the office for nearly eighty years.

The navigation act of 1663 created a naval

---

[1] *Cal. of State Pap., Col.*, 1669–1674, § 104.
[2] *Cal. of State Pap., Col.*, 1681–1685, § 241; *Cal. of Treasury Pap*, 1714–1719, 387; Hartwell, Blair, and Chilton, *Present State of Virginia*, 157.

officer to be appointed by the governor and paid by the fees of his office. The first direct mention of such an officer, however, does not appear until 1672, in connection with Barbadoes, although it is then stated that there were earlier appointees[1] The naval officers were required to make entries and keep particular accounts of all imports and exports, of shipping, burden, guns, etc., whence they came and whither they were bound, and to send quarterly reports to England.[2] They handled no customs revenue, for that was the business of the collector.

The latter official, whose work it was to collect the plantation duty established by the act of 1672, makes his first appearance in 1673 in Barbadoes and Antigua. William Dyer, husband of the Quaker Mary Dyer, was appointed collector for New York in 1674, Giles Bland for Virginia in the same year, Rousby for Maryland in 1676, Miller for Albemarle in 1677; Gibbes for "Carolina and Roanoke" before 1685, Muschamp for South Carolina in the latter year, and Walliam for Pennsylvania, as early as May, 1688.[3] Before the year 1677, there were no collectors in New England, because, as the com-

---

[1] *Colonial Entry Book*, 28, 86–93.
[2] *Cal. of State Pap., Col.*, 1677–1680, § 1590.
[3] *Declared Accounts*, MSS. in Public Record Office; *Pipe Office*, Roll 1056; *Treasury, In Letters, Indexes, Reference Book*, III., 148 (Muschamp's Petition); *Md. Archives*, V., 274; *Cal. of State Pap., Col.*, 1685–1688, § 639; *Colonial Entry Books*, 63 (MSS. Report of March 25, 1689); *Pa. Col. Records*, I., 297 (335); MSS. Instructions for Collector (British Museum, *Add. MSS.* 28089, f. 31).

missioners of the customs reported to the Lords of
Trade, the New England colonies grew none of the
enumerated commodities which were liable to the
plantation duty.[1] But in that year, as the result
of Randolph's recent visit, the office of collector,
surveyor, and searcher of customs in the colonies of
New England was established,[2] and Randolph became the first appointee. He was authorized by
his commission to search for prohibited goods and
seize such ships as traded contrary to law; he had
power to appoint deputies (who were to reside in
different parts of New England), to give them instructions, and to supervise their conduct. A similar office was held by Patrick Mien or Mein, who
in 1685 was "surveyor of his Majesties plantations
on the continent of America," and in 1687 of certain of the West Indies also.[3] In later instructions
the surveyor was empowered to inspect and control
the management of the collector's business and to
audit his accounts.[4] The collector for New England after 1681 held his office by royal letters-patent
under the great seal, but all the others were appointed by the commissioners of customs in England, and resided in the principal ports of the plantations. They were constantly quarrelling, with

---

[1] *Journal of the Lords of Trade*, I., 69.

[2] *Col. Entry Book*, Public Record Office, 60, 357–359.

[3] *Treasury, Miscellanea, King's Warrant Books* (Public Record
Office), III., 214; *ibid., In Letters, Indexes, Reference Book*, V.,
308; *Pa. Col. Records*, I., 297 (337).

[4] British Museum, *Add. MSS.*, 28089, f. 34.

governors on one side and people on the other, and on the whole do not appear to have been a very estimable class of men.

The earlier navigation acts made no provision for special courts with jurisdiction over breaches of the law. The "courts of record" mentioned in the act of 1660 refers to the common law courts in England, though there is reason to believe that the high court of admiralty, though not legally deemed a court of record at this time, occasionally tried cases that had to do with evasion of the trade laws. The colonies, however, provided themselves with such courts, some of them before the navigation acts were passed. Rhode Island erected an admiralty court in 1653, at the time of the Dutch war; Virginia passed an act in 1660 authorizing the governor and council to be a court of admiralty; Massachusetts (1673) and Connecticut (1684) authorized their respective courts of assistants to act in that capacity; Plymouth placed this power in the hands of the governor and assistants in 1684; and in the same year Pennsylvania gave the power to the president and members of the council.[1] New York declared in 1678 that in her colony admiralty cases had been tried by a special commission or by a court composed of the mayor and aldermen.[2] From the point

[1] Arnold, *Hist. of R. I.*, I., 246; Hening, *Statutes*, I., 537; *Mass. Col. Records*, IV., pt. ii., 575; *Conn. Col. Records*, III., 95; *Plymouth Col. Records*, VI., 139, 140; *Pa. Col. Records*, I., 69 (121, 122).

[2] *N. Y. Docs. Rel. to Col. Hist.*, III., 260.

of view of admiralty jurisdiction and procedure, all
these courts were irregular and illegal; and it is
noteworthy that nowhere, except in Maryland (1639)
was a regular admiralty court established till about
1697,[1] when a general system, at least on paper, was
provided.

During the first half of the seventeenth century the
English government made scarcely any attempt to
control the colonies through a system of agents. Such
colonial agents were sent over only when required.[2]
The earliest went from Virginia in 1624 to defend
the charter of that colony. Others were despatched
afterwards by various colonies to defend some
particular cause: as when Rhode Island resisted
Coddington's attempt to obtain a charter for himself as governor of Newport and Aquidneck; and
when Virginia tried to annul the grant to Arlington
and Culpeper. Agents were sometimes sent to gain
colonial privileges, as when Winthrop for Connecticut, Clarke for Rhode Island, and Increase Mather
for Massachusetts, sought to obtain charters for
those colonies. Agents were sent also to answer
charges and settle boundary disputes, as when
Maryland instructed her agents to oppose the demands of Penn. Some of the colonies—Connecticut, for example—employed English residents to do
business that did not require a special representative. Eventually, however, the Lords of Trade,

---

[1] *Md. Archives*, I., 46.
[2] Tanner, in *Political Science Quarterly*, XVI., 24–49.

warned by the difficulty of obtaining agents from Massachusetts, inserted in Penn's charter the provision, made for the first time, that an agent be appointed to reside in or near the city of London.

Equally indefinite was the attitude of the home government towards colonial legislation. No colony was allowed to make laws contrary to those of England, though at first no colony was required to transmit its acts to England for acceptance or rejection. Not until the issue of the charter to Penn was such requirement made, and then the colony was called upon to transmit its laws to England within five years after their passage, and the council was to act upon them within six months after their receipt. A similar clause was inserted in the Massachusetts charter of 1691, when the period was limited to three years and no restriction was imposed upon the action of the council. The charter corporations always denied the validity of the acts of Parliament in America unless re-enacted by their own assemblies; and Massachusetts refused to acknowledge the right of the council to invalidate her laws even when contrary to those of England.[1]

The idea of creating a uniform system of administration in the colonies, of bringing all to conform to a common type, and of rendering them more dependent on the home government by union under

[1] *Mass. Col. Records*, V., 200, 201 ; *Hutchinson Papers*, II., 232.

the crown, developed very slowly. The charter
of the Virginia company was dissolved in 1624, and
that of Massachusetts threatened in 1635–1637;
but these annulments were no part of a common
plan. The Council for Foreign Plantations, desiring to administer the navigation acts more efficiently, proposed to Charles II. in 1661 that he
take all the existing proprietary colonies into his
own hands and create no new ones in the future;[1]
but, though this plan for a uniform and centralized
colonial organization was emphasized in Noell and
Povey's "Overtures," the king allowed his personal
inclinations to override the suggestions of the committee. Between 1660 and 1670 six new charters
were issued: the four new colonies of the Carolinas,
New York, the Jerseys, and Bahamas were founded;
and Connecticut and Rhode Island received new
charters. Even as late as 1676 the council committee could say that "to consider New England so
as to bring them under taxes and impositions or to
send thither a governor to raise fortune from them
cannot be of any use or service to his Majesty." [2]

When, however, the reports of illegal trading and
of quarrels between the collectors and the colonists
began to come in, the Lords of Trade viewed the
matter differently. Breaches of the acts of trade
affected the king's income, a matter of great concern
to the committee, which existed for the very purpose

[1] *Cal. of State Pap., Col.*, 1661–1668, § 3.
[2] *Ibid.*, 1675–1676, § 813.

of safeguarding and increasing the customs revenues of the crown. The committee had already declared that the plantations could enact no laws touching the king's revenue without the king's "particular knowledge"; and had already studied how best the colonies might be brought to a closer dependency on the crown in matters of trade. After 1680 complaints came in rapidly: Maryland, the Bermudas, and Massachusetts were the first colonies to give offence in the eyes of the board: the proprietary of Maryland and the companies in Bermuda and in Massachusetts were warned that continued violations of the acts would lead to the forfeiture of their charters.

Plans were made for the issue of writs of *quo warranto* against the corporations, and in 1681 the writs were issued. The Bermuda company, resident in London, and having only a business connection with the colony, gave up its charter after a brief struggle; but the Massachusetts company died hard, staving off the inevitable result till 1684.

From the point of view of the lords who composed the committee, a union of the northern colonies had become a financial necessity, and it was carried out by the appointment of a governor-general of New England in 1686. The policy was neither arbitrary nor wilful, nor even an idea of James II., for the committee fathered it from the beginning. It was simply a part of a larger policy that subordinated the colonies to the crown and the kingdom.

Notwithstanding the great services of the committee, the last renewal of its members took place January 27, 1688, when all the lords of the Privy Council were constituted a standing committee for trade and plantations. Little business was done between October 25 and November 20, England was on the eve of a revolution. After October 17 the names of the members present are not recorded. On February 6, 1689, the last meeting was held, and it is a curious coincidence that the last minute in the journal records the receipt of letters from Andros and Randolph.

February 16, 1689, three days after William and Mary were declared king and queen of England, a new committee of twelve members was appointed to take cognizance of the affairs of trade and plantations. This body remained in control until the establishment of the permanent Board of Trade and Plantations in 1696. It is significant that the new Lords of Trade were as eager as had been their predecessors to bring the colonies into a condition of closer dependence on the crown, not so much for the sake of the revenues as to provide for adequate defence against the French.[1]

[1] *Md. Archives*, VIII., 100, 101.

CHAPTER III

REORGANIZATION OF NEW ENGLAND

(1660–1662)

AS a whole, the colonists of New England were of the same political faith, and conducted their governments according to the same general plan. So far as possible they held aloof from all connection with king, Privy Council, and Lords of Trade; and, having made their settlements without assistance from England, they were quite content to get on without the help of those who had legal authority over them. No royal governors or other appointees were present among them to arouse discontent, and between the freemen and those whom the freemen elected to represent them no serious conflict ever arose. The few royalists who lived in the colony exercised no influence in government, and were powerless to alter the convictions of the majority. The New-Englanders would make no compromise with the doctrines of divine right and passive obedience, and had as little patience with a loyal follower of the Stuarts as James II. had with a believer in the rights of a majority. They looked upon all the king's agents as tyrannical; the king in turn deemed the New-Englanders factious and rebellious. Hence any interference on the part of a Stuart, however much he might justify it from the point of view of his wars, his revenue, and his prerogative, or by the fact that the crown itself was the supreme authority over all the colonies, was sure to lead to trouble and possible revolt. The self-government which the king ignored was as the breath of life to the New England colonists.

In 1650 the commissioners of the New England Confederation, formed in 1643 by Massachusetts, Plymouth, Connecticut, and New Haven, arranged the treaty of Hartford with the Dutch, fixing the boundary between New England and New Netherland at Rye on the main-land and Oyster Bay on Long Island.[1] This truce with the Dutch lasted but two years: New Haven was angry because the Dutch had prevented her traders from settling on the Delaware; and both Connecticut and New Haven held Stuyvesant responsible for a number of Indian massacres that had taken place on the frontier near Stamford. When the "encroachments" of the Dutch and the question of a declaration of war were brought before the commissioners in 1652, seven of them declared that they felt "a call of God to make war upon the Dutch and avenge the destruc-

[1] *Plymouth Col. Records*, IX., 18–21; X., 171–190; *New Haven Col. Records*, II., 5, 6.   Cf. Tyler, *England in America*, chap. xviii.

tion of so many dear saints of God which is imputed
to the Dutch governor and fiscal."

The eighth commissioner, Bradstreet, of Massachusetts, took the ground that a majority of the commissioners had no right to authorize a declaration
of war. Bradstreet was upheld by the elders and
court of the colony. In order to avoid a war that
she did not wish and that might have imperilled
her own leadership, Massachusetts violated the
Articles of the Confederation and threatened the
existence of the union. Connecticut and New
Haven in anger threatened to withdraw, and were
appeased only when the Council of State in England,
to which they had applied for instructions, over-
ruled the decision of Massachusetts and ordered
war.[1] Cromwell, as we have seen, sent over Major
Sedgwick to co-operate with the colonists, but the
expedition was stopped by the declaration of peace.

When danger of war was over and the troops
which had been gathered for the attack had been
disbanded, Massachusetts, desirous that the Confederation should continue, reversed her former
decision and yielded the right of a majority to recommend a declaration of war.[2] Her submission
was as humble as her opposition had been vehement;
but the Confederation never regained its lost harmony. Much of its importance departed after the

---

[1] *Plymouth Col. Records*, X., 33, 54, 56 ; *Mass. Col. Records*,
IV., pt. i., 144, 165–171; *Cal. of State Pap., Col.*, 1574–1660,
pp. 386, 387.   [2] *Ibid.*, X., 75, 76, 114.

conquest of New Netherland by the English in 1664 and the incorporation of New Haven by Connecticut in the same year; and for a time it ceased to hold any meetings whatever. With the resumption of the sessions of the commissioners an attempt was made to restore the Confederation to its former state of efficiency, but without success. Opposition to it arose within the colonies themselves, and men began to say that the meetings entailed a needless expense and accomplished nothing for the good of the colonies. After languishing until 1684, the New England Confederation came to an end.

The failure of the Confederation to effect a permanent union was in no small measure due to the prominence and power of the Massachusetts Bay colony. After the crisis of 1640, when decreasing immigration threatened the prosperity of New England, Massachusetts gained pre-eminence among her neighbors because of her greater trade and riches, the number of her towns, and the wider experience and broader education of her leading men.[1] After 1650 the authorities at Boston avoided, as far as possible, all entanglement with English affairs, and resisted all attempts of Cromwell to interfere with their concerns. They refused to proclaim Richard Cromwell protector when ordered to do so, and at all times conducted themselves, to all intents and purposes, as a sovereign state. The general court

[1] Hutchinson, *Hist. of Mass. Bay*, I., 206, *n.*

of the colony levied taxes, provided for military
defence, erected inferior corporations like that of
Harvard College,[1] regulated courts of justice, controlled the right of appeal, and assumed the highest prerogatives of sovereignty in coining money
and hanging offenders, such as murderers, witches,
and Quakers.[2]

This independent position fostered among the
inhabitants of the Bay a spirit of superiority and
self-content that was not always commendable.   In
a long controversy between the Frenchmen D'Aulnay
and La Tour regarding the governorship of Acadia,
Massachusetts aided La Tour, thus again disregarding the Articles of Confederation.   In all boundary disputes with Connecticut and Rhode Island,
notably in that concerning the townships of Souther-
town and Warwick and the lands of Misquamicut,
Massachusetts was inclined to be overbearing, and
showed herself exceedingly skilful in the art of
contriving claims and disingenuous in enforcing
them.

In spite of the protests of Mason and Gorges,
who had obtained grants of lands between the
Kennebec and Merrimac rivers as early as 1622,
she extended her jurisdiction in that quarter also,
and laid claim to the entire territory.[3]   From 1651
to 1665 Kittery, Agamenticus, Wells, Saco, and
Cape Porpoise sent deputies to the general assembly

[1] *Mass. Col. Records*, IV., pt. i., 12–14.
[2] *Ibid.*, 48, 104, 118, 419.   [3] *Ibid.*, 70, 157–165.

at Boston, and the whole region was brought under the authority of the Bay. There was truth in Randolph's statement, made in 1676, that "Massachusetts having the pre-eminence takes the liberty to claim as far as their convenience and interest directs." [1]

In religious matters as in political, Massachusetts was no less determined to have her own way, and she labored unceasingly to keep herself untouched by other religious doctrines and ideas. Having driven out Roger Williams and Ann Hutchinson, the Bay authorities were certainly not likely to admit Quakers. Mary Fisher and Anne Austin, who reached New England in 1656, were promptly lodged in jail, and afterwards shipped back to Barbadoes, whence they came. Others who followed them to Massachusetts suffered a like fate. To give legal warrant for their action, the leaders at Boston persuaded the United Commissioners to recommend that each colony pass a law against the Quakers, a recommendation which the Massachusetts assembly promptly and rigorously carried out [2] and followed by a course of persecution unequalled in any of the colonies. Many Quakers were imprisoned; three—Robinson, Stevenson, and Mary Dyer—were hanged. An arrogance of power seemed to possess the colony, an intolerance that brooked no check or control. The government of "godly

[1] *Hutchinson Papers*, II., 223.
[2] *Mass. Col. Records*, IV., pt. i., 277.

men" was in its way as tyrannical as ever had been, or was to be, the government of a Stuart.

This unusual independence of Massachusetts, characterized by self-government, freedom of trade, exemption from outside interference, and a somewhat domineering way of dealing with adjoining colonies, must be taken into account if one is to understand the history of the colony from 1660 to 1689. Cromwell, engrossed by public affairs at home, and in sympathy with the religious and political views of Massachusetts, let the colony alone. The Massachusetts agent, Leverett, skilfully warded off all complaints against the colony in the period before 1660, so that it rarely came to the attention of the home authorities,[1] and, by gaining the ear of the Protector, he was able to divert the charges of Rhode Island, the Quakers, and the heirs of royalists like Mason and Gorges, whose complaints were purely individual, and in no way touched the revenue or policy of the Protector.

After the Restoration, Massachusetts could expect no such friendly treatment from Charles II. as she had received from Cromwell; nevertheless the king was inclined to be conciliatory. He and Clarendon wished to make the colonies profitable, and were not disposed to cause trouble so long as the colonists did nothing to thwart this policy. But the council for foreign plantations, which at the very outset had received a shower of complaints

[1] Hutchinson, *Hist. of Mass. Bay*, I., 190–194.

against Massachusetts from interested parties, took
a different view, and in 1662 sent a vigorous order
to Boston, bidding the general court proclaim the
king "in a most solemn manner," and apply itself
strictly to "conformity and obedience to his
Majesty."[1]

The king, however, does not appear to have been
greatly disturbed by reports of the neglect of the
colony in its duty to him; for in 1662 he wrote a
letter confirming the charter, and ascribing to the
iniquity of the times, and not to the intention of the
people, all departures from the privileges conferred
in that document.[2]   He approved of the law against
the Quakers, but broke down at one blow the ex-
clusive religious and political policy of the colony
by demanding that the Massachusetts authorities
grant full liberty of worship to all members of the
Anglican church, and concede the right to vote to
all freeholders who possessed competent estates.
During the ensuing twenty-five years the colony
made many efforts to evade these demands, and
an Anglican church was not erected in Boston till
1686; nevertheless, from this time forward the government by "godly men" gave way to a system
based on a property qualification.

Connecticut and New Haven meanwhile were
growing rapidly in size and strength.   Connecticut
accepted the advice of Sir William Boswell, Eng-

[1] *Cal. of State Pap., Col.*, 1661–1668, § 66.
[2] *Ibid.*, § 314.

lish ambassador at The Hague, to "crowd on, crowding the Dutch out of those places which they have occupied, without hostility or any act of violence."[1] By the treaty of Hartford she advanced her western frontier to Rye, and absorbed most of Long Island in 1653.

While the war with the Dutch was in progress, Connecticut seized the House of Good Hope at Hartford, and the next year annexed the Dutch lands there. In 1640 the colony took Southampton, Long Island, under its care; in 1649 and again in 1657 it received Easthampton, and in 1660 Huntington, into its jurisdiction.[3] Within the colony the number of towns increased from three to eleven, and in the decade from 1650 to 1660 the assessed value of property rose more than a fifth. In 1657, in order to prevent the admission of undesirable persons into the voting body, the franchise was for the first time limited to a property qualification. The old generation was passing away: Hooker died in 1647, Haynes in 1654, and in 1653 Ludlow went to Virginia.[4] A new generation had grown up, made of the same stuff as the old, but more aggressive and less scrupulous. Its members were actuated by the same love for the colony; but their actions, legal it may be, were wanting at times in a high-minded regard for the rights of others.

---

[1] *Conn. Col. Records*, I., 565.   [2] *Ibid.*, 254, 275.
[3] *Ibid.*, 572; *Easthampton Records*, I., 12, 140; *Huntington Records*, I., 23.   [4] Taylor, *Roger Ludlow*, 145.

That their attitude was due in part to a sense of their own insecurity, we may not doubt. Had the king desired to drive them from their territory they would have been without legal defence. They had bought their lands of the Indians, but they possessed no corporate powers of government and no land title that would stand for a moment the test of inspection. The purchase of the Warwick patent (1644)[1] was only a device designed for use in emergencies. The Connecticut colonists knew that their position was insecure, for in 1645 they joined with New Haven in sending an agent to England to obtain from the parliamentary commissioners "common privileges to both in the distinct jurisdictions." At the same time they despatched Fenwick to England "to agitate the business concerning the enlargement of the patent."[2] Neither effort was successful, and Connecticut remained without legal document of any kind to show for the money she had spent, or to defend her against royal inquiry or a writ of *quo warranto*. When Massachusetts denied her right to exact river tolls at Saybrook from the people of Springfield, situated farther up the river above Hartford, and asked uncomfortable questions regarding her claims and title, Connecticut had little to say.

[1] Hoadly, *Warwick Patent* (Acorn Club, *Publications*, No. 7); *Egerton MSS.*, in British Museum, 2648, f..1.
[2] Atwater, *Hist. of New Haven*, 569; *Conn. Col. Records*, I., 126, 128.

In July, 1660, the regicides Goffe and Whalley arrived in America. Massachusetts and Connecticut gave them welcome and aid until the king's proclamation appeared, ordering the arrest of the fugitives. After this the two colonies conducted themselves with great circumspection, and while there can be little doubt that Winthrop would have been as glad to aid the fugitives as was Davenport, he was tactful enough not to let it be known to those who were in pursuit. Kellond and Kirke, the king's messengers, could report that "the honorable governor [of Connecticut] carried himself very nobly to [them] and was very diligent to supply [them] with all manner of conveniences for the prosecution [of the fugitives] and promised that all search should be made after them, which was afterwards performed"; while they had to say that New Haven was "obstinate and pertinacious in contempt of his Majestie."[1]

The New Haven governor and magistrates anticipated trouble for the aid they had given the regicides, and six weeks after the fugitives had made their escape, solemnly proclaimed Charles II., acknowledging themselves to be "his Majesties legal and faithful subjects."[2] The New Haven authorities were not courtiers. The very issue of its proclamation shows that the colony was frightened at the outlook, and there is no doubt that many in authority

[1] *Hutchinson Papers*, II., 52–56.
[2] *New Haven Col. Records*, II., 420–423.

were discouraged because of the discontent that widely prevailed in the colony.

At the court session of New Haven, May 29, 1661, two occurrences foreshadowed the coming storm. Connecticut entered a vigorous and almost threatening protest against the work of a committee, appointed by the township of New Haven in April, 1660, to mark out the northern boundary of the town. Connecticut said that the bounds decided on were within her territory. This unexpected assertion—the first gun in the campaign for annexation—aroused the colony of New Haven to appoint a committee to treat with Connecticut regarding her "seeming right to this jurisdiction." The second occurrence was the demand of the non-freemen, once more expressed, for the privileges and liberties that were denied them. The magistrates refused to make any changes in their fundamental law, and warned "these disturbers of peace and troublers of Israel" against further "factious if not seditious" outbreaks of this character.[1]

When Charles II. came to the throne and an inquiry into franchises seemed imminent, Connecticut took definite action. In March, 1661, Winthrop draughted an address from the general court to the king, couched in those terms of intense loyalty and deep humility that Connecticut knew so well how to use when it served her purpose.[2] The general

---

[1] *New Haven Col. Records*, II., 403, 404, 409.
[2] Conn. Hist. Soc., *Collections*, I., 582, 583.

court also draughted a petition to the king, stating in frank and straightforward language exactly what it wanted. It authorized Winthrop, who was planning to go to England, to present the address and the petition and to obtain a renewal of the Warwick patent, the original of which had been lost in a fatal fire at Saybrook, or if possible to secure a charter, the terms of which it had already draughted. It appropriated for expenses a sum of £500, which Fenwick had, in 1657, bequeathed to the colony as compensation for his failure to complete the business of the patent.[1]

Thus equipped, Winthrop left New Amsterdam on July 23, 1661, and reached England by way of Holland in the autumn. His chances of success were many. He had unusual influence at the court of Charles II., through a warm personal friend in the aged Lord Say and Sele, of the Privy Council, a member of the council for plantations and a friend of Connecticut. Moreover, Winthrop was possessed of great tact and an attractive personality; he had travelled widely and had acquired the habits of courts and courtiers—in fact, so well known were his qualifications that Plymouth tried to obtain his services for a similar errand.[2]

Winthrop's cause was a good one. The home

---

[1] Trumbull, *Hist. of Conn.*, I., 542, 543; *Conn. Col. Records*, I., 327–329, 575.
[2] Mass. Hist. Soc., *Collections*, 5th series, I., 392, 394; Trumbull, *Hist. of Conn.*, I., 547.

government was well disposed towards Connecticut, a colony which dutifully proclaimed the king, was discreet in its attitude towards Whalley and Goffe, the regicides who had fled to New England, and gave no offence in matters of trade. There is nothing to show that Winthrop employed bribery, as some writers have thought, but there may be truth in the tradition that he presented to Charles II., at an opportune moment, a ring that Charles I. had given to Winthrop's father.[1] The king was, however, to no small extent guided in his decision by his advisers. The council for plantations and the legal advisers of the crown approved of Winthrop's request. The royal warrant was issued February 28, 1662, and the charter passed the great seal May 10.[2] One of the two copies which Winthrop obtained was sent home by way of Boston and "read publicly to the freemen," October 9, 1662. The other copy remained in England until after the revolution of 1689,[3] when it was brought to the colony, probably by Fitzjohn Winthrop, about 1698.

With few modifications the Connecticut charter of 1662 contained the essential features of the Fundamental Orders and such amendments to the Orders as had been made by the general court since

[1] Mather, *Magnalia* (ed. 1853), I., 158, 159.
[2] Conn. Hist. Soc., *Collections*, I., 52; and *Report*, 1899, pp. 17-20 (Hanaper office record).
[3] *Conn. Col. Records*, I., 369; A. C. Bates, in *Encyclopædia Americana*, art. "Charter Oak."

1639. The most important change concerned the representation of the towns, which henceforth, without regard to size or population, possessed practically equal representation in the legislative body.

Winthrop defined the boundaries of the colony, which he phrased in the terms of the Warwick patent,[1] giving to Connecticut all the territory from "the Narragansett River commonly called Narragansett Bay to the South Sea, bounded on the north by the Massachusetts line and on the south by the sea, with the islands thereunto adjoining"; a phrase interpreted in 1664 to include Long Island.[2]

On October 9, 1662, the court completed its organization under the charter and took measures to affirm its title to all the territory thus named. It extended its jurisdiction over Stamford, Greenwich, and Westchester, and over Southold and all other Long Island towns, thus attacking the claims of New Amsterdam on one side and New Haven on the other; and it warned Mystic and Pawtucket not to accept the jurisdiction of any other colony than itself, thus casting down the gauntlet to Rhode Island. To strengthen its position by making its liberties more attractive, it reduced the franchise qualification from £30 to £20. If there is any apology for the aggressiveness of Connecticut, it

[1] Mass. Hist. Soc., *Collections*, 5th series, IX., 33.
[2] *Conn. Col. Records*, I., 426, 427.

lies in the broader life and opportunity that her government offered to towns that had been compelled to submit, often unwillingly, to the narrower "liberties" of New Haven and Massachusetts.

CHAPTER IV

TERRITORIAL ADJUSTMENT IN NEW ENGLAND
(1662–1668)

NEW HAVEN was doomed. Not only was she legally unprotected and helpless, but she was without political or economic strength. The interests of the colony were largely mercantile, and its ventures had not proved successful. The attempt made in 1641 to establish a trading-post on the Delaware was frustrated by the Dutch and Swedes, involved a loss of £1000, and embarrassed many of the wealthiest men of the colony. Five years later the New Haven merchants, hitherto accustomed to deal with England through Boston, attempted to open a direct trade with the mother-country, and sent a ship laden with goods to the value of £5000. The ship, badly built and badly ballasted, foundered at sea, with all on board.

So great was the prevailing despondency that many New Haven colonists returned to England, and others considered favorably Cromwell's proposal to transport them to Jamaica.[1] This project was abandoned, however, and the majority of the

[1] Strong, in Amer. Hist. Assoc., *Report*, 1898, pp. 88–92. Cf. Tyler, *England in America*, chap. xv.

57

colonists remained in New England. During the year that followed, Indian attacks and massacres created additional dismay and discontent. The people of Stamford protested in vigorous language against the inefficiency of the jurisdiction, the heavy taxation, and the limitations of the government. Certain inhabitants of Southold, led by Captain John Young, showed a desire even at this time to break away from New Haven,[1] and consented to remain in the colony only after the Stamford malcontents had been fined and bound over to keep the peace.

The year 1653 was one of great excitement. Disaffected colonists spoke their minds freely regarding the narrow political privileges that New Haven offered. They objected to a government in which all political and civil and military offices were controlled by church-members, in which all judicial power was in the hands of magistrates, and trial by jury was forbidden. The unsuccessful business ventures, the decrease of population due to a falling off of immigration, the dangers from the Dutch and Indians, the quarrel with Massachusetts which threatened to break up the Confederation, the discontent due to the policy of the oligarchy that controlled the government — all these conditions contributed to New Haven's downfall as an independent colony.[2]

[1] *New Haven Col. Records*, II., 47–49, 51.
[2] See Maverick, *Description of New England*, in *N. E. Hist. and Gen. Reg.*, XXXIX., 45.

Such was the situation when in 1662 Connecticut obtained the charter giving her a legal title to
the territory of New Haven. Winthrop had drawn
the boundaries, but there is reason to believe
that he had expected to reach an arrangement
with New Haven whereby, for the sake of mutual
strength, union could be effected under the common
charter, and had even entered into an understanding with Governor Leete of that colony.[1] Winthrop probably underestimated the tenacious ad-
herence of Davenport and his party to the fundamental laws of the colony, and did not anticipate
the persistent *non possumus* that met every sug-
gestion of annexation. He probably failed to recognize also the strength of the party led by Bray
Rossiter, which demanded immediate and uncon-
ditional surrender to Connecticut.[2]

While New Haven was pondering, Connecticut
was acting. She granted the request of the people
of Stamford, Greenwich, and Southold, the latter of
whom in 1662, with entire disregard of the allegiance
they owed New Haven, asked to be admitted to
Connecticut's jurisdiction. When Rossiter and others of Guilford, on their individual accounts, without regard to the policy of town or colony, tendered
themselves and their estates to Connecticut, that colony accepted them and promised to protect them.[3]

[1] See letters in Atwater's *Hist. of New Haven*, 456-460, 484;
Steiner, in Amer. Hist. Assoc., *Report*, 1891, p. 216.

[2] *New Haven Col. Records*, II., 429, 454-456.

[3] *Conn. Col. Records*, I., 387.

This ill-judged and illegal attempt to force the issue drove the moderates of New Haven over to the side of the ultras, and led the New Haven court to decide that it would not consider the matter of union in any form unless Connecticut would order the men of Stamford and Guilford to return to their allegiance and recognize the integrity of the colony.[1] The court of New Haven addressed a temperate complaint to the United Commissioners, and, emboldened by a favorable reply,[2] took measures at once to assert authority in the colony by ordering Rossiter and his fellow-radicals to obey its commands.

A sort of deadlock ensued. Connecticut replied that if New Haven used force with Rossiter and his party, she would take it as done against herself; and New Haven could only reply, "Is this the way to union?"[3] Finally, in February, 1664, the committee appointed by Connecticut to take charge of the case promised to order the secessionists to return to allegiance, and declared that in the future all forcible actions would be "carefully shunned and all grievances would be buried."[4] This promise, however, was never ratified by the Connecticut court.

The controversy was finally ended by an unexpected event. Early in August, 1664, informa-

---

[1] *New Haven Col. Records*, II., 491, 516.
[2] *Plymouth Col. Records*, X., 308–310.
[3] *New Haven Col. Records*, II., 517–530.   [4] *Ibid.*, 516.

tion was received in New Haven that the king had granted to the duke of York the territory of New Netherland and all the region eastward to the Connecticut River. Rather than suffer the humiliation of annexation to New York, New Haven preferred to submit to Connecticut. One by one the towns withdrew, until in December only New Haven, Branford, and Guilford remained to represent the old jurisdiction. The freemen of these towns, a few from Milford, and as many others "as was pleased to come," finally met on December 13 and voted to submit "as from a necessity," but with a "*salvo jure* of former rights and claim, as a people who have not been heard in point of plea."[1] The colonial jurisdiction was dissolved; only the separate towns remained, and each independently joined Connecticut. Davenport withdrew to Boston, where he died in 1669. Many families migrated to New Jersey, and there founded the town of Newark, though it is an error to suppose that Branford or any other town migrated with its records.[2]

With Rhode Island, too, Connecticut came into controversy. That amphibious colony, numbering in 1660 not more than a thousand souls, had for thirty years struggled with its neighbors for the right to exist. Massachusetts, Plymouth, and Connecticut each laid claim to some part of its

[1] *New Haven Col. Records*, II., 551.
[2] So erroneously stated by Doyle, in *The Cambridge Modern History*, VII., 26.

territory. The union of the four towns in 1647 was but a loose compact, the conditions of which were never consistently observed by any of the settlements, to each of which the idea of a higher, sovereign power was exceedingly repugnant, "none submitting to supreme authority but as they please."[1] The inclination of the towns to reduce central authority to a minimum was as strong after 1647 as it had been before; and they looked on the general assembly and the general court of trials as inferior to their own town-meetings.

This tendency is illustrated by the career of William Coddington, who established a settlement on the island at Newport in 1639, which united with Portsmouth on the same island in 1640. The settlements increased rapidly in population and prosperity and outstripped the towns of the less fertile main-land.[2] The little community was speedily divided into parties: Coddington, Partridge, and others, chiefly of Portsmouth, composed one conservative and theocratic faction; while John Clarke, Easton, and their colleagues of Warwick and Providence, and some of Newport, liberal-minded and without definite religious affiliations, made up the other. In 1644, and again in 1648, Coddington applied for admission to the New England Confederation, but the Commissioners re-

[1] Maverick, *Description of New England*, in *N. E. Hist. and Gen. Reg.*, XXXIX., 44. Cf. Tyler, *England in America*, chap. xiv.
[2] Mass. Hist. Soc., *Collections*, 3d series, IX., 278.

fused the request, unless Rhode Island would come
in as part of Plymouth; but Newport, Warwick, and
Providence would not agree.[1]

Thwarted in his attempt to break up the colony,
Coddington appealed to England. He sailed from
Boston in January, 1649, and immediately applied
for a patent, with himself as governor. Only
Winslow, of Plymouth, opposed him,[2] and influential men worked in his favor, notably Rev.
Hugh Peters, the old enemy of Roger Williams,
with whom, Coddington wrote, "I was merry and
called him the Arch DD. of Canterbury . . . and
it passed very well."[3] Winslow could make out
no case for Plymouth, and in April, 1651, the
Council of State actually commissioned Coddington
governor of the island.[4]

He returned to the colony in triumph, only to
find the furious colonists declaring that he had
obtained his charter by falsehood, had brought upon
them "disturbances and distractions," and in getting
away the greater part of her territory had "undone
the colony."[5]

Steps were taken immediately to obtain a withdrawal of the commission, and Roger Williams and

[1] Mass. Hist. Soc., *Collections,* 3d series, IX., 23, 271; Narragansett Club, *Publications,* VI., 154.

[2] *Cal. of State Pap., Col.,* 1574 1660, pp. 335–338.

[3] Mass. Hist. Soc., *Collections,* 4th series, VII., 281–283.

[4] *Cal. of State Pap., Col.,* 1574–1660, p. 354.

[5] Narragansett Club, *Publications,* VI., 229, 267; *R. I. Col. Records,* I., 234; *Hutchinson Papers,* I., 237.

John Clarke were sent to England to secure a renewal of the patent of 1644.[1] Williams was warmly welcomed by Sir Harry Vane, who exerted himself loyally in his behalf. Inasmuch as Coddington had injured his cause by negotiating with the Dutch at New Amsterdam,[2] Williams and Clarke were successful in their mission: the patent of 1644 was confirmed and the inhabitants were ordered to "go on in the name of a colony" until a further investigation should be made.[3]

In the mean time exciting events were taking place on the island itself. Coddington's usurpation of authority was thoroughly distasteful to the men of Newport as well as to those of Warwick and Providence, and they raised the cry of treason and of conspiracy with the Dutch. In March, 1652, a party of islanders captured Partridge and hanged him. Coddington, helpless in the face of this organized discontent, appealed to Winthrop to come over and aid him; but without waiting for a reply he fled to Boston, where he surrendered the title deeds, and very unwillingly yielded all claim to the island by right of prior discovery.[4] His career as an independent governor was over, but nothing

[1] Narragansett Club, *Publications*, VI., 200, 228–232; *R. I. Col. Records*, I., 234.
[2] *N. Y. Docs. Rel. to Col. Hist.*, I., 497; Mass. Hist. Soc., *Collections*, 4th series, VII., 283.
[3] Narragansett Club, *Publications*, VI., 236, 254.
[4] Mass. Hist. Soc., *Collections*, 4th series, VII., 284; *R. I. Col. Records*, I., 50.

further was done by the authorities at home to settle the controversy.[1]

For three years Rhode Island was divided into two separate, self-governing parts,[2] and the patent of 1644 was held in abeyance. But in 1654 the main-land made overtures to the island for a union, and as the result of this appeal, in May, 1654, committees from each of the towns met at Warwick for the purpose of establishing once more a union under the old patent. Roger Williams was chosen president, and all agreed to let by-gones be by-gones. In 1656 the last trace of civil conflict was erased: Coddington made formal submission to the authority of the colony; the record of his transactions was expunged from the journal; and the incident was declared closed.[3]

The history of the united colony of Rhode Island for the next six years was in the main peaceful, though controversies among the inhabitants of the towns were not infrequent, and disputes with Massachusetts and Connecticut about boundaries were common. With the accession of Charles II, fears naturally arose that the restored Stuart might listen to the appeal of Rhode Island's neighbors and bring to an end the separate existence of the colony. The general court of Rhode Island proclaimed the king at once,

---

[1] Narragansett Club, *Publications*, VI., 254, 255.

[2] *Providence Records*, I., 76; *Portsmouth Records*, 61, 62; *R. I. Col. Records*, I., 273.

[3] Narragansett Club, *Publications*, VI., 294 and note; *R. I. Col. Records*, I., 328–333.

put on record its "unfayned humble affection" for his Majesty, and instructed John Clarke, who was still in England, to agitate for a charter.[1] Clarke sent two petitions to the king for a "more absolute, ample, and free charter of civil incorporation," and laid special stress upon the fact that Rhode Island was the guardian of that "freedom of conscience" which Charles himself had upheld in the proclamation from Breda.[2] The petitions were well received and were transmitted by the king to his council in March, 1661.

Months passed and nothing further was heard of the matter, for Winthrop, in behalf of Connecticut, brought weightier influences to bear for the establishment of boundaries that conflicted with Rhode Island's claims. But there is no reason for believing that Winthrop knew of Clarke's petition or was in any way responsible for the delay.[3] Clarke was equally ignorant at first of Winthrop's mission, and made no protest against the granting of Connecticut's charter until after it had passed the seals;[4] but he saw Winthrop before the charter was despatched to America, and made clear to him the manifest injustice of the proposed boundaries. Winthrop having agreed to leave the matter to a board of arbitrators, the question was debated pro and con, in

[1] R. I. Col. Records, I., 432, 433, 441.
[2] Cal. of State Pap., Col., 1661–1668, §§ 10, 18; R. I. Col. Records, I., 485–491.
[3] Mass. Hist. Soc., Collections, 5th series, VIII., 75; IX., 34.
[4] Ibid., IX., 33.

the presence of Clarendon, the lord chancellor, and on April 7, 1663, a decision was rendered in favor of Rhode Island.[1] The boundary - line between the two colonies was fixed at the Pawcatuck River, which henceforth was called the Narragansett, so that it might not be necessary to recall and alter Connecticut's charter.

Even with this difficulty settled, a further delay ensued. Apparently Clarendon and the king were not satisfied with certain expressions in the draught of the Rhode Island charter. They called in Winthrop, and seem to have discussed the matter with him. Whatever the exact trouble was—perhaps the question of religious toleration—the chancellor does not appear to have pressed the point, and no changes were made in the text of the document. The warrant was issued by the king, and the charter passed the seals in July, 1663, rather "upon the good opinion and confidence" that the king and Clarendon had in Winthrop than because of entire satisfaction with the provisions of the charter itself.[2]

The precious document was sent to Rhode Island by Captain Baxter, and there, November 24, 1663, was "held up on high with becoming gravity in the sight of the people."[3] The grateful deputies voted liberally their thanks to the king and Clarendon

---

[1] *R. I. Col. Records*, I., 518; Mass. Hist. Soc., *Collections*, 5th series, VIII., 82.

[2] *N. Y. Docs. Rel. to Col. Hist.*, III., 55.

[3] *R. I. Col. Records*, I., 509.

and made grants of money to Clarke and Baxter. The charter began the unification of the colony. By 1680 centralization prevailed, and the general assembly gathered to itself much of the power formerly exercised by the towns. From the circumstances of its early history, the executive in Rhode Island since that time has always been subordinate to the legislature.

The granting of the charters to Connecticut and Rhode Island made but little difference in the government and life of the colonies, but it gave them a unity and a legal standing which they had hitherto lacked. Each colony clung to its charter with remarkable tenacity and venerated it as the palladium of its liberties. The people of these colonies had good reason to cherish their fundamental instruments, for they were remarkable documents. Though clothed in the phraseology of trading charters, they were in reality constitutions of government unlike anything seen in commercial charters before; and they sanctioned principles of government that no trading company had ever possessed and no Stuart could ever have defended. They embodied the levelling doctrines of the rank and file of the army in the days of the second civil war — doctrines that had been rejected as subversive of government, not only by Charles I., but also by Cromwell and the Rump Parliament. Wittingly or unwittingly, Charles II. gave his approval of the doctrines contained in the Agreement

of the People of 1648 and 1649, and in so doing
encouraged and gave legal warrant to democratic
government in America.

While these changes were taking place in New
England, Charles II. and Clarendon were considering the advisability of sending a special commission to investigate the condition of the New
England colonies and to settle the many disputes
that had arisen regarding the boundaries and other
matters of controversy there. In April, 1664, a
commission was created, consisting of Colonel Richard Nicolls, the governor appointed for the as yet
uncaptured New Netherland; Colonel Robert Carr,
a burly and tactless English officer; Colonel George
Cartwright, a well-meaning soldier, unversed in the
arts of diplomacy; and Samuel Maverick, an old
resident of Boston and *persona ingrata* to the men
of Massachusetts Bay.

The three colonels, fully instructed and intrusted
with a business of unusual delicacy, embarked in
June on the ships commissioned by the king to
seize New Netherland. They were sent to effect the
capture of that colony; to induce New England to
submit peacefully to the king; to heal factional
strife; to settle boundary questions, to inquire into
the laws, manners, and customs of the various
governments; and to find out how to make the
colonies more profitable to the crown.[1]

Had Clarendon selected his men as shrewdly as

[1] *N. Y. Docs. Rel. to Col. Hist.*, III., 55 61.

he drew up their instructions, the undertaking might have been moderately successful; but Nicolls was the only one of the four with any sense of the situation. Carr and Cartwright possessed neither tact nor statesmanship, and Maverick was not likely to have much influence in New England. So far as Connecticut and Rhode Island were concerned, the commissioners had no reason to anticipate trouble, for the recent grant of the charters smoothed their path with the authorities in those colonies. Plymouth also was certain to be friendly, for that colony was hoping for a charter of its own and could not afford to offend the king. The result justified these expectations. Each of these colonies welcomed the commissioners with "great expressions of loyalty," and suffered them to hear complaints and settle disputes "to the great satisfaction of all."[1] In their report the commissioners spoke highly of these colonies, declaring that among them they had had as great success as the most sanguine could have hoped for.[2]

With Massachusetts the case was different. Nicolls and Cartwright presented their credentials in Boston in July, 1664; and as their demand was only for troops and the repeal of the franchise law, they got on well enough, Massachusetts evidently expecting soon to be rid of them. But in February, 1665, Cartwright and Carr returned, and the first

[1] *Mass. Col. Records*, IV., pt. i., 174–176.
[2] *N. Y. Docs. Rel. to Col. Hist.*, III., 96, 97.

interviews were stormy, Massachusetts vehemently
denying their right to hear appeals or to exercise
any jurisdiction whatever, on the ground that such
acts conflicted with the colony's right under the
charter. In May, Nicolls came on from New York,
and for more than three weeks the matter in question was debated between the commissioners on
one side and the general court on the other. The
magistrates argued every point at length, refusing
to recognize any abuses in their government or the
right of the commissioners to assume any of their
prerogatives.[1] Finally, the commissioners, angry
and baffled, brought the conferences to an end, and,
leaving everything unsettled, journeyed northward
to Piscataway and soon afterwards returned to England.

The colony had saved its rights of government
at the expense of its reputation in England, and the
impression gained ground that Massachusetts was on
the eve of rebellion. In their report the commissioners advised the king to adopt a policy of coercion,
and Charles II., in his reply to the commissioners,
took occasion to rebuke the colony sharply for its
want of respect to those whom he had sent intrusted
with his commands. But the king went no further,
for Clarendon, suspecting that the commissioners
had not used as much tact as they ought, bade the

---

[1] *Mass. Col. Records*, IV., pt. i., 177–234; *N. Y. Docs. Rel.
to Col. Hist.*, III., 93–100; Hutchinson, *Hist. of Mass. Bay*, I.,
230–250.

colony send agents to England with authority to settle there the questions in dispute.[1] Though for the moment Massachusetts escaped an attack upon her prerogatives, the slight which she had inflicted upon the king's representatives was not easily or soon forgotten.

The fall of Clarendon in 1667 probably saved the colony. The king was appeased by extraordinary protestations of loyalty from the Massachusetts general court and the present of twenty-six "great masts," which the colony sent as evidence of its affection.[2] Taking advantage of this lull in the storm, Massachusetts resumed control over the county of York, that portion of Maine claimed by the heirs of Sir Ferdinando Gorges, which the commissioners, as almost their last act, had removed from the jurisdiction of the colony. A special committee was appointed by the Lords of Trade to investigate this piece of presumption,[3] but eventually Massachusetts was left in full possession of the territory. Never did the colony seem more secure than at this time: its authority extended from Sagadahoc to Hingham and into the interior westward as far as the Connecticut River; the French and Indians were quiet; trade was unchecked by any serious attempt to enforce the navigation acts;

---

[1] *Cal. of State Pap., Col.*, 1661–1668, §§ 1171, 1174.
[2] *Ibid.*, § 1797.
[3] *Mass. Col. Records*, IV., pt. i., 371; *Cal. of State Pap., Col.*, 1669–1674, §§ 59, 82, 184, 439, 512.

and a spirit of industry and contentment brooded over the colony.[1] Resistance to the king's commissioners seemed to have been a wise and successful policy.

[1] Hutchinson, *Hist. of Mass. Bay*, I., 269.

CHAPTER V

NEW AMSTERDAM BECOMES NEW YORK

(1652–1672)

THE re-adjustment of affairs in New England was only one phase of that revived interest in trade and colonization which characterized the period of the Restoration in England and attracted the attention, not only of the merchants, but also of men of high rank and official prominence. Preeminently important at this time were the commercial supremacy of the Dutch and the presence of a Dutch colony in America lying midway between New England and Maryland. On the eastern seaboard, the Dutch occupied the most advantageous position, and their claims stretched eastward to Cape Cod and southward to Cape Henlopen on the farther side of Delaware Bay.[1] In one direction they came into conflict with New Haven, Connecticut, and Rhode Island, and in the other with the Swedes and Lord Baltimore; they controlled the trade of the Five Nations; and, from England's point of view, they offered a tempting opportunity to planters and

[1] *Plymouth Col. Records*, IX., 146, 147, 210–214; *N. Y. Docs. Rel. to Col. Hist.*, I., 288–292.

traders to sell tobacco contrary to the navigation acts and to defraud the king of his revenues. To deprive the Dutch of their power and their opportunity in America was, therefore, a necessary part of England's policy as shaped by Cromwell and carried out by Charles II.

Had the expedition of Major Sedgwick against New Amsterdam in 1652 been carried out, the Dutch must surely have been beaten then and there; for the Dutch colony had taken no firm root in America, and lacking both political and social unity, was in no condition at that time to resist an attacking force from England and her colonies. Peter Stuyvesant, who became director of the colony in 1647, was an energetic ruler, but he alienated the burghers by his domineering methods and by his attempts to keep the control of government in the hands of himself and the council. His inability to carry out his plans made his own position weak. At the very beginning of his administration the need of financial support forced him to listen to the burghers' demand for a share in their government and to establish a board of nine men representing the people, who should confer with him in all matters concerning the city (1647).[1] This board became a centre of municipal discontent, and the quarrels which ensued ended in 1653 in the grant

---

[1] Jameson, "Government of New York City" (*Magazine of Amer. Hist.*, VIII., pt. i., 326); text of charter in O'Callaghan, *Hist. of New Neth.*, I., 37–39.

of a municipal charter for the city, which made New Amsterdam independent of the government of the rest of the island of Manhattan.

Yet Stuyvesant's policy rendered any efficient self-government for the city impossible, and the burgomaster and schepens exercised very little actual authority, their functions being chiefly judicial.[1] Opposed by his own countrymen, Stuyvesant came to depend on the English residents within the colony; but they, forbidden by the States-General of Holland to hold office, were never a certain support. The fort on the southern point of the city fell into decay; the burghers, phlegmatic in temperament, refused to listen to Stuyvesant's passionate appeals for aid in defending the town; and the Dutch West India Company seemed wholly unwilling to spend any money in behalf of its colony. Consequently, the last years of Dutch rule were characterized by friction in political and social matters, by neglect of military defence, and a gradual waning of Dutch colonial prestige.

Stuyvesant watched with great concern the gradual advance of the English. After the grant of the charter of 1662 Connecticut, notwithstanding the treaty of Hartford of 1650, claimed all the territory between Stamford and Westchester, as well as the whole of Long Island.[2] Stuyvesant

[1] *Records of New Amsterdam*, I., 49.
[2] *Conn. Col. Records*, I., 406; *N. Y. Docs. Rel. to Col. Hist.*, II., 217.

truly said in reply to the demands of Connecticut that, even if New Netherland should cede Westchester and all Long Island, it would not satisfy the aggressors, whose object was to drive the Dutch entirely from America.[1] For ten years the Dutch and the English, though nominally at peace, were actually engaged in a persistent commercial and colonial war.[2] Englishmen never forgot the massacre of Amboyna in 1623, whereby the Dutch had driven them out of the Spice Islands; and complaints by the score came from English residents of Long Island for injuries done to English trade and revenue by the Dutch in New Amsterdam.[3] Influential men like Sir George Downing kept up a fire of criticism and comment hostile to Holland; and the founding of the Royal African Company in 1661 gave rise to new conflicts at Cabo-Corso castle (Cape Verd) and on the Guinea coast.[4]

Impressed with the belief that the Dutch were injuring England's commerce, the council for plantations took the matter in hand, and in July, 1663, with Sir John Berkeley as its presiding officer, bade the complainants bring in a report proving their charges, and appointed a special committee, composed of Berkeley, Carteret, and William Coventry, secretary to the duke of York, to report re-

---

[1] Thurloe, *State Papers*, V., 81.
[2] *N. Y. Docs. Rel. to Col. Hist.*, II., 385–393; III., 230–231; *Plymouth Col. Records*, X., 302–304.
[3] *N. Y. Docs. Rel. to Col. Hist.*, III., 46.
[4] *Cal. of State Pap., Col.*, 1661–1668, § 618, 1668–1674, § 936.

garding the feasibility of an attack on the Dutch territory in America. The committee made inquiry of residents of Long Island who were in London, and in January, 1664, reported that the overthrow of the colony could be easily effected. The following six months furnish a remarkable chapter in the history of English aggression. English statesmen and merchants were thoroughly aroused against the Dutch. The duke of York and his personal friends—Clarendon, Carteret, and Berkeley—were leaders of the movement, the duke showing his active interest by frequently conferring with the merchants, encouraging the merchant companies, and doing all in his power to hinder the Dutch trade.[1]

Under the guidance of these men the conspiracy against the Dutch made rapid progress. Berkeley and Carteret submitted their report in January, 1664; in February James obtained of his brother a grant of £4000 to undertake the conquest, and on March 12, 1664, received a royal charter of the territory, which by the king's special instruction was rushed through the seals with extraordinary rapidity in less than two weeks, the forms which usually preceded the king's warrant in this case not being necessary.[2] On March 26 the House of Commons resolved that an investigation should be made into the causes of the decay of trade, and authorized

[1] Clark, *Life of James Second*, I., 399–401.
[2] *Cal. of State Pap., Col.*, 1661–1668, §§ 675, 685.

the committee of trade to look into the matter.[1]
The committee bade the merchant companies state
their grievances and propose a remedy;[2] and on
April 1, 1664, the merchants declared that the
Dutch were the greatest enemies to the trade of
the kingdom.

On April 2, James commissioned Richard Nicolls,
groom of his bedchamber, to be lieutenant-governor
of the yet unconquered territory in America;[3] and on
April 21, Parliament accepted the report of the committee based on the statements of the merchants,
and justified the king's assertion that both houses
were in "good humor" and ready to "pawn their
estates to maintain a war."[4] The king opposed
war with Holland, but believed that the Dutch were
the aggressors and that he had a legitimate complaint
against the Dutch East and West India companies,
particularly in America, for, he said, New Amsterdam "did belong to England heretofore, but the
Duch by degrees drove our people out of it."[5]
On April 23 he sent to the government of New
England an announcement of his determination to
conquer New Netherland, and appointed the commission, consisting of Nicolls, Cartwright, Carr, and
Maverick, to go to America to investigate the

[1] *Cal. of State Pap., Dom.*, 1663–1664, § 531.
[2] *Ibid.*, § 541.
[3] *Cal. of State Pap., Col.*, 1661–1668, § 695.
[4] *Cal. of State Pap., Dom.*, 1663 – 1664, § 562; Cartwright,
Madame, Memoirs of the Princess Henrietta, 158, 160.
[5] Cartwright, *Madame*, 176.

situation.[1]   In June James, probably at the urgent
request of his friends, divided the territory granted
him by the king, and gave the region between the
Hudson and the Delaware to Carteret and Berkeley.
A month later, though England and Holland were
at peace, Nicolls and his fleet of four vessels started
for America to conquer the territory thus summarily
disposed of.   A more unprincipled series of secret
actions against a friendly nation, whose only
offence was greater success in commerce, can hardly
be imagined.

The territory thus assigned included all the area
"beginning at a certain place called St. Croix, next
adjoining to New Scotland in America," and extending westward to the Kennebec River and northward to Canada; also, all the territory lying between the Connecticut and Delaware rivers, together
with Long Island, Martha's Vineyard, and Nan-
tucket.   For ten years the islands last named
had been independent of any outside jurisdiction,
having been governed by a certain Thomas Mayhew
and his son, who derived their authority from
Stirling and Gorges, original patentees of the New
England council.   Of the entire territory the portion occupied by the Dutch, extending from Fort
Orange on the north to Delaware Bay on the south,
was by far the most important, and its centre and
key was the city of New Amsterdam.

As the duke of York and his colleagues must have

[1] *N. Y. Docs. Rel. to Col. Hist.*, II., 237; III., 51–61, 63.

anticipated from their preliminary study of the
situation, the city fell an easy prey to the fleet.
Stuyvesant wished to fight. When he received from
Nicolls the letter demanding the surrender of the
city he tore it in pieces and in a storm of wrath
stamped upon the torn fragments, and declared to
the members of the council that he would never
yield. But the phlegmatic burghers refused to support him, and, gathering the pieces of the letter,
they read the communication and answered it with
a flag of truce. August 26, 1664, the English occupied the city.[1] Cartwright was sent to capture
Fort Orange, and Carr was despatched to the
Delaware to capture Fort Amstel, which he did in
an unnecessarily brutal manner. Nicolls, the only
efficient statesman among the four commissioners,
made every effort to conciliate the defeated burghers
and to build up the colony, for by the terms of the
capitulation the Dutch were allowed to keep their
property and to remain in the colony if they chose,
to have liberty of conscience and worship, to retain
their own customs, and to enjoy all the privileges
of English subjects.[2]

Towards Connecticut Nicolls displayed the same
liberality; instead of attempting to carry out
literally the terms of the duke of York's patent,

---

[1] *Records of New Amsterdam*, V., 114–116; Brodhead, *Hist.
of New York*, I., 20–37.
[2] *N. Y. Docs. Rel. to Col. Hist.*, II., 250–253; Munsell, *Annals
of Albany*, IV., 28; Smith, *Hist. of New York*, I., 28.

which would have cost Connecticut all her territory west of the Connecticut River, he compromised
on a line drawn north-northwest from a point on
the coast twelve miles east of the Hudson River.
Though the Connecticut men who accepted this
arrangement lost Long Island, they managed to
add a few miles of territory west of the line previously agreed to by the Dutch, and, had the northwest line ever been allowed, would have carried
their frontier across the Hudson River. The line
was subjected to severe scrutiny at a later time, and
Connecticut was forced eventually to retire within
the boundary provided for in the treaty of Hartford.[1]

The duke of York, as proprietary of the new
colony, was intrusted with full and absolute power
to govern and administer his province according to
such laws and ordinances as he might choose to
establish, but on condition that all laws be agreeable to those of England and appeals allowed to the
king in council from all judgments of the colonial
courts. The proprietary could appoint a governor
and other officers authorized to administer the
province under such laws and methods of government as seemed to him fit and suitable and not
contrary to the laws of England, and he could
regulate trade as he pleased within the territory of

[1] Bowen, *Boundary Disputes of Connecticut*, 69, 70; Smith,
Hist. of New York, I., 36; N. Y. State Library, *Bulletin, History*
No. 2, p. 135; N. Y. State Historian, *Report*, 1896, pp. 143, 144.

the grant. That James himself determined the leading points of this patent we cannot doubt.

Under the provisions of the grant, Nicolls governed with fairness and wisdom. He promptly Anglicized the different portions of his colony, calling New Amsterdam New York, Fort Orange Albany, New Amstel New Castle, the region west of the Hudson River Albania; and erecting Long Island, Staten Island, and Westchester into the district of Yorkshire. He organized a system of judicial districts, or ridings, but it was not until 1683 that the province was divided into counties.[1]

He attempted to increase the population of Albania by offering favorable conditions to settlers; he encouraged the trade of the colony by increasing merchant shipping; he made treaties with the Indians; and he urged the Long Island people to settle their boundary difficulties, and to live peacefully among themselves. Even the Dutch testified to the "gentleness, wisdom, and intelligence" with which he managed the government,[2] and his fellow - commissioner Maverick wrote to Arlington that Nicolls had acquired "great repute and honor," and had "kept persons of different judgments and divers nations in place when a great part of the world was in wars." "As to the Indians," he added, "they were never brought into such a peaceful

---

[1] *Colonial Laws of New York*, I., 121.
[2] *Records of New Amsterdam*, V., 160–162.

posture and fair correspondence as they now are."[1]

In all that related to law and government Nicolls was restricted by definite instructions from the duke, who was opposed to self-government in any form, and not only caused any mention of a representative assembly to be omitted from the royal charter, but specially instructed his governor to model the government of the city of New York after that of a municipal corporation in England. Under these instructions Nicolls had to establish a government in city and province in which the people as a whole had no share. In 1665 he granted a charter to the city, inaugurating a government of the familiar English type, in accordance with which mayor, aldermen, and sheriff were appointed by the lieutenant-governor, but were given power to make by-laws, to name inferior officers, and to sit as a final court in all cases involving forty shillings or less. Though the charter favored the freemen of the city by bestowing upon them a monopoly of trade, it made the lieutenant-governor the supreme authority under the duke and denied to the people the privilege of self-government.[2]

Inasmuch as the royal charter made no provision for representative government such as appeared in other proprietary charters, Nicolls was unable to

[1] *N. Y. Docs. Rel. to Col. Hist.*, III., 173, 174.
[2] Jameson, "Government of New York City" (*Magazine of Amer. Hist.*, VIII., pt. ii., 598–611).

place the draughting of a code of laws in the hands
of an elected legislative body, and was compelled
himself to draw up as fairly as possible such laws
as seemed to him reasonable and necessary. These
laws, later known as the Duke's Laws, were intended mainly for the residents of Westchester and
Long Island, where a majority of the inhabitants
were Englishmen. In carrying out his task Nicolls
copied many provisions from the codes of New
Haven and Massachusetts, introduced many Dutch
customs, and added some peculiarities of his own.
The laws made no provision for town-meetings, freemen, and schools; and instead of the "townsmen"
whom the English had been accustomed to choose to
manage their prudential affairs, elective officers were
established—a constable and eight overseers—with
limited powers, somewhat after the fashion of the
Dutch village communities. Absolute toleration in
matters of religion was allowed, and land-holding instead of church membership was made the qualification of voters.[1] Thus the code, admirably drawn
in many particulars and liberal in all that concerned
religion and the suffrage, distinctly curtailed the
political privileges which the inhabitants of the
English towns had hitherto enjoyed. Such an in-
novation was certain in the end to make trouble.

After draughting his laws, Nicolls, in February,
1665, issued a proclamation bidding the people of the
towns of Long Island send deputies to Hempstead,

[1] McKinley, in *Amer. Hist. Review*, VI., 704-718.

promising them "freedom and immunities" equal to those possessed by the New England colonies.[1] When the deputies came together they discovered for the first time that their business was simply to sanction without addition or amendment a body of laws already drawn up. Some demurred, but opposition was useless; all eventually gave their consent and scattered to their homes without further protest. Afterwards, roused by the criticisms of their townspeople, they issued a "narrative and remonstrance," in which they demanded a reconsideration of those provisions of the code which concerned the election of magistrates, the levying of taxes, and the control of the militia— the provisions most objectionable to the Long-Islanders.[2] Nicolls answered that he could do nothing for them and that they would have to go to the king if they wanted further privileges; a reply with which the deputies seem to have been content.

The people did not view the matter in quite the same light as the deputies. The towns of western as of eastern Long Island understood "immunities" to mean political liberties.[3] Hence, after the Hempstead meeting discontent prevailed widely. Many of the people refused to pay taxes; towns

[1] *N. Y. Docs. Rel. to Col. Hist.*, XIV., 564, 565; N. Y. State Library, *Bulletin, History* No. 2, 154, 155; *Southold Records*, I., 357, 358.

[2] Thompson, *Hist. of Long Island*, II., 323–326.

[3] N. Y. State Historian, *Report*, 1897, pp. 241, 242; *Southold Records*, I., 358, 359.

refused to elect officers according to the provisions
of the Duke's Laws; trouble arose over the officering
of the militia, and some prominent Long-Islanders
spoke their minds so freely as to bring upon them
penalties for seditious utterances.[1]   When Nicolls
was succeeded by Governor Lovelace, in 1668, the
towns of western Long Island renewed the attack,
and sent in a petition craving redress of grievances
and asking that their "deputies be joined with the
governor and council in making the laws of the
government"; but Lovelace, with less tact than
Nicolls had displayed, bade them remember that he
had no authority to grant their request, and that
it was their business to be obedient and submissive
to the authority of the duke.[2]

The Puritans, however, were not inclined to accept
this advice, and a further opportunity soon arose
for them to show their spirit. The fort in New
York had fallen into decay, and in 1670 Lovelace
and the court of assizes took into consideration the
question of how it could best be repaired "to the
ease and satisfaction of the inhabitants."[3]   Before
any tax was levied for this purpose Flushing, Hempstead, and Jamaica — and later Huntington — took
fright and called town meetings, which draughted
strongly worded protests against any attempt to
impose taxes upon them without their consent.[4]

[1] N. Y. Docs. Rel. to Col. Hist., XIV., 576, 578, 579; Waller,
Hist. of Flushing, 62–66; Brodhead, Hist. of New York, I., 108.
[2] N. Y. Docs. Rel. to Col. Hist., XIV., 631, 632.
[3] Ibid., 646.   [4] Huntington Records, I., 163, 164.

Lovelace was so angry at receiving these "scandalous, illegal, and seditious addresses" that he ordered them to be openly and publicly burned before the town - house in New York, an action to which the council and the justices of the peace gave their approval.[1] Nevertheless, the addresses were not without their effect; for, two years later, when the same question came up again, Lovelace sent to the towns a very temperate address asking for voluntary contributions.[2] The western towns, appeased, responded promptly and liberally, but the eastern towns remained obdurate.

Both Southampton and Southold refused to renew their patents in 1669;[3] and when Lovelace, in October, 1670, declared that unless they did so their lands would be forfeited, they joined with Easthampton and sent a petition to the king begging that they might be annexed to Connecticut. Hearing nothing from this petition, the three towns, in June, 1672, drew up a statement agreeing to contribute to the repairing of the fort "if they might have the privileges that other of his majesty's subjects in these parts have and do enjoy."[4] Evidently the towns sent some contribution to New York with their statement, for when their letter was read Lovelace promised to answer it and "to take notice of the meanness of their contribution and the

[1] *N. Y. Docs Rel. to Col. Hist.*, XIV., 646, 647.   [2] *Ibid.*, 667.

[3] N. Y. State Historian, *Report*, 1896, p. 356; *N. Y. Docs. Rel. to Col. Hist.*, III., 197, 198.

[4] *Easthampton Records*, I., 346.

seeming condition of it." [1] Thus ended the first attempt of the people of New York to obtain redress of grievances before granting supplies.

In 1673 war again broke out between England and Holland, and in August of that year a Dutch fleet recaptured New York and restored, though only temporarily, the authority of the Dutch. This event gave to the three Long Island towns a new opportunity to obtain the desired liberties. They refused to take the oath of fidelity to the Dutch government, and an attempt of the governor, Colve, to subdue them by force failed because of the intervention of Connecticut. The towns remained independent of all higher jurisdiction until in May, 1674, the court at Hartford appointed a commission with "magistratical power" to hold a county court for them on Long Island. [2] In June, anticipating a return to the jurisdiction of the duke of York, they drew up a petition to the king, begging to be allowed to remain as they were, [3] but it is doubtful if the petition was ever sent, for in December, 1674, a month after the English had again taken possession of New York, they were compelled, very much against their will, to submit to the authority of the duke of York's government. [4] Thus Southampton, Easthampton, and Southold failed in their attempt to secure the greater political privileges that the colony of Connecticut enjoyed.

[1] N. Y. Docs. Rel. to Col. Hist., XIV., 668.
[2] Conn. Col. Records, II., 229.   [3] Easthampton Records, I., 370.
[4] N. Y. Docs. Rel. to Col. Hist., XIV., 681–685.

CHAPTER VI

THE PROVINCE OF NEW YORK
(1674–1686)

THE capture and occupation of the province by the Dutch proved only an interlude in the history of the colony. Colve, the Dutch governor, was an able man, and had he been supported by the Dutch authorities at home, might have held New Orange (as he called New York) against the English. But the fate of the province was settled in Europe and not in America. News of the conquest and of the hopeful condition of the city was late in reaching The Hague.[1] On February 19, 1674, by the treaty of Westminster, the province was returned to Charles II., and in October was formally surrendered to Major Edmund Andros, who had been appointed governor by the duke of York. Andros, the son of a Guernsey gentleman belonging to the household of Charles I., was at this time a young man thirty-seven years of age. Having spent his life in the environment of camp and court in the service of the king, he brought to New York the habits of a soldier and the sympathies of a Stuart devotee. He was

---

[1] *N. Y. Docs. Rel. to Col. Hist.*, II., 526–530.

a kindly man in his personal and domestic relations, but narrow in his views of government and
limited in his abilities as an executive. Like his
superior, the duke of York, he had no sense of
humor, no appreciation of the condition of the
English in America, and no tolerance for political
views that differed from his own.

Like his predecessors, Nicolls and Lovelace,
Andros was the governor of a wide-stretching,
irregularly shaped province, without unity, either
territorial or ethnic. It was peopled by English,
Dutch, and Swedes, and, though adapted to trade,
was not suited for compact and uniform administration or for rapid growth in population and in
well-rooted political institutions. Though ten years
of association had done something to harmonize the
customs and practices of the varied regions included
in New York, uniformity was impossible. The
colony, deprived of the broad lands of Connecticut
and the Jerseys, and cut off from rapid expansion
northward by the Indians, was hindered in its
growth, and remained for half a century backward
in its development.

Andros did what he could to unite the scattered
portions of his colony. He reduced the towns of
eastern Long Island in December, 1674, and in June
following carried out the express instructions of the
duke by attempting to seize that portion of Connecticut named in the duke's charter as within his
jurisdiction. Connecticut met charter with charter,

and when Andros persisted in his claim and with three vessels went to Saybrook ostensibly to protect the colony, he found a Connecticut force there. Though he felt that Connecticut ought to be annexed to New York, he did no more than state the duke's claim and sail away to Southold and the eastern islands.[1] He made a similar attempt to annex the Jerseys, but with no better success.

Though he failed in these two ventures, which have laid him open, very unjustly, to the charge of playing the tyrant, he succeeded remarkably well in his efforts to guard his province against attacks of the Indians during King Philip's War. Not only did he prevent inroads upon New York, but he sent powder to Rhode Island and a sloop to Maine, and would have aided Massachusetts and Connecticut had not these colonies, suspicious of his intentions, refused his proffered assistance.[2]

Andros was the appointee of an able but narrow-minded prince, who had no sympathy for popular government, but who for the sake of his revenues was anxious to promote the prosperity of his colony. James instructed his governor to use his power "for the protection and benefit of the province, for the encouragement of planters and plantations and the improvement of trade and commerce, and for the preservation of religion, justice, and equity among

[1] *Documentary Hist. of New York*, I., 153, 187; *Conn. Col. Records*, II., 569–574.
[2] *N. Y. Docs. Rel. to Col. Hist.*, III., 254.

them,"[1] instructions which Andros fully carried out.
He repaired and beautified houses and streets,
improved the social, moral, and religious condition
of the people, and gave time and attention to the
problems of excise, revenue, currency, and, above
all, of trade. The more his career is studied the
more the conviction grows that, as compared with
many other colonial governors, he was upright,
sympathetic, and faithful. He certainly was not
a great man, or, like Nicolls, he would have won
the respect of the people whom he governed; but
he never lost the confidence of his superiors, and elsewhere and at other times would doubtless have
earned an honorable reputation as a soldier and
administrator.

Nor was Andros an enemy of representative assemblies, but he probably viewed the matter, as did
many other English statesmen of his time, from
the practical rather than from the theoretical stand-
point. At the outset of his administration the people of Jamaica — and probably of other towns—
asked that deputies from the towns should be
summoned at least once a year to sit with the
governor and council in New York.[2] In his letters
to the duke, Andros urged the desirability of granting
these requests, but James would hear nothing of it;
he had his own ideas of what good government
ought to be, and was satisfied with the New York

[1] *N. Y. Docs. Rel. to Col. Hist.*, III., 216.
[2] N. Y. State Historian, *Report*, 1897, pp. 240-242.

system as it was. A representative assembly, he answered, was inconsistent with the form of government established for New York, and to summon one would be a dangerous matter, "nothing being more known than the aptness of such bodies to assume to themselves many privileges which prove destructive to or very oft disturb the peace of the government wherein they are allowed." [1] New York, therefore, remained for six years longer the only colony in which the people had no share in their government.

In 1681 James was compelled to reconsider his decision because of the danger of loss of revenue. The merchants of New York took advantage of his neglect to renew the customs duties, which had been in force since 1674, and refused to pay them. Fenwick in West New Jersey refused in like manner to pay the five per cent. duty which Andros levied on all goods brought up the Delaware; and Philip Carteret denied his right to levy duties in the harbors of East New Jersey for the benefit of the proprietary. Reports began to come in that the receipts of the province were falling off, and immediately James ordered Andros to return to England to answer these reports. Under the weak rule of the deputy, Brockholls, the province fell into further disorder; trade continued to decline and the duke's revenues to decrease, and every indication seemed to show that as a producer of profit to the propri-

[1] *N. Y. Docs. Rel. to Col. Hist.*, III., 230, 235.

etary the autocratic system of government had failed.[1]

The revolt of the merchants was accompanied with wide - spread disaffection among the people. Penn's grant of self-government and free-trade to the colonists of Pennsylvania in 1682 increased the discontent in New York and stimulated emigration. The council, aldermen, and justices petitioned for a representative assembly,[2] and meetings were called in the towns of Long Island to agitate for a redress of public grievances. In England, Andros, Nicolls, and Dyer urged the duke to allow an assembly as the only means whereby money could be raised to pay the expenses of government; and, confronted with bankruptcy, the duke yielded. He wrote to Brockholls bidding him retain the government for the present, and saying that he would grant an assembly on the condition that it would raise a revenue for the province.[3]

This promise the duke fulfilled. In 1682, when he appointed Thomas Dongan governor of New York, he authorized him to call at once on his arrival a general representative assembly of the freeholders, with free liberty of debate, to consult with the governor and council regarding the levying of taxes and the making of laws.[4] Dongan, an Irish Roman Catholic and a man of warm heart and

---

[1] Brodhead, *Hist. of New York*, II., 354, 355.
[2] Text of the petition, *ibid.*, 658.
[3] *N. Y. Docs. Rel. to Col. Hist.*, III., 317, 318.   [4] *Ibid.*, 331.

large powers; caused the writs to be issued, and on October 17, 1683, there met in New York for the first time in the history of the province a general popular assembly. The representatives, seventeen in number, passed several laws, but all other measures were insignificant when compared with the Charter of Franchises and Liberties,[1] in which they embodied all the political claims and privileges for which the people had been agitating for eighteen years. The charter contained provisions from Magna Carta, the Confirmation of the Charters, and the Petition of Right, set forth all the privileges that Parliament had won in the days of Elizabeth, and in grandly calling the "people" the "electoral body," used a word unknown in colonial charters, where "freemen" was the invariable term. Well might James, when he received this statute for his approval, have repeated his remark that "representative assemblies were apt to assume to themselves privileges." Yet he signed and sealed the charter, and October 4, 1684, ordered that it be despatched to New York.[2]

For some reason the charter was not sent over as ordered. Probably the document was held back that it might be "perfected," but in the interim Charles II. died, February 6, 1685, and the duke of York became king of England. The whole

[1] *Colonial Laws of New York*, I., 111–116.
[2] *Cal. of State Pap., Col.*, 1681–1685, § 1885; *Historical Magazine*, 1st series, VI., 233.

situation was altered: the proprietary had become
the king, and New York thereby a royal province
under the direct charge of the Lords of Trade, who
from this time forward were responsible for its
management. King James rejected the charter
which he had signed as proprietary, and at once
took up a plan which the Lords of Trade had been
formulating since 1675 for bringing all the proprietary and charter colonies into a closer dependence on the crown. Nicolls, Andros, and Dongan
had shown that New York could never prosper
unless the adjoining colonies were annexed to it.[1]
Troubles with Connecticut, Long Island, and the
Jerseys were all largely trade troubles. Tales of
evasion of duties, of smuggling, and of diversion of
Indian traffic kept coming to the ears of the home
authorities, and there seemed to be no other remedy
than consolidation.

James and his councillors had no appreciation
of the political and racial differences among the
colonies, or of the deep-rooted instinct for self-
government and love of independence which the
colonists possessed. There is no evidence to show
that he ever took these characteristics into consideration; and he probably could not have understood them, for James was always blind to
popular moods and convictions. He was now king
and could enforce his plan. On March 4, 1685,
when the matter was brought before the committee

---

[1] *N. Y. Docs. Rel. to Col. Hist.*, III., 361–364, 392, 394.

of his council sitting in his presence, he declared that he would not confirm the charter, but desired to bring New York under the constitution which was to be draughted for the newly organized dominion of New England.[1] In 1686, when a new commission was sent to Dongan, all reference to a representative assembly was omitted, and all powers of legislation and taxation were once more vested in the governor and council.

Dongan proved an admirable governor, better even than Nicolls and Andros. He not only showed his sympathy with the representative body that sat during his administration, but he granted a new charter to the city of New York (1683) and another to Albany, conferring many additional privileges of self-government.[2] The charter to New York, according to which mayor, recorder, and sheriff were appointed by the governor, and aldermen were chosen by the people, fixed the municipal officers of New York for one hundred and thirty-five years. Dongan opposed an attempt of Penn to purchase the Susquehanna territory from the Indians. He wished to draw the boundary-line between New York and Pennsylvania at 41° 40′, so that Penn might not secure jurisdiction over the Five Nations and control of the whole peltry trade west of Albany;[3] likewise, when Connecticut tried to establish her boundary, according to the arrangement with

[1] *N. Y. Docs. Rel. to Col. Hist.*, III., 357.   [2] *Ibid.*, 347.
[3] *Cal. of State Pap., Col.*, 1685–1688, 327, 328.

Nicolls, at a point twelve miles from the Hudson, Dongan compelled her to withdraw to the twenty-mile mark of the treaty of Hartford, under penalty of a revival of the duke's claim to all the lands west of the Connecticut River.[1] He refused to lessen New York's commerce by allowing Perth Amboy to become a port of entry, and demanded that all vessels bound for East New Jersey should touch at New York. On every side he upheld the interests of the duke and protected the trade and enhanced the prosperity of the province. For the year 1683 the duke's profits rose to £2000, and before 1689 had become £5000.

Dongan's greatest service, not only to New York but to all the colonies, lay in his dealings with the Indians. The time was critical, for the French were aiming to extend their conquests southward and to control the Hudson as they were already controlling the St. Lawrence and the Mississippi, and thus to obtain a third outlet to the ocean, which would divide the English colonies into two parts as completely as in the time of the Dutch province. But Dongan took up the policy which Andros had successfully applied, and made a famous treaty with the Iroquois, July 30, 1684, fastening the duke of York's arms to the Indian wigwams as a sign of their subjection to the king of England. Henceforth the Iroquois looked on their lands as the

[1] *Conn. Col. Records*, III., 326-333.

duke's territory and protected the valley of the
Hudson from all invasions of the French.[1]

Thus, through the influence and activity of three
able colonial governors, a territory in the beginning
unjustly acquired became a stable and profitable
province, forming a powerful link in the chain of
English colonies from Massachusetts Bay to South
Carolina. Controlled by a king who was blind to
the significance of popular government, New York
began its career as a colony governed wholly from
above; for the people, though well cared for, were denied the right of representation. Admirably situated
for purposes of trade, with a harbor unequalled on
the eastern seaboard, the colony was hampered in
its economic growth by heavy duties, a narrow
policy of trade monopoly, and a limited area of
supply. Peace with the Indians and favorable
treaty relations were necessary, not only to guard
against the French, but also to open up the interior
to the north and northwest for agriculture and trade,
and so to prepare the colony for its great future.
Another quarter of a century was destined to show
great changes for the better in the history of the
colony of New York.

[1] *N. Y. Docs. Rel. to Col. Hist.*, III., 347, 364, 394–396, 428–490;
Colden, *Hist. of the Five Nations* (1727).

CHAPTER VII

FOUNDATION OF THE JERSEYS

(1660-1677)

THE prosperity of the colony of New York was
impaired at the very outset by a serious loss
of territory lying west of the Hudson River. June
24, 1664, three months after the issue of the royal
patent, and before the Dutch had actually surrendered the territory to the English crown, the
duke of York, by a peculiar form of English con-
veyancing known as "lease and release," granted to
Berkeley and Carteret all the land between the
Hudson and the Delaware from about the fortieth
parallel of latitude on the north to Cape May on
the south.[1] The region received in the deed the
name of Nova Cæsaria, or New Jersey, a title
serving to show that the new land was a sort of
compensation for Carteret's former office as governor
of the island of Jersey. The land was broad and
fertile, stretching from the mountainous districts of
the north to the low sandy and marshy flats of the
south. In a letter to the duke of York, Nicolls declared that it was the best part of the entire grant;

[1] *N. J. Archives*, I., 8-14.

and both he and Dongan frequently asserted that the duke made a great mistake in giving away so promising a region and in creating another small government between New England and Maryland.[1] Protests were all too late, for the new proprietaries forthwith took steps to organize their grant. After 1674 the question arose whether the "lease and release" by implication conveyed to them the right to rule as well as to own the land;[2] but there is no doubt that the proprietaries believed that they had been vested with powers as full as those granted to them and their associates the year before as proprietaries of Carolina.

This grant of New Jersey was made by the duke of York to two of his favorites, Sir George Carteret and Sir John Berkeley, who, during the years after 1649, stood nearer to the exiled Stuart princes than any other English refugees except Clarendon. Carteret as governor of the island of Jersey provided a home for them in 1649, and in 1653 loyally defended the island against the parliamentarians. Berkeley became the governor of the household of the duke and the manager of his affairs after 1652, and sought by such means as he could employ to increase the revenues of the prince, who, like all the royal exiles, was in great need of money.

After 1660 these men secured their reward: each

[1] *Clarendon Papers*, 115; *N. Y. Docs. Rel. to Col. Hist.*, III., 105.

[2] Whitehead, *Civil and Judicial Hist. of N. J.*, 30–32.

became a member of the Privy Council and of the councils of trade and plantations; each became a patentee of the lands monopolized by the Royal African Company, and one of the lords proprietors of Carolina and the Bahamas. Carteret became vice-chamberlain and treasurer of the navy, was appointed one of the lords of the admiralty under the duke of York as lord high admiral, and actively promoted all matters connected with trade and navigation from 1660 to his death in 1679. As early as 1650 he planned a colonizing expedition to Virginia, where he had received the grant of an island, but owing to the failure of the royalist cause he gave up the project. Berkeley was equally favored. He became Baron Berkeley of Stratton, a member of the council, one of the lords of the admiralty, a member of the committee for foreign plantations in 1660, and a member of the council committee appointed in 1671. He was one of the patentees who received from Charles, September 18, 1649, "in the first year of his reign," a grant of a portion of Virginia. Thus both Carteret and Berkeley stood not only in an intimate relation to the king and the duke of York, "deserving much by their great services and sufferings," but, by virtue of the offices which they held, were in very close connection with the colonies and all that concerned them.

It is not clear who influenced Carteret and Berkeley to ask for the territory in America. Clarendon kept himself informed regarding the situation in New England and New Netherland,[1] and Berkeley desired to recoup himself for a purchase for £3500 of a part interest in certain claims to lands in New England by the earl of Sterling, under a grant of 1625 by the Council of New England.[2]

Carteret and Berkeley both served on the committee to investigate the conditions in New Netherland; and as late as January, 1664, they were discoursing "with several persons well acquainted with the affairs of New England, some having lately inhabited on Long Island, where they have yet an interest."[3] Both were deeply implicated in the plot for the seizure of New Netherland, and received a part of the conquered territory as their share of the spoils.

For the government of the new colony a body of "Concessions" was drawn up (by whom we do not know), and issued by the proprietaries in January and February, 1665, to the colonies of New Jersey and Carolina, defining the form of the government, outlining the conditions under which lands were to be allotted, and guaranteeing liberty of religion, of property, and of elections. This document became the foundation and model of government during the proprietary period and later. The people clung

[1] *Clarendon Papers* (N. Y. Hist. Soc., *Collections*, 1869), 1–14.

[2] "Blathwayt's Report on the Case of the Earl of Sterling," MS. in Public Record Office, *Treasury*, etc., XXIII., 24.

[3] *Cal. of State Pap., Col.*, 1661–1668, § 647.

to it, they quarrelled with their governor because they thought he disregarded its provisions, and they made it the basis of their demands in all the exigencies of their colonial history. Its liberal provisions were utilized by all those who tried to attract settlers to the colony. Scot said that, as the result of this guarantee of religion and property, the province was "considerably peopled and many resorted there from the neighboring colonies"; and again, comparing New Jersey and Carolina in 1685, he said that any man in Carolina who had money could have honor and trust though he were the "arrantest Blockhead in nature," while in New Jersey office was based on merit;[1] and Budd wrote that the government was settled by concessions and fundamental laws "by which every man's liberty and property, both as men and Christians, are preserved, so that none shall be hurt in his person, estate, or liberty for his religious persuasions or practice in worship towards God."[2]

The region for which a government was thus provided was already partly settled. The Dutch had planted trading-posts on the left bank of the Hudson at a very early date, and named them Bergen, after Bergen-op-Zoom, in Holland, Hobuc, Wiehawken, and the like. In the south, on the east bank of the Delaware, and also at New Castle (New Amstel) on the west, were many Finns, Swedes, and

---

[1] Whitehead, *East Jersey*, App., 397, 398, 446.
[2] Budd, *Good Order Established* (1685).

Dutch, relics of the Swedish and Dutch settlements there, who willingly accepted the English rule and were left in undisturbed possession of their lands.[1]

Governor Nicolls began his broad-minded and liberal rule in New York by making strenuous efforts to people the colony. At the time of his coming he knew nothing of the grant to Berkeley and Carteret, and in the summer of 1664 he issued a proclamation making liberal offers to settlers.[2] As a result a number of families came from Jamaica, Long Island—which by descent was a Connecticut and New Haven colony—purchased land from the Indians, and settled within a wide tract covering the later townships of Elizabeth, Woodbridge, and Piscataway.[3] Here, during 1665, appear to have gathered somewhere about two hundred people.[4] In April of the same year Nicolls issued the "Monmouth" patent to certain people from Gravesend, who had previously bought the land of the Indians; and thus gave legal warrant, and such measure of self-government as he was able, to the settlers of the new towns of Middletown and Shrewsbury. He likewise granted "free liberty of conscience without any molestation or disturbance whatsoever in the way of worship.[5] These grants were partly responsible for the trouble that arose in later years be-

[1] *N. Y. Docs. Rel. to Col. Hist.*, III., 71.
[2] Text in Whitehead, *Civil and Judicial Hist. of N. J.*, 54, 55.
[3] *N. J. Archives*, I., 14–19.
[4] Whitehead, *Civil and Judicial Hist. of N. J.*, 102, 103.
[5] *N. J. Archives*, I., 43–46.

tween the governor and the towns of northern New Jersey.

When Philip Carteret (probably a younger brother of Sir George)[1] arrived in August, 1665, with a commission from the new proprietaries as governor of the colony, he found a goodly number of people already settled in his province. He was a young man, only twenty-six years of age, of an arbitrary and dictatorial temperament. With him came about thirty people in all, of whom two only, Captain Bollen and Robert Vanquillon, were gentlemen. The remainder were servants, French inhabitants of the island of Jersey, who in appearance and manners were in strange contrast to the strict Puritans among whom they settled. The governor took up his residence in the town, which in honor of the wife of the proprietary he called Elizabeth; but he and his little band of French immigrants found a rather scant welcome from the New Englanders, who looked upon him with distrust as a cavalier from the court of Charles II. and a relative of the gay courtier Sir George Carteret.

The influx of New England settlers did not cease with the settlement of Elizabeth. The New Haven colony was a prolific mother of towns.[2] In June, 1666, families from New Haven and Milford set sail for the Passaic; three months later more families left

[1] Edmundson (*Baronagium Genealogicum*, III., 209) mentions such a younger brother.

[2] *New Haven Col. Records*, II., 552; *N. J. Archives*, I., 51–54.

Branford and Guilford for the same place.[1] Each
group drew up its "fundamental articles," its
plantation covenant redolent of the narrow spirit of
the old Fundamental Articles of New Haven. That
signed by the family heads of Branford and Guilford,
on October 30, 1666, declared that no one was to
be a freeman or burgess, no one was to be a magis-
trate or to hold office, and no one was to take part
in elections, except such as were members of the
Congregational church; and that the purity of the
religion of this polity was to be maintained with
diligence and care.[2] These agreements stand in
striking contrast with the liberal provisions of the
Concessions. The New-Englanders established their
plantation on the Passaic, and there, in June, 1667,
founded the town of Newark, "alias Milford," a
typical New England settlement with its town-
meeting, its divided lands, and its theocratic polity
like that of Davenport and the New Haven colony.[3]

From this time colonists continued to pour in
both from England and from New England. Emigrants from Newburyport, Massachusetts, led probably by Daniel Pierce, settled in Woodbridge. To
these settlers Philip Carteret granted a very liberal
charter, conferring "perfect self-government, perfect
tolerance," trial by jury, and the like, a charter

[1] Levermore, *Republic of New Haven*, 114–120; *Records of
Newark* (N. J. Hist. Soc., *Collections*, VI.), 1, 2.

[2] *Records of Newark*, 2.

[3] *Ibid.*, 3–9; Whitehead, *East Jersey*, App., 405.

which was afterwards confirmed by Berkeley and
Carteret.[1]   Thus New Jersey became a little
model of New England, animated by the spirit of
the Puritan commonwealth, the intolerance of the
"saints," and the sturdy independence of the town-
meeting; and it is not strange that the proprietaries'
governor, Carteret, a representative of the Restoration, should have had but little sympathy with the
views of those over whom he ruled.

At first no regular government was established
for the province, although in 1667 the patentees and
delegates of Middletown, Shrewsbury, and Portland
Point set up a little assembly, which passed laws and
appointed officers for the towns, but in a limited
jurisdiction.   In April, 1668, Carteret issued a call
for a general assembly of the whole province to
meet at Elizabethtown in May.[2]   The meeting
contained no representatives from Middletown and
Shrewsbury, and did not sit long, but it passed a
"Levitical Code" so "blue" as to make it clear
that the New Haven spirit and faith in the Mosaic
law governed the Newark delegates and ruled the
assembly.[3]

To the adjourned meeting in October Middletown and Shrewsbury sent delegates, who were
not allowed to sit.   Trouble was brewing.   Carteret

[1] Text of this charter in Whitehead, *Civil and Judicial Hist.
of N. J.*, 108, 109.
[2] *N. J. Archives*, I., 56, 57; Whitehead, *East Jersey*, 188.
[3] Leaming and Spicer, *Grants of New Jersey*, 77–84.

was inclined to be aggressive, and the colonists were suspicious and unconciliatory. The governor claimed the right to preside at town-meetings and to establish his French emigrants in the towns on an equality with the New-Englanders. The latter, deeming him an ungodly autocrat appointed in England, resented his interference, and guarded jealously what they considered their rights. No agreement could be reached by men of such conflicting opinions. The assembly broke up in disorder (November 7) and did not come together again for seven years.

During the years from 1668 to 1670 the governor with his council ruled without disturbance, until the time came when, according to the terms of the Concessions, the quit-rents fell due. These the colonists flatly refused to pay, claiming that they had the lands from the Indians and by grant from Nicolls, and that they owed nothing to the proprietaries. The Newark town-meeting expressed the opinion of the time when it said: "They do hold and possess their lands and rights in said town, both by civil and divine right, as by their legal purchase and articles may and doth show." In this refusal there was some justification for those individuals who had not taken oaths of allegiance, but none for those who had; yet nearly all joined in the revolt, a fact that disclosed a discontent deeper than that due to the quit-rent of a halfpenny an acre. Outbreaks took place, riots ensued, and for two years the colony was in a state of confusion.

Finally, the discontent took the form of rebellion, and all the towns except Middletown and Shrewsbury set up a separate government and sent delegates to an assembly of their own in March and May, 1672. Inasmuch as Philip Carteret would have nothing to do with this unauthorized body, they fastened on a certain James Carteret, supposed to be an illegitimate son of the proprietary, and made him governor.[1] But the tenure of this personage was brief. The proprietaries sustained Philip Carteret,[2] modified somewhat the former Concessions, and repudiated the grants which Nicolls had made; and King Charles II. upheld to the full the authority of the proprietaries.[3] The populace and their representatives withdrew from the struggle, accepting the terms offered them.

Trouble with the Indians undoubtedly had something to do with this peaceful settlement, but the seizure of New York by the Dutch in 1673 had a more potent influence. In that year New Jersey, along with New York and Long Island, passed for the second time under the rule of the States-General of Holland, with Colve as governor; but except for the obligation to swear a new allegiance,[4] this event brought little change into the colony.

[1] *N. J. Archives*, I., 89–91, 95.
[2] *Ibid.*, 91–97.
[3] N. Y. State Historian, *Report*, 1896, p. 364; *Harleian MSS.* in British Museum, 7001, f. 299.
[4] *N. J. Archives*, I., 121–152, espec. 123, 128, 133, 134.

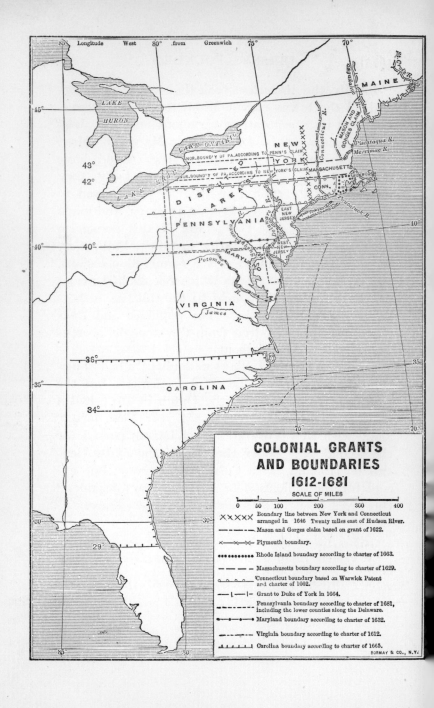

COLONIAL GRANTS
AND BOUNDARIES
1612-1681

SCALE OF MILES

0   50   100   200   300   400

×××× Boundary line between New York and Connecticut
arranged in 1646 Twenty miles east of Hudson River.

------ Mason and Gorges claim based on grant of 1622.

—×—×— Plymouth boundary.

•••••••••• Rhode Island boundary according to charter of 1663.

—-—-—- Massachusetts boundary according to charter of 1629.

ₒ ₒ ₒ ₒ Connecticut boundary based on Warwick Patent
and charter of 1662.

—|—|— Grant to Duke of York in 1664.

—·—·— Pennsylvania boundary according to charter of 1681,
including the lower counties along the Delaware.

•—•—•—• Maryland boundary according to charter of 1632.

———— Virginia boundary according to charter of 1612.

↧↧↧↧↧ Carolina boundary according to charter of 1665.

BORMAY & CO., N.Y.

CHAPTER VIII

DEVELOPMENT OF THE JERSEYS

(1674–1689)

WHEN, in 1674, by the treaty of Westminster, the Jerseys were restored to the English, it became necessary to issue a new grant to the duke of York, a new lease to the proprietaries, and new directions and instructions to the colonists, owing to the fact that "the property of this tract of land was by some persons of that time supposed to be altered by its having been taken and possessed by a foreign power."[1] Therefore, in the summer of 1674, when Philip Carteret returned with a new commission as governor and new directions for the government of the province,[2] he was received very graciously by both people and assembly.[3]

Until 1674 New Jersey remained an undivided province. To be sure, the term West New Jersey was used for the settlements on the Delaware;[4] but

---

[1] *Short Account of the First Settlement* (1735), 16; another view in *N. J. Archives*, I., 290.
[2] *N. J. Archives*, I., 167–175.
[3] Whitehead, *Civil and Judicial Hist. of N. J.*, 132, 133.
[4] *N. J. Archives*, I., 118.

the colonists there obtained the titles to many
of their lands from Philip Carteret,[1] and were represented in the assembly which met in Elizabethtown in October, 1668. Still, they took but little
part in the events thus far recounted, and, though
numbering a thousand people, were not called upon
to pay quit-rents and did not share in the uprising
against Carteret. In 1674 a change came about
when Berkeley, wearying of his proprietary relation
to New Jersey, sold his share of the province for
£1000 to Edward Byllynge, a member of the Society of Friends, a brewer of London, a friend of
Berkeley's, and a former officer in Cromwell's army.
Byllynge placed the management of the business in
the hands of a Quaker friend, Major John Fenwick,
who, in consideration of a portion of the property,
offered to settle the colony and look after the lands
and the revenues.[2]

The entrance of the Quakers upon the scene was
no sudden nor unpremeditated event. For some
time members of the society had been looking for
a home in America where they might be free from
persecution, and many of them went to New England, Long Island, New Jersey, and Carolina.
Eighteen were reported at Shrewsbury in 1673.[3]
In that year George Fox, the founder of the society,

[1] *Pa. Magazine*, XVII., 84, 85.
[2] Dankers and Sluyter, *Journal*, 241, 242; *N. J. Archives*, I.,
185, *n.*, 209; *Pa. Magazine*, V., 312.
[3] *N. J. Archives*, I., 133, 134, 184; *N. Y. Docs. Rel. to Col.
Hist.*, II., 607, 619.

returned from a tour in America, and, understanding the circumstances and opportunities there, he may have been influential in persuading Byllynge to purchase Berkeley's rights. Whether William Penn, son of Admiral Penn, and one of the most important members in England, had any share in the undertaking at this time cannot be determined. He met Fox on his return, and during the year that followed must have discussed with him the situation in America. The desire for an independent colony where they might establish a government embodying their own ideas had long been in the minds of the Quakers, and there is reason to believe that the purchase of Berkeley's share by Byllynge was made in the interest of the whole society.

At first the experiment did not succeed. Byllynge and Fenwick could not agree as to the division of the property; and Penn, who lived near Fenwick in England was called in as arbiter. "The present difference between thee and E. B. fills the hearts of Friends with grief," he wrote to Fenwick, who had evidently refused to accept Penn's first award of one-tenth as his share. "I took care to hide the pretences on both hands as to the original of the thing, because it reflects on you both and which is worse on the truth." Fenwick took the case into chancery, with what results we do not know, but he finally accepted the allotment of one-tenth and began to make preparations for crossing to

America.[1]   No sooner was this difficulty met than
another arose.   Byllynge became involved in business, and to satisfy his creditors, was compelled to
convey his rights (February 14, 1675) to Penn and
two distinguished fellow - Quakers, Gawen Lawrie
and Nicholas Lucas.[2]   Fenwick, too, leased his one-
tenth to Eldridge and Warner, as security for money
borrowed.[3]

The title to West New Jersey, already sufficiently
involved by these transactions, was further com-
plicated by the attitude of the duke of York, who
appears at this point to have sought to take back
his grant and to avoid a reconveyance.   In a letter
from Charles II., of June, 1674, Carteret was mentioned as if sole proprietary and all others were
ignored.[4]   In the new "lease and release" which
the duke finally executed, the province was for the
first time divided by a straight line from Barnegat
Creek to Rankokus Kill, near Burlington on the
Delaware,[5] but no mention is anywhere made of
Berkeley's rights or of those to whom these rights
had been sold.   Whitehead says that he "hesitated,
dallied, played fast and loose, equivocated, and held
back," and even though he signed the lease to
Carteret in 1674, he did not recognize Berkeley's

[1] Letters in Bowden, *Hist. of Friends*, I., 391, 392; *Harleian
MSS.*, in British Museum, 7001, ff. 300, 301.
[2] Johnson, *Hist. of Salem*, 56–63; *Pa. Magazine*, V., 327–329.
[3] List of these grants in Penn's letter, *N. J. Archives*, I.,
232, 233.
[4] *N. J. Archives*, I., 153, 154.   [5] *Ibid.*, 161.

sale till August 6, 1680.[1]　This equivocation had
the disastrous effect of clouding the title to West
New Jersey and hindering colonization there.

There is no reason to believe that Berkeley and
Carteret deliberately planned to divide their grant,
but the withdrawal of the former from the enter-
prise and the coming of the Quakers altered the
situation.　Penn had no desire to join with Carteret
in the government of a single province; he wished
rather to have a free field wherein to test his own
plan of government.　The division named in the
duke's warrant of 1674 was not equitable, and
consequently, in 1676, "after no little labor, trouble,
and cost,"[2] a new arrangement was agreed upon.
By a "quintipartite" deed (executed by Carteret
on one side, and Penn, Lawrie, Lucas, and Byllynge
on the other),[3] which rehearsed all the acts thus
far determined in the establishment of title, a line
was drawn from the "most southwardly point of the
east side of Little Egg Harbor" through the province
northwestwardly to the junction of the Delaware
River with the forty-first parallel of latitude.　One
part was to be called East New Jersey and the other
West New Jersey.[4]　In the mean time, Eldridge
and Warner had conveyed their rights in Fenwick's
tenth to Penn, Lucas, and Lawrie, "the better to

---

[1] Whitehead, *Civil and Judicial Hist. of N. J.*, 77, 78; *N. J.
Archives*, II., 163–167, 324; cf. *Cal. of State Pap., Col.*, 1677–
1680, § 778.　　　　　　　　[2] *N. J. Archives*, I., 232, 233.
[3] *Ibid.*, 327.　　　　　　　　[4] *Ibid.*, 205–219.

enable them to make a partition of the entire
premises with Sir George Carteret." In the years
that followed there was much controversy over
this line and many changes were made, so that
the boundary question was not permanently settled till an act of assembly of New Jersey in
1718.

Each colony was now free to pursue its own career,
but a new trouble, or, rather, an old trouble in a new
form, arose from an unexpected quarter. When
Andros was commissioned governor of New York,
July 1, 1674, he was instructed to govern, not only
the other lands granted to the duke in 1664, but
also "all the land from the west side of Connecticut
River to the east side of Delaware Bay."[1] This fact
seems to indicate that James was attempting to
recover his control of New Jersey by denying that
the right of government had been conveyed by the
"lease and release." Andros, acting under his instructions, made his first attempt to recover New
Jersey for the duke by attacking the claims in West
New Jersey, where Fenwick, apparently disregarding his lease to Eldridge and Warner, had issued
proposals in March, 1675, for the settlement and
government of "my colony."[2] Getting together a
body of one hundred and fifty emigrants in the same
year, he set sail in the *Griffith* and landed at Swamp

---

[1] *N. Y. Docs. Rel. to Col. Hist.*, III., 215.
[2] *Pa. Magazine*, VI., 86–90; cf. Dankers and Sluyter, *Journal*, 242, 243; *Harleian MSS.*, in British Museum, 7001, f. 301.

Town, which because of its peaceful appearance he called New Salem.[1]

Andros, aroused by this invasion, took immediate action. He denied Fenwick's right to grant patents of land, and when Fenwick refused to obey his orders, caused him to be brought to New York by an armed force and only released him after he produced his title-deeds.[2] Andros had no case against Fenwick, as he soon discovered, for even the duke of York acknowledged that Fenwick's patents of land gave good title.[3]

Andros was not content with his attack on West New Jersey; he was already coming into conflict with Governor Carteret over commerce and trade. As in the Delaware, so in the East New Jersey harbors, he proposed to levy duties for the benefit of the proprietary. Taking advantage of the death of Sir George Carteret in 1679, Andros wrote forbidding Philip Carteret to exercise jurisdiction in New Jersey.[4] Carteret replied in kind, warning Andros not to trespass in East New Jersey. Thereupon the latter, in 1680, seized Carteret and brought him to New York, where he had him tried by special court for presuming to exercise jurisdiction and government over the subjects of King Charles.[5] The

<hr />

[1] *N. J. Archives*, I., 185, 186; *Harleian MSS.*, in British Museum, 7001, f. 302.   [2] *N. J. Archives*, I., 187–204.

[3] *Cal. of State Pap., Col.*, 1677–1680, § 778.

[4] *N. J. Archives*, I., 292–299.

[5] *Ibid.*, 299–306, 316–318; Leaming and Spicer, *Grants*, 677–691.

jury, to the great wrath of Andros, acquitted Carteret; the East New Jersey assembly upheld their governor; the towns refused the commissions issued by Andros; and the next year (1681), when the legal authorities showed that he had no case, not even against the Quakers, the duke gave up the struggle, confirmed Philip Carteret in the government, and forbade Andros to take further action.[1] In East New Jersey as in West New Jersey the efforts of the duke to recover possession proved a failure.

In the mean time, West New Jersey was receiving new settlers. While Fenwick was in possession of his one-tenth, Penn, Lawrie, and Lucas, acting as trustees for Byllynge, disposed of the nine-tenths to two companies of Quakers (one resident in Hull and other towns in Yorkshire, the other in London), who at once displayed great energy in the work of settling the territory.[2] In 1677 the ship *Kent* arrived in New York harbor with two hundred colonists, who reported their intentions and displayed their titles. Although the duke of York was at that time contesting their claims, they received permission to settle on the Delaware, provided they would submit to the government at New York.[3] They then proceeded on their way, arrived at the Delaware, and laid the foundation of the town of Bridlington or Burlington.

[1] *N. J. Archives*, I., 323, 345–347; *Cal. of State Pap., Col.*, 1677–1680, § 1479; *N. Y. Docs. Rel. to Col. Hist.*, III., 284.
[2] *N. J. Archives*, I., 233.   [3] *Ibid.*, 239, 240.

These colonists brought with them a famous body of "Concessions and Agreements," the broadest, sanest, and most equitable charter draughted for any body of colonists up to this time. This document assured privileges and rights to men of that day which must have seemed almost Utopian. It contains the best that the political thinkers of the period could furnish, and looks ahead to the time when men stated in forcible terms what they considered the fundamental rights of man. It was a true constitution; not octroyed, as had been the Concessions of 1665, but agreed upon and signed in England by emigrants, one hundred and fifty-one in number.[1]

The Concessions and Agreements provided for a government by a board of commissioners—a directory appointed by the proprietaries, who, however, soon substituted a single executive—and an assembly freely chosen by the inhabitants to sit for a year, the members of which were to be paid and to have full liberty of speech and all parliamentary prerogatives. This body was to have entire control over the passing and the repealing of laws, agreeable to the Concessions and the laws of England. The commissioners were to impose no tallages, subsidies, or assessments, and the assembly was to levy only such taxes as were necessary. The fundamental rights of the people are very definitely and strongly expressed—absolute religious freedom,

[1] *N. J. Archives*, I., 422.

right of trial by jury, no arbitrary imprisonment for debt, no capital punishment even for treason, unless the assembly so decreed, publicity of courts of justice, and right of petition. Save for the appointment of the executive and the reserve of quit-rents, this constitution is thoroughly democratic, subordinating the executive to the legislative and making the latter responsible to the people.[1] That this document was in large part draughted by William Penn seems highly probable; its spirit of forgiveness, justice, and brotherly love testifies to its origin.

For three years the settlers made no effort to put the Concessions into operation, as the question of their right to rule was still undetermined. But after persistent efforts Byllynge obtained a grant from the duke of York, August 6, 1680, recognizing the rights and title of the proprietaries and vesting in himself the government of the province.[2] He then sent over Samuel Jennings as his deputy, and the first assembly met November 21, 1681, lasting until the following January. The deputies acknowledged the authority of Jennings to act as their governor, provided he would assent to a bill of rights consisting of a preamble and ten clauses, still further restricting the power of the governor.[3] Fenwick sold his lands,[4] with a reservation, in 1682 to Penn, now proprietary and governor of

---

[1] *N. J. Archives*, I., 241–270.   [2] *Ibid.*, 323–333.
[3] Text in Smith, *Hist. of N. J.*, 126–129.
[4] See his "Remonstrance," March 12, 1679, *ibid.*, VI.

Pennsylvania, and accepted election to the assembly at Burlington in 1683, thus recognizing its jurisdiction over his portion.[1]   During the next four years the only serious difficulty that arose in the province concerned the right of the people to elect their own governor,[2] a right that was certainly not found in the Concessions and that Byllynge was unwilling to concede.

Byllynge died in 1687, after an unsuccessful and troubled business career, and his interest in West New Jersey was bought by Daniel Coxe, a London merchant, and one of the most sanguine of colonial promoters.   Coxe acquired large quantities of land, not only in New Jersey, but in New York and Long Island also,[3] and made strenuous efforts to build up his colony.   He issued alluring prospectuses for the purpose of attracting emigrants, started whale and cod fisheries, planned to tap the fur trade of the Northwest, and to establish a "circular trade" between New Jersey, the other colonies, and Jamaica and Barbadoes in the West Indies.   He started a fruit plantation at Cape May and a pottery at Burlington for "white and chiney ware," of which £1200 worth was sold in the neighboring colonies and the West Indies.[4]   He was greatly

---

[1] Shroud, *Hist. and Genealogy of Fenwick's Colony*, 12.

[2] *N. J. Archives*, I., 421.

[3] "Account of the Quantity and Value of Coxe's Land," *Rawlinson MSS.*, in Bod. Lib., C 128, f. 42.

[4] "Daniel Coxe's Account of New Jersey," *Pa. Magazine*, VII., 327–337.

impressed with the possibilities of West New Jersey for supplying masts and boards, and speaks of a proposal made to him to furnish cedar-trees for the "roof and inward work" of St. Paul's cathedral, rebuilding at that time (1675-1697) under the guidance of Sir Christopher Wren.[1] Though making every concession that he could in the way of political privileges to the people,[2] he retained, as had Byllynge, control of the governorship; and by transferring the seat of government to Burlington, raised that place to a position of first importance in the colony.[3] The brick houses, market-places, fairs, wharves, large timber yards, and extensive trade made it for some years a rival of Philadelphia.

In 1685 the colony was threatened with a writ of *quo warranto* by Edward Randolph,[4] and in 1688 was taken under the jurisdiction of Andros, governor of the Dominion of New England; but after the revolution of 1688 it was returned to Governor Coxe, who, disturbed by the attitude of the crown and somewhat embarrassed in his affairs, resolved to sell his interest in the colony. The property and rights were bought by a group of proprietaries called the West New Jersey Society, of which Coxe himself remained a member and for which he drew up a plan of management.[5] This

---

[1] "Coxe's Account of New Jersey," *Pa. Magazine*, VII., 329.
[2] See Coxe's letter of Sept. 5, 1687, in Smith, *Hist. of N. J.*, 190, note *k*.   [3] Thomas, *Account of West New Jersey*, 15, 16.
[4] *Cal. of State Pap., Col.*, 1685-1688, §§ 304, 309, 2112.
[5] Smith, *Hist. of N. J.*, 207; *Proposals Made by Coxe*,

society controlled the government and lands of the colony, but agreed that Fletcher, governor of New York, should retain command of the militia.[1] Under these proprietaries West New Jersey remained until its final surrender to the crown in 1702.

In East New Jersey Philip Carteret won his victory over Andros in 1681; but his career as governor was almost over. Scarcely had the assembly convened in October, 1681, when the deputies charged Carteret with violating the Concessions "by interpretations contrary to the literal sense of the same."[2] In the year 1682 he resigned his government, and the board of trustees, to whom Sir George Carteret had devised his rights in New Jersey for the payment of his debts and legacies in 1679,[3] offered these rights at once to whosoever would purchase them.

They were disposed of at public sale to twelve Quakers, with William Penn at the head, who organized themselves as a body of proprietaries for the government of the province.[4] Soon afterwards this body of twelve became associated in a business partnership with the earl of Perth, Robert Barclay, a famous Quaker apologist, and his brother David, and nine others, some of whom were Scottish Presbyterians, who thus became tenants in common

Rawlinson MSS., in Bod. Lib., C 128, ff. 46, 47 (undated, but probably 1691).

[1] *Cal. of State Pap., Col.*, 1689–1692, § 2250.
[2] *N. J. Archives*, I., 356.   [3] *Ibid.*, 388.
[4] *Ibid.*, 366–369, 373–375.

with the first twelve. A majority of the twenty-four were Quakers, so that both the Jerseys came under Quaker control. It is not difficult to see in all these transactions a definite attempt of the Society of Friends to obtain a home for its members in America.

For the benefit of the twenty-four proprietaries the duke of York executed a deed of release, dated March 14, 1683, investing them with rights of government as well as with title to the soil.[1] Already had Robert Barclay been named as governor, and he remained in England, governing the province by deputy. A new frame of government, much less democratic than the old Concessions, was sent over in 1683, signed by sixteen of the twenty-four proprietaries.[2] The new code was distinctly lacking in directness and simplicity, and could hardly have done anything to improve the government of the colony or to lessen the complication growing out of the numerous proprietary rights in the provinces. Fortunately, it was never put into force.

Rudyard, the first deputy governor under Barclay, was recalled in 1683, and Gawen Lawrie, who had been interested in New Jersey since 1675, came over as governor. "Here wants nothing but people," he wrote back; "there is not a poor body in the province."[3] Strenuous efforts were made to

[1] N. J. Archives, I., 383–394.   [2] Ibid., 395–410.
[3] Whitehead, East Jersey, App., 418; Smith, Hist. of N. J., 177.

promote settlement. Scot, of Pitlockie, prepared
an elaborate prospectus, quoting evidence from the
province to prove its desirability; while the proprietaries—notably Barclay—organized bodies of
emigrants and started them on their way. Gradually the colony began to fill with a sober and industrious people. Lawrie called for able-bodied
men to plough and till the soil, and the general
sentiment seemed to be that riches lay in corn and
cattle rather than in trade and commerce.[1]

The attempt of the proprietaries to promote trade
and to obtain the recognition of Perth Amboy as a
port of entry led to a long controversy with New
York, which probably had much to do with the
inauguration of the *quo warranto* proceedings against
them. In 1688 they handed over all rights of
government to the duke of York, reserving only the
title to the soil, and East New Jersey was annexed
to New York. Though restored to the proprietaries
after 1689, the colony continued to be a source of
trouble to them, owing to disputes with New York
on one side and the inhabitants of the colony on
the other, and was finally surrendered to the crown
in 1702.

The weakness of the Jerseys lay in the fact that
from the first grant to Carteret and Berkeley to the
final surrender they were utilized by their pro-

---

[1] Historical Manuscripts Commission, *Report*, VI., pt. i.,
484, VII., 485; Smith, *Hist. of N. J.*, 181, 182; Whitehead, *East
Jersey*, App., 401.

prietaries as sources of profit and revenue. Proprietary rights in both the colonies were bought and sold so frequently and controlled by so many stockholders that the management of the colonies was neither systematic nor efficient. Controversies among the proprietaries themselves, between the proprietaries and the inhabitants, and between the colonies and their neighbors rendered a rapid and prosperous growth practically impossible.

CHAPTER IX

FOUNDATION OF THE CAROLINAS

(1663–1671)

WHILE New England, New York, and New Jersey were working out the problems of colonization and reorganization, settlement was also in progress in the vacant or sparsely settled regions of the southern coast. There the low land, differing essentially from the coast formations of New England, constituted a plateau but a few feet above the level of the sea, which was traversed by wide - mouthed rivers and skirted by islands often large in extent and identical in soil and verdure with the main-land. The broken and indented coast formed natural harbors, and the rivers, which were navigable from the sea back to the rapids and falls of the second terrace or lower pine belt, made transportation easy. By furnishing a means of internal communication unknown to the people of the northern colonies, they made possible the scattered settlements which characterized the southern colonies, notably Virginia.

To the south of Virginia lay a wide and empty territory stretching indefinitely towards the Spanish

settlement at St. Augustine. After the revoking
of the charter of the London Company in 1624
the king was free to make such grant of this southern
territory as he pleased, and in 1629 he gave to Sir
Robert Heath all the region lying between the
thirty-first and thirty-sixth parallels of latitude.
Heath's plans fell still-born among colonial ventures.
The land was not easily accessible either overland
or by sea, and such was its reputation for unwhole-
someness that few men from other colonies ventured
to explore it. Moreover, it was claimed in part by
Spain, and hence was looked upon askance by
Englishmen who were seeking homes in the New
World.

After the failure of Raleigh's unfortunate ex-
peditions, the first Englishman, so far as we know,
to reach Carolina was Henry Taverner, a ship
captain employed by English promoters, Vassell
and Kingswell, to carry passengers to Virginia. In
1632 Taverner made a voyage of discovery in his
ship, the *Mayflower*, and entered the St. Helena
River. In 1634 he came from England in a new
ship, the *Thomas*, with servants, clothing, and
provisions for the purpose of taking Kingswell and
his company from Virginia to settle in Carolina,
but for some reason the plan failed.[1] Between
1632 and 1660 only one journey is recorded.[2] About

[1] MSS. in Public Record Office, *Admiralty Court, Instance and
Prize, Examinations*, 51, Dec. 12, 17, 1634, April 14, 1635.
[2] *N. C. Col. Records*, I., 19, 20.

1660, however, two efforts were made at settlement, one by colonists from Virginia, who planted a community at Albemarle, on the Chowan River, destined to become the nucleus of the colony of North Carolina; the other by New England traders from Massachusetts, who, after inspecting the lands at the mouth of the Cape Fear River—then known as the Charles—departed, leaving behind them, attached to a post, a warning in which they denounced the country.[1]

Thus far, therefore, the territory south of Virginia was unoccupied except in the northern border, at a point some seventy miles from the James. Just at this time discontent and uneasiness were rife in Barbadoes. The land there was originally allotted in small parcels, the largest of which seems to have been thirty acres in size, and proved only sufficient for the maintenance of a man and his family:[2] and when the necessities of sugar-planting led to the consolidating of these small estates, many landholders were forced to emigrate to other colonies. In addition, the return of Charles II. to the English throne was followed by restrictive measures which created dissatisfaction, because they were deemed contrary to the liberal terms given to the royalists by the charter of 1652, in consequence of their surrendering the island to the fleet of Parliament.

Among those directly interested in the develop-

---

[1] N. C. Col. Records, I., 36–38.
[2] Davis, Cavaliers and Roundheads of Barbadoes, 80.

ment of the island was Colonel John Colleton, major - general in Barbadoes, a member of the Barbadian council under the protectorate,[1] and a man of influence and authority in the island. Colleton returned to England in 1660 and was made a member of the newly appointed Council for Foreign Plantations,[2] where he came into friendly relations with Anthony Ashley Cooper (soon after created Lord Ashley), a member of the committee of the Council of State in 1653.[3] Both Colleton and Ashley knew of the unoccupied lands of Carolina, and there can be little doubt that when the discontent of many of the Barbadians gave rise to a new project for a settlement elsewhere, Colleton suggested applying to the king for a grant of these continental territories.

As both Colleton and Ashley had served the protectorate, they deemed it wise to associate with themselves others who, by their loyalty to the king in exile, had a greater claim on the king's bounty and were at the same time thoroughly interested in colonial affairs. Of these Clarendon and Carteret stand out most prominently. Consequently, April 3, 1663, probably at the request[4] of Ashley and

---

[1] *Cal. of State Pap., Col.*, 1574–1660, pp. 456, 476.
[2] *Ibid.*, 1661–1668, §§ 91, 470; *N. Y. Docs. Rel. to Col. Hist.*, III., 48, 49.   [3] *Cal. of State Pap., Col.*, 1574–1660, p. 412.
[4] Ashley's influence seems likely from the known facts as to his procuring the grant of the Bahamas in 1670.   See *Shaftesbury Papers* (S. C. Hist. Soc., *Collections*, V.), 153, 180, 207–210; *Cal. of State Pap., Col.*, 1669–1674, § 311, 1675–1676, § 384.

others of his colleagues, Charles II. caused the first
charter of Carolina to be issued to eight proprietaries
—Clarendon, Craven, Albemarle (who as General
Monck had saved England from a third civil war),
Carteret, Lord John Berkeley, Sir William Berkeley
(governor of Virginia), Ashley, and Colleton, now
Sir John Colleton. Craven, Carteret, and John
Berkeley were faithful members of the council com-
mittee known as the Lords of Trade.

The Carolina charter[1] was modelled after preceding charters, and in nearly all its parts was
identical with the grants made to Robert Heath and
Lord Baltimore, except that the patentees were a
group instead of a single proprietary. The territory
granted extended north and south from the thirty-
sixth to the .thirty-first parallel and westward to
the south seas. In matters of administration and
government the charter reproduced the rights,
jurisdictions, and immunities of the palatinate of
Durham, that independent, self-governing fief
on the northern border of England which until
1536 remained outside the control of the kings of
England and formed a petty state by itself.[2] The
patentees of Carolina and their heirs were made true
and absolute lords, and the territory was called a
province. The lands were to be held in free and
common socage at a fixed rent of twenty marks.

---

[1] N. C. Col. Records, I., 20–23.
[2] Lapsley, The Palatinate of Durham (Harvard Historical
Studies, VIII.).

The proprietaries could grant titles of rank, were endowed with the patronage and advowson of churches, and could erect forts, fortresses, cities, towns, and boroughs. In matters of government they were granted full and absolute power to make laws, with the advice and assent of the freemen or their delegates, whom they could summon when they desired. They were empowered to issue ordinances, to execute all laws, to receive customs duties, to erect courts of judicature, and to establish a militia. They could allow full freedom of conscience if they wished, and free-trade as far as it was not forbidden by English statute.

Inasmuch as the original purpose of the grant was to provide a refuge for the discontented Barbadians, it was expected that they would be among the first colonists in the new territory. At the outset, however, certain claims had to be quieted. The old Heath title began to show signs of life; and about the same time a group of London adventurers who had subscribed funds to aid some New England undertaking (perhaps that of 1660) put in a claim to the territory about Cape Fear, based on the right of first discovery.[1] These claims were swept aside by an order of the Privy Council, and the way was thus cleared for the Barbadians.

Sir John Colleton was treasurer of the proprietaries, and through his friends in Barbadoes was already urging planters to come to Carolina. August

---

[1] *N. C. Col. Records*, I., 34–38.

10, 1663, an expedition under Captain Hilton
started from Barbadoes to spy out the new land,
financed by a large body of planters led by Henry
Evans and John Vassall, who drew up a plan of settlement, which they submitted to the proprietaries,
providing for the erection of a "county or corporation" on the soil of Carolina, with full powers of
local government.[1] The proprietaries did not like
the Barbadian draught and suggested another plan,
which bears the date of August 21, 1663.[2] This
interesting document provided for a governor and
council to be chosen by the proprietaries.

Nevertheless, they did not insist on their own
scheme, but allowed their agents, Peter Colleton and
Modyford, to exercise their discretion in a series of
proposals or concessions issued probably some time
after January 6, 1664. Their work is important, as,
indeed, are all these various draughts, in showing
the trend of political thought at that time. During
the years from 1640 to 1660, both in England and the
colonies, men were seeking for fundamental principles
of government and were endeavoring to put them
into practice. The charter of Barbadoes of 1652
emphasized freedom of conscience, assemblies freely
and voluntarily elected, and freedom of trade; and
it forbade monopolies and taxation without the

[1] *N. C. Col. Records*, I., 34, 35, 39-42; *Cal. of State Pap., Col.*,
1661-1668, § 457; Hilton, *Relation* (1664), reprinted in *Charleston Year-Book*, 1884, pp. 227-255; *Shaftesbury Papers*, 10, 11.

[2] Rivers, *Sketch of South Carolina*, 335-337; *N. C. Col.
Records*, I., 43, 153; *Cal. of State Pap., Col.*, 1675-1676, § 377.

consent of the taxed.[1] It was therefore natural that Modyford, who had helped to negotiate the Barbadoes treaty, should have joined with Colleton in promising liberty of conscience, immunity from customs, freedom of trade as far as the charter allowed, a free assembly, and laws which, if once accepted by the proprietaries, could not be repealed except by the power that enacted them.[2]

It is clear that in England the necessity was felt of granting prospective colonists the most liberal terms possible, and of allowing principles to have utterance in America that were no longer advocated at home. Yet for some reason, not entirely clear, the proprietaries refused to confirm the terms offered by Modyford and Peter Colleton, and consequently the first migration from Barbadoes was given up.

The proprietaries, lest they might seem to sleep on their patent, kept up an intermittent activity during the summer of 1664,[3] and in the winter began new negotiations with Sir John Yeamans and eighty-five associates in Barbadoes. A formal agreement was carefully drawn up under which the new settlement was to be made, and on January 7, 1665, a new body of Concessions was presented.[4]

This plan of government is the one already familiar to the student of the history of the Jerseys, for six weeks afterwards it was granted by Berkeley and

[1] Schomburgk, *Hist. of Barbadoes*, 280–283.
[2] *Charleston Year-Book*, 1884, pp. 255–266.
[3] *Cal. of State Pap., Col.*, 1661–1668, § 1192.
[4] *N. C. Col. Records*, I., 75–92.

Carteret to those about to settle in that special propriety. Though the Concessions were liberal in allowing toleration, free elections, naturalization, and the right of petition, they lacked the simplicity of the earlier privileges, and were thoroughly dominated by the all-pervading authority of the proprietaries. They were approved by the settlers of New Jersey— at least by those who wrote the alluring descriptions of that province for the purpose of attracting emigrants; but they never had much influence in Carolina, and, compared with the systems already in force in Maryland and New England, they have the character of a constitution based on theory and good intentions rather than on practical experience.

Yeamans's expedition left Barbadoes in October, 1665, and after many vicissitudes reached the mouth of the Charles River, within the region already set off by the proprietaries as the county of Clarendon, and, according to Sanford's account, "newly begun to be peopled." This statement may refer to a settlement said to have been made by Englishmen some time in 1663 or 1664, to which Sir William Berkeley also may have referred when he wrote that "two hundred families from New England, we hear, are seated a little to the south of us."[1] Whether or not the Yeamans party found

[1] Sanford, *The Port Royal Discovery*, *N. C. Col. Records*, I., 119; *A Brief Description of the Province of Carolina*, *ibid.*, 156 ; *Egerton MSS.*, in British Museum, 2395, ff. 362–364.

settlers already on the ground, the settlement lan-
guished from the beginning. Relief was vainly
sought from Virginia, and a second charter was obtained in 1665, according to which the boundaries
were extended to include the territory southward.
To open up that region, Sanford undertook an ad-
venturous voyage, and, having rediscovered Port Royal in July, 1666, took formal possession of that country
by turf and twig. But this discovery availed little.
Deserted by their leader, Yeamans, who returned to
Barbadoes, the settlers became desperate. Clothing
and necessaries failed, the Indians became threatening, the conditions of land-settling embodied in the
Concessions proved to be exceedingly irksome, and
no new settlers arrived either from Barbadoes or
from the adjoining colonies.[1] Finally, the colonists
broke up the settlement in the fall of 1667 and scattered, some going to Albemarle and Virginia, others
to Boston. Once more, save for the single colony
on the Chowan River, Carolina was without a settlement within its borders.

The plan of colonizing Carolina from Barbadoes
having failed, a change in policy seemed necessary. Ashley now came forward more prominently
than before as the true leader of the undertaking.
The new patent of 1665 included the Albemarle
settlement on the north, which by this time was
fairly well established. In 1664 William Drummond

---

[1] Letter of John Vassall, *N. C. Col. Records*, I., 160. Cf. *Cal.
of State Pap., Col.*, 1675–1676, § 390.

was sent over as governor,[1] and a general assembly
met in 1665, which may have been composed, as the
Concessions demanded, of a governor, council, and
twelve delegates. It is noteworthy that the first
recorded action of the body is a petition to the lords
proprietaries begging for easier methods of allotting
lands, on the ground that the existing conditions
discouraged many who might otherwise have come
there from Virginia. The assembly also protested
against the proprietaries' attempt to make the people settle in towns.[2] In 1667, under the Concessions
of 1665, the assembly successfully petitioned that
the colony might have its lands on the same
terms as were allowed in Virginia:[3] according to
a contemporary, "rather than to be stinted with
small proportions at a great rent."

When the colony at Albemarle was thus fairly
started on its way, Ashley renewed his attempt to
settle the southern portion of the province, and,
stimulated by the reports of Sanford, determined
to plant the next colony at Port Royal. In the
mean time, dissatisfied with all the proposals for
government that had thus far been draughted, he
planned an entirely new scheme, and called upon
John Locke to draw up a frame of government
suitable for a palatinate. This extraordinary docu-

[1] Bassett, *Constitutional Beginnings of North Carolina; N. C.
Col. Records*, I., 93; *Cal. of State Pap., Col.*, 1661 – 1668,
§§ 908, 1005, 1192, 1222.
[2] *Cal. of State Pap., Col.*, 1661–1668, § 1005.
[3] *N. C. Col. Records*, I., 175, 176.

ment, known as the Fundamental Constitutions,[1] was completed in 1669, and is a notable instance of a constitution made to order without regard to the needs of the people for whom it was intended. The proprietaries were to become a group of palatine officials—palatine, admiral, chamberlain, and the like—each in full and absolute control of some part of what was intended to be the administrative business of the province. Within the territory itself an hereditary nobility was to be created, consisting of landgraves and casiques, and colonies of freeholders were to constitute the mass of the people. The whole territory was to be divided into counties, and these into seignories to be held by the proprietaries; baronies and manors to be held by the nobility; and precincts within which "colonies" were to be planted at the rate of four to a precinct.

Elaborate rules based on feudal law touched inheritance, alienation, devolution, and escheat, and gave rise at once to great discontent. The freeholders were to have their lands in the precincts and to pay quit-rent; to occupy sundry offices, provided they possessed a sufficient amount of freehold land; and to vote for delegates to the parliament. Lowest of all, except slaves, were to be the class of leet-men and women—a faint survival of English villeinage—

---

[1] *N. C. Col. Records*, I., 187–205. The original draught, with Locke's corrections, in Deputy Keeper of the Public Records, 33d *Report* (1872), App. iii., 258–269; and in *Shaftesbury Papers*. Cf. *Cal. of State Pap., Col.*, 1669–1674, §§ 84, 157; for proprietaries' point of view, see *ibid.*, 1685–1688, § 1162.

tenants settled in villages on the baronies and manors and bound to the soil. There were to be a grand council, eight proprietors' courts, county courts with justices and sheriffs, precinct courts with justices and stewards, a grand jury, itinerant judges, petty juries, and finally a parliament composed of the nobility, and freeholders elected under a considerable property franchise.

This constitution, except in a few instances, where baronies were actually laid out for settlers, was never applied in Carolina, but the attempt of the proprietaries to force its use for more than twenty years had an important influence on the development of the colony. It is chiefly interesting as showing what Locke, Ashley, and the others thought a palatinate ought to be. They wished to avoid too numerous a democracy and to introduce aristocracy and rich men, but they wished also to give expression to the prevailing ideas of the day by admitting full religious toleration,[1] trial by jury, and a limited measure of self-government. Planned as a general scheme for all the colonies that Ashley was to promote — eventually three — its provisions seemed to him the best that had ever been stated anywhere, its conditions the fairest, and its laws the "equalest" that a people could have. "We have no other aim," he said in 1671, "in the framing of our laws but to make every one as safe and happy

[1] *Shaftesbury Papers*, 312; *Shaftesbury Papers*, MSS. in Public Record Office, X., 8 (iv.).

as the state of human affairs is capable of." [1]
Locke and Ashley were very earnest in their work;
the former spoke of the colonies as his "darlings"
and did a vast amount of clerical labor in their
behalf, while the latter gave thought, time, and
money to their development.

While Locke was providing a form of government Ashley was promoting a new settlement.
Funds were provided by the proprietaries,[2] vessels
were purchased, some ninety-two immigrant-freemen
and servants were obtained, and careful instructions
were drawn up.[3] The expedition sailed in August,
1669, for Barbadoes,[4] where it arrived at the very
end of October; and with some sixty additional
settlers[5] the fleet started late in November for
Carolina.

After a stormy voyage and many hardships the
voyagers reached the Bermudas. There Sir John
Yeamans, who was to be the governor of the new
settlement, turned back, handing over the governorship to a certain William Sayle, a Bermudian and a
Dissenter, as were most of the emigrants,[6] and
"a man of no great sufficiency." [7] The expedition

---

[1] *Shaftesbury Papers*, 208–210, 314; *Cal. of State Pap., Col.*,
1669–1674, § 492.

[2] *Cal. of State Pap., Col.*, 1669–1674, §§ 54, 55.

[3] *Shaftesbury Papers*, 117–132.   [4] *Ibid.*, 133–156.

[5] Accounts vary a little. Cf. *Shaftesbury Papers*, 157, 163,
178; *Cal. of State Pap., Col.*, 1669–1674, § 163.

[6] Rivers, *South Carolina*, App., 462; *Shaftesbury Papers*, 171.

[7] *Ibid.*, 217, 218; cf. *ibid.*, 163, 189, 291; *N. C. Col. Records*,
I., 207.

went first to Port Royal, following the instructions of the proprietaries, but finally turned northward and landed near the mouth of the Kiawha, a river to which the settlers gave the name of Ashley, after their proprietary.[1] Here was established the settlement of old Charles Town.

For the first year the colony can hardly be said to have prospered. The town was laid out, lands near by were distributed, and some attempt was made to plant corn and potatoes, but early frosts spoiled the crops, and provisions soon became scarce. Through the efforts of Dr. Henry Woodward, who was familiar with the Indian language, friendly relations were entered into with the adjacent tribes, and some help was obtained; but it became necessary to send to Virginia for new supplies and to Barbadoes and New England for horses, cows, and more settlers. The place proved healthful, and of the few that died only one was from England; later, however, fever and ague became frequent complaints.

Political troubles arose early. Sayle was an old man and in bad health and had "much lost himself in his government."[2] At the beginning, acting under the instructions, he caused five councillors to be elected by the people, but he called no "parliament" because there were not enough freemen to

---

[1] Carteret, *Relation*, reprinted in *Charleston Year-Book*, 1883, p. 370; *Shaftesbury Papers*, 165–168; Mathews, *Relation*, *ibid.*, 169–171.   [2] *Shaftesbury Papers*, 203, 204.

elect representatives. Trouble having arisen over the observance of Sunday, Sayle called the freemen together and read them a series of orders drawn up by the council on this and one or two other matters. At this point William Owens, "a Magna Charta and Petition of Rights man," told the people that they could have no laws without a parliament, and in some way persuaded them to elect delegates;[1] but this body, irregularly chosen and irregularly called, accomplished nothing. After Sayle's death, March 4, 1671, West was elected governor by the colonists, "because they stood in great need of a head at once," but he issued the same orders somewhat revised. Owens declared that they were illegal "because the great seal of the province was not in the colony,"[2] and West had some difficulty in quieting the colonists, who feared lest the titles to their lands might be endangered because the great seal of the province remained in England.[3]

[1] *Shaftesbury Papers*, 291, 292, 300.   [2] *Ibid.*, 294.
[3] See *Cal. of State Pap., Col.*, 1681–1685, § 1733.

CHAPTER X

GOVERNMENTAL PROBLEMS IN THE CAROLINAS
(1671 1691)

THE situation at Charles Town was not satisfactory to Ashley, who was in the full flush of his colonial undertaking, and was determined that his plans should not be thwarted. Urged on by the governor and council of Carolina, and by certain merchants of Bermuda, he "got of his Majestie," on November 1, 1670, a grant of the Bahamas for himself and the other remaining proprietaries.[1] He placed the colony under the government of the Fundamental Constitutions, with Hugh Wentworth as governor, and planned to build up a system of co-operation and trade among the three colonies situated at Albemarle, Charles Town, and New Providence in the Bahamas.[2] A later attempt to plant a colony on the Edisto seems to indicate that he meant to include other settlements also in the union. To let the Charles Town settlement die would endanger the entire scheme, so that in the summer of 1670 Ashley ordered

---

[1] Ante, 132, n.
[2] *Shaftesbury Papers*, 207. Cf. *N. C. Col. Records*, I., 228.

Sayle to issue a proclamation offering all sorts of inducements to the people of Barbadoes to come to Carolina. Thomas Colleton, son of the late Sir John and brother of the present proprietary, Sir Peter, took the matter in hand and sent from Barbadoes the *John and Thomas* with forty-two passengers, who reached Charles Town February 16, 1671. Eight days later the *Carolina* arrived with sixty-four passengers.[1]

The new settlers were welcomed by the colonists and received homes near the town. The leader of the Barbadians was Captain Godfrey, Sir Peter Colleton's deputy and an experienced soldier and planter. The colony needed men of this type to take places in the council and to build up agricultural life, for the earlier settlers had been chiefly tradesmen by profession. In the same year Ashley sent another ship from England, the *Blessing*, which arrived May 14, 1671, and he declared that he proposed to continue sending ships until a thousand people were in the colony and the place was established.

The active proprietaries were now only four— Ashley (made earl of Shaftesbury April 23, 1672), Craven, Carteret, and Colleton. Seemingly they realized that their Grand Model could not be made immediately practicable, for they had erected a temporary form of government in the commission and instructions issued to Sayle in 1669;[2] and now

---

[1] *Shaftesbury Papers*, 266–268.
[2] *Ibid.*, 117–119; Rivers, *South Carolina*, App., 340, 347.

did the same in a new body of instructions and
a set of temporary laws sent over on the *Blessing.*
Again urging settlement in towns as safer and more
conducive to trade, they sent over a description of
a town organization such as they would like to see
established.[1]

As the settlers increased in number, the government of the colony began to take definite form. After
the death of Sayles, West became governor, but
Yeamans, arriving from Barbadoes in July, 1671,
claimed the office, because under the Fundamental
Constitutions only landgraves could be governors,
and he was the only person in the colony with such a
title.   West retained the governorship, however, for
seven months longer, and managed the colony successfully.   The council, composed of the deputies
of the proprietaries and five elected by the people, met regularly and prepared bills for the parliament which began to sit for the first time in August,
1671.   Several important measures were passed, one
of which, authorizing the payment of the Lords
Proprietaries' debts, was received with great ap
proval in England, for profits were as yet unknown
to the proprietaries.   They must have spent the
equivalent of $250,000 to $300,000 upon the
colony,[2] and neither at this time nor afterwards
received any return for their expenditure.   In later

---

[1] *Cal. of State Pap., Col.,* 1669–1674, § 514.   Cf. *Shaftesbury
Papers,* 343.

[2] *Ibid.,* 358; McCrady, *Hist. of S. C.,* I., 273, 274.

years the stockholders' rights depreciated greatly in value and were often sold for almost nothing, a fact that will explain the inferior character of some of the later proprietaries.

Yeamans finally got his commission and arrived in April, 1672, but he soon made it clear that he had sought the office only for his own good. He represented the Barbadians in the colony, and, as the proprietaries finally discovered, took advantage of his position to benefit himself.[1] They discovered, too, that instead of trying to pay the debt of the colony, due to the proprietaries, as West had proposed, he was constantly calling for new expenditures. They therefore revoked his commission, and in April, 1674, created West a landgrave and appointed him governor.[2] The colony now entered on a period of prosperous rule for eight years.

During this period and down to 1690 the number of colonists increased rapidly. In 1672 there were four hundred and six men, women, and children in the colony;[3] by 1685 the population had risen to at least two thousand five hundred, if we may accept Ashe's estimate of one thousand to twelve hundred in 1682.[4] The first considerable body of new-comers consisted of more than a hundred French Protestants. The commissioners of customs op-

[1] Cal. of State Pap., Col., 1669–1674, 325, §§ 861, 971; Shaftesbury Papers, 416–419.   [2] N. C. Col. Records, I., 220.
[3] Cal. of State Pap., Col., 1669–1674, § 736.
[4] Carroll, Hist. Collections, II., 82.

posed their departure, thinking that they should be
encouraged to remain in England; but both the king
and the proprietaries favored the scheme, a subscrip-
tion was raised, and the consent of the Lords of
Trade and Plantations was obtained.[1] Many men
of estates recommended by the proprietaries to the
governor of Carolina went out also and received lands
in the colony. Additional settlers came from Barbadoes and other colonies, and for a decade after
1680 the influx was rapid.

The uneasiness and popular unrest in England
during the years from 1679 to 1685 sent large
numbers of Protestants to America, many of whom
came to Carolina. Five hundred from western
England are said to have arrived in one month,
thus doubling the population of the settlement.[2]
A large colony of Scots, who at first intended to go
to New York, changed their minds and went to
Port Royal in 1683, and other Scots would have
followed had they not been prevented.[3]

For several years the proprietaries had been
urging the transfer of the centre of settlement
from the old town to a place better adapted for
trade and capable of defence. The site selected

---

[1] *N. C. Col. Records*, I., 242, 243; *Cal. of State Pap., Col.,*
1677–1680, §§ 875, 888, 918–920, 930, 967, 1000, 1006, 1149,
1167, 1233.

[2] McCrady, *Hist. of S. C.*, 193, 194; Archdale and Oldmixon,
in Carroll, *Hist. Collections*, II.

[3] *Cal. of State Pap., Col.*, 1681–1685, §§ 809, 1774; Hist.
MSS. Commission, *Report*, VII., 407; XIV., pt. iii., 113.

was across the river at Oyster Point, at the junction of the Ashley and Cooper rivers. Here in 1680 new Charles Town arose, and before a decade passed became the largest centre of trade and the most important settlement south of Philadelphia. In 1682 the settlement began to expand somewhat towards the interior.[1]

Progress from the sea-coast into the back country was, however, slow, and the difficulties which attended the occupation of the uplands, where lay the best soil in the colony, proved a serious obstacle to the growth of the settlement. Though in the main relations with the Indians were peaceful, trouble began in 1681 with the Westoes, whom Thomas Newe spoke of as "a tribe of barbarous Indians, being not above sixty in number, but by reason of their great growth and cruelty in feeding on all their neighbors, terrible to all other Indians, of which there are about forty other kingdoms." The colonists were determined to exterminate this body of "man - eaters," who had killed two "eminent planters"; and not only went out themselves in small bands, but aroused and armed the peaceful Indians to discover the settlement of the Westoes and to destroy the tribe. This attack aroused a general excitement along the frontier, and for three years an intermittent Indian warfare continued.

To danger from the Indians was soon added

[1] *Cal. of State Pap., Col.*, 1677 – 1680, § 1233; 1681 – 1685, § 497.

danger from the Spaniards settled at St. Augustine since 1565: "a place," as Newe wrote, "belonging to our proprietors about one hundred and fifty miles to the south of us, where the Spaniards are seated and have a pretty strong town."[1] The colonists prepared for defence, and desired a just pretext to undertake an aggressive war, but the proprietaries rigidly forbade them to take any offensive action, inasmuch as England and Spain were at peace.[2] In 1685 the Spaniards appeared in force before the English settlements and burned many homes. The colonists retaliated by arranging with two French privateers to attack St. Augustine, but changed their plans because of peremptory orders which came from the proprietaries. In 1686 the Spaniards appeared again, and destroyed Stewart's Town, the seat of the Scottish settlement of Lord Cardross at Port Royal.

Thus far the colonists had suffered but little from proprietary interference in matters of government. To be sure, Shaftesbury declared that "the compass you are to steer by is the Fundamental Constitutions, the Temporary Laws, and the Instructions," and bade his deputy, Mathews, "obstinately to stick to those rules and to oppose all deviations."[3] Nevertheless, at no time during his period of control

---

[1] Newe to his father, *Rawlinson MSS.*, in Bod. Lib., D 810, f. 54.
[2] *Cal. of State Pap., Col.*, 1681–1685, § 1651; cf. 1685–1688, § 1167.
[3] *Shaftesbury Papers*, 397 – 399; *Cal. of State Pap., Col.*, 1669–1674, § 862.

did he seek to force on the colonists more of the Fundamentals than "were capable of being put into practice." The government was in the main simple and satisfactory, the colonists minding but little the appointment of nominal landgraves and casiques, the proprietaries' control of patronage, and the creation of baronies.

From 1672 to 1682 the life of the colony flowed on smoothly. But after the latter year Morton, who had aided the emigration of Dissenters from western England, was superseded by West; and frequent changes in government followed, which mark a period of unrest and of friction between proprietaries and colonists. Nearly all the original patentees were dead: Shaftesbury was disgraced; and only John Berkeley and Craven remained. The others were new men, with less knowledge and less tact than their predecessors, and their task was made heavier by the increase in the size of the colony, the presence among the colonists of men of great independence and experience, and the frequent recurrence of intricate and difficult problems. Proprietary interference from 1682 to 1689 was of such a character as to drive the colonists almost to open rebellion.

At first the proprietaries attempted to tamper with the freedom of trade in the colony; and Thomas Newe reports that he found the colonists in a state of great excitement in 1682, because of the attempt of a few men to monopolize the Indian traffic in

furs. Then arose a difficulty with the Fundamental
Constitutions, which the colonists had always refused to confirm by any act of their own parliament. By the same vessel that brought Newe to
the colony the proprietaries sent over a revised
draught of the Fundamentals, with some slight additions which evidently were designed to encourage
emigration of Dissenters from western England.[1]
Before they could hear from the colonists regarding
this draught they decided to revise the Fundamentals still further; and on August 17, 1682, sent over
another draught, at the special request of the Scots
and "some other considerable men," who were already
planning to emigrate to Carolina, and who declared
that the articles contained too few guarantees
against oppression by the governors and other
officials of the colony.[2]

The new constitution placed more power in the
hands of the people and limited to a small extent
the authority of the proprietaries; but the colonists
rejected these articles as they had the others. These
repeated rejections irritated the proprietaries, who
now declared that they would not permit the
Constitutions to be "used again till the people were
fit to enjoy them and till they petition for that
which they now reject."[3]

From this time forward the proprietaries became

---

[1] *Cal. of State Pap., Col.*, 1681-1685, § 496.
[2] *Ibid.*, §§ 807, 1780, and p. 510; 1689-1692, § 1117.
[3] *Ibid.*, 1681-1685, § 1780.

more imperative. They charged the settlers with
disregard of their interest and contempt of their
orders, and were irritated by the unfriendly treatment accorded Lord Cardross and his Scots, and
by the failure of the Charles Town government to
deliver certain cannon for the protection of the
Scottish settlement (Stewart's Town) at Port
Royal.[1] They changed the system of granting
land by patent to granting by indenture, which
required payment of quit-rent in money;[2] they
complained of the selling of Indians as slaves, which
brought about war and interfered with trade and
their profits; they rebuked Governor West sharply
for acting against their orders, saying, "Pray, are
you to govern the people or the people you?"[3]
Their letters became so peremptory that West,
appointed governor for the third time in 1684,
resigned in despair, and in 1685 Morton for the
second time was appointed to succeed him.

Times had changed; the days of Shaftesbury were
gone; the days of James II. and Jeffreys were come,
and the colonists readily perceived the difference.
When the colonial parliament met, November 19,
1685, Governor Morton, carrying out the orders
given him, declared that every one must swear
allegiance to the new king, fidelity to the proprietaries, and acceptance of the Fundamentals.

[1] *Cal. of State Pap., Col.*, 1685–1688, § 1163; 1689–1692, § 1117.
[2] *Ibid.*, 1685–1688, § 639.
[3] *Ibid.*, 1685–1688, § 59; cf. §§ 363, 364, 365.

Twelve members refused to do this and withdrew, and next day were excluded from the parliament.

In the mean time, Morton, who had fallen under the displeasure of the proprietaries, was dismissed, and in the summer of 1686 James Colleton, son of the old Sir John and an unworthy scion of the Colleton house, was commissioned in his stead, apparently for reasons connected with the attitude of the colonists towards the navigation acts. When George Muschamp was appointed king's collector of customs in Carolina in 1685, he was not well received by the colony. Reports of illegal trading came to the knowledge of the Lords of Trade, and were transmitted to the proprietaries, who warned Morton against suffering any ships to trade contrary to law.[1] The matter gave them great concern, for already the Lords of Trade were recommending the annulment of all the proprietary and corporate charters, and the Carolina proprietaries were anxious to do everything in their power to prevent the prosecution of a writ of *quo warranto* against theirs.[2]

Colleton arrived in the colony late in the year 1687; and soon after his arrival a committee was appointed to examine the Fundamentals, in the hope of suggesting such changes as would make possible

[1] *Cal. of State Pap., Col.*, 1685–1688, § 639; *Journal of the Lords of Trade*, VI., 97–98. The proprietaries disclaimed all responsibility, see *Cal. of State Pap., Col.*, 1685–1688, § 1417.
[2] *N. C. Col. Records*, I., 263; *Cal. of State Pap., Col.*, 1685–1688, §§ 767, 1417; Rivers, *South Carolina*, App., 393.

an agreement with the proprietaries.[1] The work dragged on until February 14, 1688, when Colleton, in anger, produced the letter of the proprietaries stating that the Fundamentals of 1669 had no official standing. Thereupon a deadlock ensued; the governor and council adhered to the orders from England, while the delegates of the people stood by their former decision not to recognize any other constitution than that of 1669. They went further and voted that the government ought to be conducted according to the charters and not the Fundamentals, and denied that any bill need necessarily pass the council before it was read in parliament.[2] Legislation stopped. The colony, already stirred to its depths by the Spanish inroad of 1686, by the controversy over illegal trading, and by the difficulties with privateers and pirates, and now exasperated by the attitude of the proprietaries, was almost on the eve of revolt.

Colleton began to govern with a high hand. At the request of certain colonists he proclaimed martial law, and refused to call another parliament. Seth Sothell, who had become a proprietary by buying out Lord Clarendon's share, but for misgovernment had been banished from Albemarle by the people of that colony, came to Charles Town and claimed the governorship according to the terms of the

---

[1] Oldmixon, in Carroll, *Hist. Collections*, II., 411, 412.
[2] Abstract in *Cal. of State Pap., Col.*, 1685–1688, § 1962, full text in Rivers, *South Carolina*, 423.

Fundamental Constitutions. He was welcomed by the opposition party, and in December, 1690, after seizing the records, called a parliament (which in all probability was the first to meet since February, 1688). In March, 1691, he convened another parliament and obtained the passage of acts banishing Colleton and his friends.[1]

The proprietaries refused to sanction such lawless proceedings. Having charged Sothell with disobedience of their orders, with seizure of their letters and deputations, with holding illegal parliaments, and with supporting acts offensive in themselves and illegally passed, they suspended him from the governorship on November 8, 1691, and appointed Philip Ludwell in his place. Although eleven years passed before the Fundamental Constitutions were officially abandoned, it is evident that they were already a dead letter, owing to the determination of the colonists not to receive them; that in many important particulars the authority of the proprietaries was strenuously resisted; and that English practices and English customs, whether in government, parliamentary distribution, or forms of land tenure, in so far as they did not conform to the needs of the colonists or to their sense of fairness and equity, could not be enforced in the Carolinas.

In the county of Albemarle in the northern part of the province similar issues were working themselves out in a rather more tumultuous way.

[1] *Cal. of State Pap. Col.*, 1689–1692, §§ 1488–1490, 1535, 1539.

Stephens was made governor in 1667, but for ten years we hear little of the life of the colony. The inhabitants were composed of wanderers from Virginia who had obtained lands under patent from Berkeley before 1663. In that year and the year following a large number of Quakers came into the province, forming an influential body among the inhabitants. Though the lands were fertile the settlement never had much encouragement from the proprietaries. It was not exactly neglected, but occupied a minor place in their thoughts. The people were poor, the assignments of land small, and the quit-rents high, though the conditions were somewhat modified by the proprietaries.[1] There was no clergyman in the colony in 1670, and laws passed in that year indicate the difficulties confronting a settlement without sufficient support, and isolated from the world outside.[2] Life was purely agricultural, the only export being furs and tobacco, shipped in vessels from New England, whose merchants seem, to the vexation of the proprietaries, to have monopolized their business.

The proprietaries repeatedly urged the Albemarle colonists to open up negotiations with the southern settlement and to send their products directly to England instead of allowing them to fall into the hands of the New-Englanders. They also urged them to expand their settlement and to colonize not only the shores of the Pamlico but the valley

[1] Ante, 139.   [2] N. C. Col. Records, I., 183-187.

of the Neuse as well. The colony showed little eagerness to please the proprietaries, and the latter could say in reply that "the neglect of these two [instructions] has been the cause that hitherto we have had no more regard for you as looking upon you as a people that neither understood your own nor regarded our interests."[1]

Stephens was succeeded in 1670 by Peter Carteret, Sir George Carteret's deputy in the colony and president of the council. To him were sent the Fundamental Constitutions and a body of temporary laws and instructions defining the form the government should take until the Fundamentals could be put into practice.[2] But his government was not successful, for what reason it is not easy to determine. In all probability his connection with the Indian trade and the illicit trade with New England brought him into disfavor with the proprietaries.[3] Carteret was dismissed, and in 1677 Eastchurch, speaker of the Albemarle assembly, who had gone to England to lay the matter before the proprietaries, was appointed in his stead; but he appointed Miller, collector of customs, to act as governor in his place.

Miller was hardly the man to meet the situation, and no sooner had he arrived than trouble broke out. Some hundred or more of the colonists, who

---

[1] *N. C. Col. Records*, I., 228.   [2] *Ibid.*, 181–183.
[3] The instructions of 1676 seem to show this. See *ibid.*, 228–230.

were determined that they would not pay the penny a pound on all tobacco exported to the other colonies, rose against the government, and having imprisoned governor, president of the assembly, and all but one of the deputies, they usurped the power and controlled the colony for a year. While to personal grievances and questions of trade may be traced some of the causes of this movement, there can be little doubt, if one may judge from the Pasquotank appeal for a "free parliament," that poverty and dislike of misgovernment lay at the bottom of the popular support of the uprising. The matter was soon ended. Miller was charged with holding his office without legal authority and was ejected by the proprietaries.

In the mean time, Sothell, already mentioned in connection with Charles Town, was appointed governor by the proprietaries. Having been captured by Algerine pirates, he did not reach the colony till 1683, when he found the condition of affairs hopelessly confused. The authority of the proprietaries availed little, land titles were doubtful, the question of pirates and privateers was becoming a burning one in the colony, and a feeling of unrest seemed prevalent among the colonists.

Sothell only made matters worse, and was sharply called to account by the proprietaries,[1] who were already bending to the storm of the *quo warranto*

---

[1] *N. C. Col. Records*, I., 350-352; for charges against Sothell, see 368-371.

inquiries. But the people saved them further trouble. Seizing Sothell, they banished him from the colony, and though he was one of the " true and absolute lords of the province," the proprietaries acquiesced in this act on the ground that he had acted contrary to the Fundamental Constitutions. They appointed Philip Ludwell governor, first of Albemarle, and in 1691 of the southern province also, and henceforth Albemarle was governed by a deputy sent from the southern colony.

Few colonies could show a more consistent discontent, more bitter party feeling and personal hostility than did Albemarle. Even more than its neighbor it suffered from foolish laws and injudicious instructions, as well as from bad governors. To the proprietaries and the Lords of Trade it must have seemed a hot-bed of bickering and discontent, yet, were the full truth known, as it cannot be because of lack of indisputable evidence, it might be seen that the discontent was due to the attempts of a body of poor though honest settlers to get the most out of the circumstances in which they were placed, despite the policy of the proprietaries and the self-seeking activities of their appointees.

CHAPTER XI

FOUNDATION OF PENNSYLVANIA
(1680–1691)

ALMOST twenty years passed after the conquest of New Netherland before the southern portion of the territory claimed by the Dutch was colonized by the English. The settlement of Pennsylvania was due to the deep interest already aroused among the members of the Society of Friends in the colonization of the New World. In 1653 members of this religious body began to come to America, and at one time or another sought refuge in each of the colonies there established. They came first as missionaries, and in their outspoken defence of their faith roused against themselves the hostility of the New England Puritans, who had no intention of building up a home for people who differed in religious belief from themselves.

In the years from 1653 to 1660 the Puritans banished some of the Quakers, imprisoned many, and hanged three—Robinson, Stevenson, and Mary Dyer. The commissioners of the New England Confederation recommended in 1656 that all Quakers should be kept out of the colonies, and the legislat-

162

ures of Massachusetts Bay, Plymouth, and Connecticut enacted laws to this effect.   Only Rhode Island gave them a welcome: the assembly wrote a letter to the United Commissioners, declaring that freedom of conscience was "the greatest happiness that men can possess in the world."   But Long Island and New Amsterdam, following the example of Massachusetts Bay, flogged and imprisoned the Quaker preachers.   Only in Shelter Island, far removed from the populous towns of western Long Island, and existing for the time being independent of any higher jurisdiction, lived a small body of Quakers unmolested by the colonial authorities.

After 1660 the number of Quakers in America rapidly increased, owing to the persecutions that began in England soon after the outbreak of the Fifth Monarchy men in 1660.[1]   The harrying of the Nonconformists that followed the Conventicle Acts of 1664 and 1670 fell with exceptional severity upon members of the Society of Friends, because of their practice of holding meetings at stated times and places, and because of their refusal to change their practice in order to avoid arrest and imprisonment.   Persecution followed them to America, and efforts, less prolonged, but none the less determined, were made there to crush out the new religious body.   In Maryland they were fined and imprisoned, not only because they held an unwelcome faith, but also because they refused to

[1] Fox, *Journal* (ed. 1694), 337.

bear arms and to take the oath that the colony required.

Oppressed in Virginia, a body of Friends pushed southward into the wilderness and joined the colony at Albemarle; while in the north others left New England and settled at Shrewsbury in the region afterwards to be known as East New Jersey. Thus in Rhode Island, Shelter Island, New Jersey, Maryland, Virginia, and Carolina, communities of Quaker colonists existed, whose life was characterized by humility, simplicity, and agricultural thrift. George Fox, the founder of the society, made a noteworthy journey among them in 1672, visiting all the communities from Rhode Island to Carolina, holding meetings and encouraging his followers. His journal gives a vivid picture of the extent of Quaker settlement in America before the appearance of William Penn as a promoter of Quaker colonization.[1]

This situation was far from satisfactory to those interested in the future of Quaker settlement in America; the communities were widely scattered and without unity. Save in Rhode Island, where Quakers obtained control of the government from 1673 to 1677 and furnished the governors and most of the deputies, they were without political influence, and had to be content to dwell under a government not of their own making. It became eminently desirable that a place should be found

[1] Fox, *Journal*, 362–383.

where they could be free to live in peace and to erect a government of their own.

As early as 1660 George Fox thought of purchasing land in America for a Quaker settlement, and made inquiries of Josiah Coale regarding a suitable territory in Maryland. The region suggested lay at the head of Chesapeake Bay along the Susquehanna River, back to the Susquehanna fort. But the conditions were not favorable, and the project was given up.[1] Nothing more was done until after 1666, when Penn became a member of the society and a large number of well-to-do and influential men became associated with the movement. To obtain territory in America was no easy matter, for the seaboard was already occupied, and an inland region would not be favorable to commerce, which was likely to be the chief activity of the colony.

William Penn, the founder of Pennsylvania, was the son of Admiral Penn, a leading naval officer of his day and one of the commanders of the expedition which captured Jamaica in 1655. He was brought up at Wanstead, in Essex, and matriculated at Oxford in 1660, when sixteen years of age. Even at that early date he was intimate with John Owen, the Puritan divine, and listened with sympathy to the discourses of Thomas Loe, the Quaker. When the admiral learned of his son's interest in Nonconformist ideas and preachings, he sent him

---

[1] Coale to Fox, in Bowden, *Hist. of Friends*, I., 389, 390.

off to the Continent, where young Penn entered into the gayeties of the French court, travelled in Italy, and a little later took service in the Dutch war, donning the armor which, in strange contradiction to Quaker principles, appears in the only authentic portrait that exists of the great Quaker leader. On his return to England he entered Lincoln's Inn to prepare himself for the profession of law; but in 1666, while visiting his father's estate in Ireland, he met Thomas Loe at Cork and was converted to Quakerism. His father, angry at this thwarting of his plans for Penn's future career, turned against him, but before his own death in 1670 he became reconciled with his son and aided him when with other Quakers he was persecuted for his faith.

Admiral Penn left to his son what was then considered the large income of £1500 a year;[1] yet towards the end of the decade Penn appears to have been financially embarrassed.[2] Admiral Penn had left an important claim upon the king, consisting of arrears of pay and of money which had been advanced from time to time to supply the navy. This debt was repudiated in 1672 by the Stop of the Exchequer, and the royal promise of interest was unfulfilled till 1677, and then was paid only in part. This loss of interest for five years raised Penn's claim from £11,000 to £16,000, and, taken in

[1] *Memorials of Sir William Penn*, II., 560, 570, 571, 617–619.
[2] Preamble to petition, Hazard, *Annals*, 474.

conjunction with losses in Ireland, reduced very materially the value of Penn's estate. It was at this time, therefore, that Penn determined to petition the king for a grant of land in America.

The thought was not new to him. Before he became a Quaker he had been eager to discover a region where he might experiment with certain theories of government which he had begun to formulate as early as 1661 at Oxford. That he was familiar with the writings of More and Harrington we may well believe; that he was a friend of Henry and Algernon Sydney we know; and that he was an observer of "mischiefs in government" and desired "to settle one" of his own his letters tell us.[1] But it was not until after 1673 that he began seriously to consider the plan of colonization, and, as we have already seen, not until 1674 that he joined with others of his faith in attempting to obtain an interest in the Jerseys.

Just when Penn first formed the plan of building up a colony of his own in America we do not know. As a favorite in the royal household, a friend of the duke of York, and intimate with many of the men interested in colonization in America, he must early have become aware that the territory taken from the Dutch on the west side of the Delaware was desirable. Nicolls, in his letters to the duke, to Clarendon, and to Bennett, later Lord Arlington, called attention to the region, and recommended it

[1] Penn, in Pa. Hist. Soc., *Memoirs*, I., 210, 211.

as a substitute for what he considered the duke's unfortunate grant of East New Jersey to Carteret.[1]

Penn's New Jersey venture must have made him familiar with the region, and in the years from 1676 to 1680 he was trying to obtain the removal of the five per cent. tax which Andros, in the name of the duke of York, imposed on all goods entering the Delaware, and in his remonstrances displayed thorough knowledge of the legal questions involved;[2] while his description of the region in his later account of his province, issued before he left England, shows a like knowledge of the ground.[3] Penn differed from the other proprietaries in that he made profit a subordinate motive. He wished to found a colony for his fellow-Quakers, to try a new and holy experiment in government, and in person to build up the new settlement. Since the days of the Massachusetts Bay colony there had been among the various proprietaries and patentees no examples of motives such as these.

In June, 1680, Penn petitioned the king to grant him "letters-patent for a tract of land in America lying north of Maryland, on the east bounded by the Delaware River, on the west limited as Maryland, and northward to extend as far as plantable."[4] Penn did not ask for the territory

[1] N. J. Archives, I., 48, 55, 56; Clarendon Papers, 115.
[2] Pa. Magazine, V., 323–325.
[3] Hazard, Annals, 509, 510.
[4] Journal of the Lords of Trade, III., 173; Hazard, Annals, 474.

as payment for the debt, but rather that he might thereby restore his fortunes, believing that by a profitable conduct of the plantation he would be able to meet financial indebtedness incurred in consequence of his Irish losses and the repudiation of the amount owed him by the king. In a letter written in 1689 he said, "Had I pressed my own debts with King James, that his brother owed me, there had been sixteen thousand pounds." Evidently he still nominally claimed the debt, of which he was willing to remit the whole or a part.[1] The grant was to be made in consideration of the circumstances in which the debt had placed him, not in settlement of the debt itself.

The petition which was sent to the king was handed over to the Lords of Trade, and received by them June 14, 1680. It does not appear that in Penn's case the committee hesitated to increase the number of proprieties in America, a fact due undoubtedly to the influence of Penn at court and his friendship with Charles II. and the duke of York. So far as the minutes of its deliberations show, the committee in Penn's case was concerned chiefly with the difficulty of making the grant without detriment to the other proprietaries, the duke of York on the northeast and Lord Baltimore on the south.

The discussion showed great uncertainty as to

[1] *The Friend*, VII., 67; *Friends' Review*, I. 33, 34; *Journal of the Lords of Trade*, III., 174; *Pa. Magazine*, VI., 313.

the position of the fortieth parallel, which was fixed upon as Penn's southern boundary. The duke cared nothing for the boundaries north and west, but he wished to retain the New Castle colony. His agent, Sir John Werden, at once protested against the inclusion of that settlement, and Penn was required by the committee to reach an agreement with the duke privately on this point.[1] Werden proposed a southern line twenty or thirty miles north of New Castle, but Penn, who wished to control as much of the Delaware as possible, asked that the distance be reduced to twelve miles.[2] Sir John Werden dismissed the matter by saying, "I confess I do not understand why it is precisely necessary to insist on just such a number of miles, more or less, in a country of which we know so little."[3] Dutch and Burke, the agents of Baltimore, in their statement to the committee, requested that the line be drawn north of Susquehanna fort (which was supposed to mark the fortieth parallel), and to run thence eastward to the Delaware. Penn agreed to this line, and we are told that " Sir John Werden and my Lord Baltimore's agent attended my Lord Chief-Justice North at his chamber, and upon laying before his lordship their respective interests and both of them acquiescing in the bounds

[1] *Cal. of State Pap., Col.*, 1677–1680, §§ 1390, 1403; Hazard, *Annals*, 475, 476.

[2] Hazard, *Annals*, 482, 483; *Cal. of State Pap., Col.*, 1677–1680, §§ 1404, 1409, 1544, 1599.

[3] *Cal. of State Pap., Col.*, 1677–1680, § 1603.

as they stand now described, they were presented to
the committee and agreed upon by their lordships."[1]
All obstacles to the issue of the patent having thus
been removed, the committee reported favorably to
the king, and the charter was signed March 4, 1681.

The territory thus granted was bounded on the
east by the Delaware River and by a line drawn
from the head of that river to the forty-third
degree of northern latitude; on the south by a
semicircle whose periphery lay twelve miles distant
from New Castle north and northwest, intersecting
with the fortieth parallel, along which the boundary-
line ran through five degrees of longitude. These
boundaries involved two serious difficulties that became the subject of long and painful controversies.

In the first place, the critical phrase "three and
fortieth degree of northern latitude" (elsewhere in
the same charter called the "beginning of the three
and fortieth degree") might mean either the line
known as the forty-third degree or the zone between the forty-second and forty-third degrees.
If the former meaning were accepted, as Penn afterwards insisted and Governor Dongan thought would
be the case,[2] then Penn's grant would have extended
north of Albany and have controlled the Indian
trade of the Mohawk valley; and the five degrees
westward would have given to him a part of Lake

---

[1] "Letter to Mr. Lewen at New York concerning Mr. Pen's
Patent," *Egerton MSS.*, in British Museum, 2395, ff. 593, 594.

[2] *N. Y. Docs. Rel. to Col. Hist.*, III., 392, 394.

Erie and a share of the trade with Canada. By the latter interpretation, which was accepted a century later, the northern line of Pennsylvania would coincide with the forty-second degree or parallel.[1]

On the south the question was even more perplexing. Baltimore was entitled to territory extending as far north as the fortieth parallel, and possessed a legal title to the region covering the Dutch and Swedish settlements on the west bank of the Delaware. In the charter this territory was spoken of as "hitherto uncultivated," and the question was raised as to whether this statement did not exclude such portions as had been actually settled since 1632. Baltimore had never attempted to exercise jurisdiction over these northern settlements, which since 1664 had been under the government of the duke of York. Penn's charter confused matters still further, for the twelve-mile circle around New Castle did not intersect the fortieth parallel by at least eight miles. A settlement of the difficulty between Penn and Baltimore, based on a literal interpretation of the two charters, was manifestly out of the question.

The fault lies in the first instance with those who draughted Penn's charter. Penn was seeking ports, not land, because his province had no ocean front, a fact that is evident from his offer in 1683 to buy of Baltimore control of the Susquehanna River to its

---

[1] Regents' Commission, *Report on the New York and Pennsylvania Boundary* (1886).

mouth in order to gain an outlet on the Chesapeake. Baltimore, though possessing the whole of the Chesapeake and having an outlet to the ocean through the Potomac, declined Penn's offer.[1] Penn was justified in attempting to save his capital, Philadelphia, which was building before the controversy began, and in seeking to obtain a waterway for the commerce he planned to develop. Had all of Baltimore's claims been allowed, the value of Penn's grant would have been destroyed, whereas the province of Maryland as it then existed would have profited little, for Baltimore had never concerned himself with the lands northeast of Chesapeake Bay.

The question of the fortieth parallel and of the Chesapeake port was not the only cause of the long quarrel that followed. Penn became anxious regarding his control of Delaware Bay, and in 1681 applied to the duke of York for a grant of New Castle, the islands of the Delaware, and eventually for all the territory on the right bank of the Delaware to its mouth.[2] The duke demurred at first, but eventually yielded, and in August, 1682, deeded both New Castle and the lower territory to Penn.[3] But the duke's title was not itself clear, inasmuch as he had never received from the king any territory

---

[1] *Cal. of State Pap., Col.*, 1681–1685, §§ 356, 444; *Pa. Magazine*, VI., 423.

[2] Nicolls first suggested this in *N. Y. Docs. Rel. to Col. Hist.*, III., 70, 290.   [3] Hazard, *Annals*, 587–593.

on the west side of the Delaware, and exercised jurisdiction over Upland and New Castle rather by sufferance than by any legal warrant. It was necessary, therefore, that the duke of York get a release from the king.

Before this release was signed, Baltimore, in consternation at this further encroachment on his charter limits, appealed to the Lords of Trade, praying for an investigation.[1] Penn and the duke of York's counsel insisted that the Delaware water-front had never been possessed by Lord Baltimore; that the land had been originally inhabited by Dutch and Swedes, and that the grant to Baltimore had been only of lands not inhabited by Christians. They also insisted that all lands occupied by the Dutch had been surrendered to the king in 1664, and that such as had not been granted away since that time had remained in the king's possession.

For a year and a half the matter remained undecided, the committee postponing consideration of it, probably because of the anticipated *quo warranto* proceedings against Lord Baltimore's charter. When Penn showed that the question was, as he put it, one of "title to soil and not of power," the lords took up the matter in earnest, and on October 17, 1685, reached a first decision that the "tract of land in dispute did not belong to Lord Baltimore." Shortly

[1] *Journal of the Lords of Trade*, IV., 155, 156; *N. Y. Docs. Rel. to Col. Hist.*, III., 339, 340.

afterwards the committee modified this statement in a final decision, and in view of the uncertainty of the boundary divided the territory into equal parts by a north and south line from the New Castle circle to a point between the thirty-eighth and thirty-ninth parallels. This line became the basis of the final western boundary of the state of Delaware, and by this decision Baltimore retained possession of a large part of the "Eastern Shore."[1] He refused, however, to accept the decision of the committee and reopened the controversy in 1694; even as late as 1755 the proprietary of Maryland was still claiming the three lower counties.[2]

By the charter of 1681 Penn and his heirs became the true and absolute lords of a province or seignory, with rights and privileges similar to those granted to other proprietaries. The province was called Pennsylvania, though Penn expressly endeavored to have it called New Wales, and that failing, Sylvania. Secretary Blathwayt, a Welshman, refused to have it called New Wales; the king would not interfere; and though Penn offered the under-secretaries twenty guineas, they would not alter the name which had been inserted in the charter in honor of the admiral.[3] This province was to be held by Penn in free and common socage—that is,

[1] *Journal of the Lords of Trade*, V., 116, 179, 180, 188, 198, 199, 207, 208, 211, 225, 226.

[2] *Calvert Papers* (Md. Hist. Soc., *Fund Publication*, No. 34), 133.

[3] Letter from Penn, in Pa. Hist. Soc., *Memoirs*, I., 202–209.

by fealty and a fixed rent of two beaver skins. The proprietary was to make laws with the advice and consent of his freemen, though in his hands lay the execution of the laws and the issue of occasional ordinances. He could, furthermore, appoint judges and magistrates, remit, release, and pardon, and erect towns, boroughs, and manors.

The fact that the charter was the last save one of the great proprietary patents gave the king and his council opportunity to profit by experience, and to hedge the new proprietary in by limitations unknown to the earlier documents. It was a witness to Penn's influence that at this time such a charter should have been issued at all. Penn was required, as were some of the other proprietaries, to send all laws to England for approval, though if the Privy Council did not act upon them within six months after their receipt they were to be valid. He was given no control over cases of treason or wilful and malicious murder. His ordinances were under no circumstances to bind any one or to take away the rights of any one to life, limbs, goods, or chattels; while the people of the province were to have full right to appeal to the king in council. He was to maintain an agent in England, to observe the navigation acts and all customs regulations, and to have no correspondence with other sovereigns or states who were at war with the king of England. Especial stress was laid upon the observance of the navigation acts, and a breach of them carried a liability to forfeiture of the government. Even Penn could not be allowed to do anything that would diminish the revenues of the crown. April 2, 1681, the king announced to Lord Baltimore and the inhabitants and planters already in the province that the charter had been issued.[1]

Having received his charter, Penn immediately set about organizing his colony. After long waiting he had obtained an opportunity of giving practical shape to his ideas upon government. "Thou mayst communicate to friends," he wrote Robert Turner, "and expect shortly my proposals; 'tis a clear and just thing, and my God that has given it me through many difficulties wih, I believe, bless and make it the seed of a nation. I shall have a tender care to the government that it be well laid at first."[2] He began at once to draught an account of the province for the information of those who might desire to emigrate. This pamphlet, which presented the advantages of the colony and outlined very briefly "the privileges and powers necessary to the well-governing thereof,"[3] was a treatise not only on Pennsylvania, but also on the advantages of colonies in general; and it was circulated widely among those who would be likely to respond to it not only in England but in Ireland, Wales,

---

[1] *Cal. of State Pap., Col.*, 1661–1685, §§ 62, 63; Hazard, *Annals*, 502.   [2] Pa. Hist. Soc., *Memoirs*, I., 209.
[3] Hazard, *Annals*, 505–513; Winsor, *Narr. and Crit. Hist.* III., 496.

Holland, and Germany. It seems to have had considerable influence in inducing emigration from countries where Penn had already travelled and to which he had written letters in anticipation of the opportunity that had now come. Many Friends in Ireland and Wales were ready to come to America; Mennonites and other religious bodies in Germany looked favorably on the scheme; and Penn, greatly encouraged by the welcome his pamphlet received, looked forward with confident anticipation to a rapid colonization of his province.

In the mean time, he was busily engaged in drawing up another document, an agreement between himself and those who were to be the purchasers of his lands. He began by selling shares to those who wished to buy five thousand acres for a price of £100, with an annual quit-rent of fifty shillings or a commutation of all quit-rent for £20 in cash.[1] To regulate these purchases and to arrange for distributing land to those who could not afford to buy, he issued, July 11, 1681, his body of Conditions and Concessions.[2] These proposals dealt chiefly with the division and settlement of his province and laid down certain regulations to cover all dealings with the Indians. The Concessions were not intended to define the particular form of govern-

[1] Claypoole's Letter-Book, *Pa. Magazine*, X., 190, 191; letters from Penn to James Harrison, in Hazard, *Annals*, 522, 523, 538; *Pa. Archives*, 1st series, I., 39–46.
[2] Hazard, *Annals*, 516–520; Proud, *Hist. of Pennsylvania*, II., App.; Poore, *Constitutions*, 1516.

ment. Penn's purpose in this regard was set forth
in a letter to the people in Pennsylvania which he
wrote in 1681. "You shall be governed," he said,
"by laws of your own making, and live a free and,
if you will, a sober and industrious people. I shall
not usurp the right of any or oppress his person.
Whatever sober and free men can reasonably desire
for the security and improvement of their own
happiness I shall heartily comply with." [1]

In April, 1681, Penn commissioned his cousin,
William Markham, to go out at once as deputy
governor, promising to follow himself in five months'
time, a promise that he was unable to fulfil. Markham was given a body of instructions, and authority
to call a council to receive the allegiance of the
people in the territory, to settle the boundaries
with Baltimore, to survey and distribute lands,
to keep the peace and punish vice, and to issue
ordinances, but not to summon an assembly. [2]
He arrived in America in June, probably touched
first at Boston, then at New York, where Brockholls
recognized his authority, and afterwards sailed for
the Delaware. Up the river, beyond the head of
the bay, lay New Castle, at that time still retained
under the jurisdiction of the duke of York. Farther
on was Upland, the first town in Penn's jurisdiction,
occupied largely by Swedes and Dutch; while extending to the mouth of the Schuylkill were settlements of Dutch and Swedish farmers, containing

[1] Hazard, *Annals*, 502.   [2] *Ibid.*, 503, 504.

also a few Englishmen who had crossed over from Fenwick's colony and Burlington in West New Jersey. Since 1664 these people had been under the jurisdiction of the duke of York's laws, with a seat of justice at Upland.

Thither Markham went with his letter from Penn and his proclamation from Brockholls, and received the allegiance of the inhabitants. Having reorganized the court, and established the authority of the proprietary there,[1] he crossed in August to the head of the Chesapeake and took the long sail south to Maryland, hoping to arrange the boundary difficulty with Lord Baltimore; but he returned to Upland by the way he had come, having accomplished nothing.[2]

While Markham was at St. Mary's, three men— Crispin, Bezar, and Allen—were commissioned by Penn to go to America with the first body of colonists and to assist Markham in the work of laying out the colony. They were instructed to choose a site for a town where, as Penn said, "it is most navigable, dry, and healthy—that is, where most ships may best ride, of deepest draught of water, if possible to load or unload at the bank or keyside, without boating or lightering of it"; to lay out ten thousand acres for the town, and to arrange that every purchaser should have one hundred of his five thousand acres within this area. Minute

---

[1] *Records of Upland*, 195, 196; Hazard, *Annals*, 525, 526.
[2] *Pa. Magazine*, VI., 415, 416.

directions were given regarding the laying out of
streets, the location of houses, each "in the middle
of its plat, that it may be a green country town,
which will never be burned and always be wholesome," and particularly regarding the treatment
of the Indians, to whom a very friendly letter was
sent.[1] These instructions were afterwards modified by Penn, who enlarged the original plat and
reduced the hundred - acre share within the city
to a small home lot.   In April, 1682, he sent out
Thomas Holme in the *Amity* to be surveyor-general.
Under the latter's guidance the city of Philadelphia
was laid out, lots were assigned to purchasers, and
amid much confusion the erecting of a stately town
was begun.   The symmetry and regularity of Philadelphia are due to the plan, but little changed,
which Holme made at this time.[2]

While others were thus shaping the settlement in
America, Penn himself was busy promoting the
undertaking in England and completing the organization of the trade and government of his
colony.   First he granted a charter to a trading
and land company known as the Free Society of
Traders.   To this body, of which a majority of
the members were Quakers, he gave elaborate
trading privileges, twenty thousand acres of land,
and the right to send three representatives to
the provincial assembly.   Penn had already refused

[1] Hazard, *Annals*, 527–533.
[2] *Pa. Magazine*, XIX., 421, 422.

a very advantageous offer from a trader in Maryland
for a monopoly of the Indian trade in the province.[1]
"I did refuse a great temptation last second day,"
he wrote to Turner, "which was £6000, . . . but
. . . I would not . . . defile what came to me
clean."[2]   It would have been for him financially
better had he accepted the offer, for the Free
Society of Traders never prospered. It early came
into conflict with the colonial authorities, and,
though successful in disposing of its goods, was
unsuccessful in collecting its debts. As its members were Quakers, who were averse to law-suits,
the company soon found itself without credit or
money.[3]

As yet Penn had constructed no frame of government such as he was entitled to issue under the
terms of his charter, but he had clearly in mind the
chief principles of the government that he desired to
establish, and had already given expression to his
plan in the noble body of Concessions under which
the West New Jersey settlers were at this time living. In draughting the government that he wished
to establish in Pennsylvania he refused to defend
any particular form, democratic or other. "The
age is too nice and difficult for it," he said, "there
being nothing the wits of men are more busy and

[1] Claypoole's Letter-Book, *ibid.*, X., 189.

[2] Pa. Hist. Soc., *Memoirs*, I., 212.

[3] Claypoole's Letter-Book, *Pa. Magazine*, X., 411; Baldwin,
Amer. Hist. Review, VIII., 453–456.

divided upon. I choose to solve the controversy with this small distinction: any government is free to the people under it, whatever be the frame, where the laws rule and the people are a party to those laws, and more than this is tyranny, oligarchy, or confusion. . . . Let men be good and the government cannot be bad; if it be ill they will cure it. But if men be bad, let the government be ever so good, they will endeavor to warp and spoil it to their own turn."

Whatever the form, there was to Penn but one great end of government — namely, " to support power in reverence with the people, and to secure the people from the abuse of power, that they may be free by their just obedience, and the magistrates honorable for their just administration; for liberty without obedience is confusion and obedience without liberty is slavery." [1]

That Penn reaches in these *dicta* a very high level of political principles is evident when we compare his ideals with those of other men of his day. Many were, as he says, seeking for the solution of the great problem of government, but no one struck out higher truths than these. Penn issued his scheme of government with fear and uncertainty, but he enunciated the principles on which it was based without hesitation or questioning.

Penn's Frame of Government bears the date April

[1] Preface to the Frame of Government.

25, 1682,[1] and was the first constitution for the colony of Pennsylvania. The government established was in all essential particulars similar to those of the other colonies. There were a governor and a deputy governor, a provincial council and an assembly, both elected by the people; and the powers of executive and legislature were carefully and minutely defined. Appended to the Frame of Government, and bearing date May 5, were certain "laws agreed upon in England," which deal with the liberties of the individual, and therefore partake of the character of a bill of rights. The government thus established is noteworthy for the importance given to the provincial council, an elective body of seventy-two members with power to prepare bills and adjourn the assembly, and for the minor position occupied by the governor, who, having no powers independent of the council, was more or less of a figurehead.

[1] Proud, *Hist. of Pennsylvania*, II., App.; Hazard, *Annals*, 561–568; Poore, *Constitutions*, 1518; Shepherd, *Proprietary Government in Pennsylvania*, 235–243.

CHAPTER XII

GOVERNMENTAL PROBLEMS IN PENNSYLVANIA
(1681–1696)

PENN was now ready to sail to America, where his city was already founded and his colony was awaiting his coming. September 2, 1682, the London *Gazette* reported that "two days since sailed out of the Downs three ships bound for Pensilvania on board of which was Mr. Pen with a great many Quakers who go to settle there." [1] After he had sailed, many malicious rumors were circulated in England, some stating that he had become a Jesuit, others that he was dead. These reports caused him considerable uneasiness and pain. "I am still alive," he wrote from America to the Free Society of Traders, " and no *Jesuit*, and I thank God very well."

The voyage to America required more than six weeks and proved very distressing, owing to the outbreak of small-pox on board the *Welcome*, and the death of nearly one-third of the passengers. On October 27, the vessel lay off New Castle. "As they sailed up the river they received visits and

[1] *Pa. Magazine*, VI., 175.

invitations from the inhabitants, the people being joyful to see him, both Swedes, Dutch, and English coming up to New Castle. They received and entertained him with great expressions of joy after their sort." [1]   He summoned the people of New Castle, and in taking possession addressed them regarding his object in coming to America and the government that he proposed to establish. The next day (October 29, O.S., November 8, N.S.) he went to Upland, which, according to tradition, [2] he renamed Chester, and he there entered for the first time upon the soil of Pennsylvania.

Penn now instructed the sheriffs to issue writs summoning the people to the polls to elect delegates to an assembly that was to meet December 4. The assembly passed a series of important measures that laid broadly and deeply the constitutional foundations of the colony. The first measure formally annexed New Castle and the lower territories to Pennsylvania; a second naturalized the Swedes and other foreigners who had come within the jurisdiction of Penn's government; a third, known as the Great Law, accepted the laws that had been agreed upon in England, and added a number of others. It stands as the exponent of Penn's ideas and principles and inaugurated the Holy Experiment. It provided for liberty of conscience, for lofty standards of moral and religious

[1] Penn to Philip Ford, *Pa. Magazine*, VI., 179.
[2] Clarkson, *Life of Penn*, I., 259.

life, and for capital punishment in but two cases, murder and treason, a noteworthy clause when one remembers the two hundred capital crimes in England at this time. The entire body of sixty-nine capitularies is characterized by temperance, love, and justice. The Agreement of West New Jersey and the Great Law of Pennsylvania emanate from the same source. Well might Penn say that "such an assembly for Love, Unity, and Concord scarcely ever was known in and about outward things in those parts."[1]

Penn went from Chester to Philadelphia and stepped ashore at the primitive wharf that stood in front of the Blue Anchor tavern, probably erected some years before for the people of New Castle and others on the river. During the winter and spring that followed he was busy laying the material foundations of the colony. Shortly after landing he sent two persons to confer with Lord Baltimore about the boundaries, and himself undertook a trip to Maryland in December,[2] which was the first of a series of extended and painful interviews between the two proprietaries. He journeyed to New York to pay his respects to the governor of the colony of the duke of York, and in March, 1683, he visited East New Jersey and sat for five days as a pro-

[1] *Pa. Magazine*, VI., 180; Great Law, in Hazard, *Annals*, 619–634.
[2] Penn to the Lords of Trade, *Cal. of State Pap., Col.*, 1681–1685, § 1179.

prietary in the council of the deputy governor,
Rudyard.[1]   At home he was busy with the new
city and in making a tour of his own province. He
watched with great care the building of Philadelphia, and during the first year after his landing saw
it grow to be a town of "four-score houses and cot-
tages, where merchants and handicrafts are following their vocations as fast as they can, while the
countrymen are close at their farms."   "With the
help of God," he wrote to Lord Sunderland, "I will
show a province in seven years equal to her neighbors of forty years' planting."[2]   Of the journey
that he made throughout the province no other evidence remains than the long letter which he wrote
to the Free Society of Traders describing the colony.   He declared that he was fully satisfied with
the country, although the labor of settlement was
arduous, and vexing problems were constantly arising.[3]

With the Indians from the first his relations were
governed by motives of the highest character.   He
had already made known the policy that he proposed to follow in his Conditions and Concessions,
and sent over several letters to be read to the
Indians, expressing his desire for their friendship
and good-will.   During his first year he held many

[1] *N. J. Archives*, XIII., 6, 8, 11, 13, 15.
[2] Pa. Hist. Soc., *Memoirs*, II., 246.   Descriptions of the
province, in (1682), *Pa. Magazine*, XIII., 227; (1685) *ibid.*,
IX., 64–81, and Pa. Hist. Soc., *Memoirs*, I., 446.
[3] Clarkson, *Life of Penn*, I., 292–315.

meetings with them and evidently impressed upon
them, as he impressed upon all purchasers of land
in the province, his desire for perfect amity and
justice in the relations between the white and the
red man. He planned a kind of arbitration tribunal, consisting of six planters and six natives, to
settle all differences, and there is reason to believe
that some such tribunal was actually set up. In
June, 1683, he made a great treaty with the Indians,
probably at Shackamaxon, now Kensington, under
an elm, that long afterwards bore the name of the
"Treaty Elm." This scene has gained the attention
of the poet and the artist, and has long stood as
symbolic of a noble purpose successfully carried out.

Meanwhile the number of settlers in the province
was rapidly increasing. Before 1682 a thousand
people were established in the region, and between
1682 and 1685 the number was increased to more
than eight thousand. First on the ground after
the Swedes, Dutch, and Finns were the Welsh
Quakers from Merionethshire, who arrived in August, 1682, and settled on the "Welsh Tract," west
of Philadelphia.[1] In October, 1683, came a company of Mennonites from Crefeld, on the Rhine,
led by their pastor, Pastorius, who took up their
divisions of land northwest of Philadelphia, naming
their settlement German Town. It is noteworthy
that five years later four of this company drew
up a protest which they sent to the Friends meeting

[1] Glenn, *Merion in the Welsh Tract.*

against the holding of slaves. "And those who steal or rob men and those who buy or purchase them, are they not all alicke? Here is liberty of conscience, which is right and reasonable, here ought to be lickewise liberty of ye body, except of evil doers, wch is another case. But to bring men hither or to robb and sell them against their will we stand against."[1] Other race elements were French, Danes, Scots, Irish, forming a strangely cosmopolitan organization; yet all lived like the people of one country, prosperous and contented.

Pennsylvania continued to receive settlers more rapidly than any other colony in America at this time, and only about half of these were Englishmen. Philadelphia was pleasantly situated; its houses, frequently three stories high, were large and well built, having good cellars and in some cases balconies. Its fertility was such that its streets were named "from things that spontaneously" grew in the country. Markets were held twice a week and fairs twice a year; a good meal could be had for sixpence; hours for work and meals for laborers were indicated by the ringing of a bell; and no one was allowed at a public-house at night who was not a lodger. The drink was chiefly beer and a punch made of rum and water;—so Penn wrote in 1685.[2] At that time three counties—Philadelphia, Bucks, and Chester—had been laid out and fifty townships

[1] Text in *Pa. Magazine*, IV., 1–41. Cf. with the Rhode Island law, *R. I. Col. Records*, I., 243.   [2] *Pa. Magazine*, IX., 65.

settled. A weekly post was established,[1] a school
was opened,[2] and a printing-press was set up.

Trade began with the neighboring colonies and
with the West Indies, ships and wharves were
built, and Philadelphia entered on her career as a
prosperous commercial city. No town on the colonial seaboard had leaped into prominence with
such rapidity as had this Quaker community. It
possessed a tannery, saw-mill, brick kiln, and a glass-
house, erected for the Free Society;[3] mills of other
kinds were built, Irish Quakers introduced the
manufacture of linen; and flour, pipe-staves, and
horses began to be exported. So rapidly did the
settlement grow that Penn could write in 1684,
"I have led the greatest colony into America that
ever any man did upon a private credit, and the
most prosperous beginnings that ever were in it
are to be found among us."[4] To his own sagacity
and energy this result must be in large part ascribed.

Notwithstanding this rapid growth, provisions of
the Frame of Government touching council and
assembly were drawn on too large a scale. A
council of seventy-two members, in addition to a
general assembly of two hundred members, all
elected, proved to be beyond the resources of the
colony. In December, 1682, Penn agreed with

[1] Proud, *Hist. of Pennsylvania*, I., 345.
[2] *Pemberton MSS.*, quoted in Watson, *Annals*, 626.
[3] Penn in Clarkson, *Life of Penn*, I., 314, § 33.
[4] Penn in Pa. Hist. Soc., *Memoirs*, I., 448, 449.

Markham that the seventy - two persons chosen by the six counties should suffice—eighteen for the council and fifty - four for the assembly.[1] This arrangement was carried out by the council in March, 1683, and when a member expressed fear lest this alteration should injure their other privileges under the charter, Penn replied that the assembly might amend, alter, or add for the public good, and that he was ready to settle such foundations as might be for their happiness and the good of their posterities, according to the powers vested in him.[2]

Penn's desire to meet the wishes of the people appears not to have pleased his wealthier associates, notably those connected with the Free Society, many of whom were large landholders in the colony and probably expected as members of the council to play a prominent part in government. The president of the society, Nicholas Moore, was charged with having said in a public - house that governor and council had broken the charter and deserved to be impeached for treason. For this rash comment he was summoned before the council, and though he defended himself by saying that he had rather raised the question than asserted the fact, he was reprimanded and told that his discourse was unreasonable and impudent.[3]

---

[1] *Pa. Magazine*, VI., 466, 467; see Hazard, *Annals*, 603, 604; and British Museum, *Additional MSS.*, 35909, f. 2.
[2] *Pa. Col. Records* (1838), I., 2; (1852), I., 57, 58.
[3] *Ibid.*, 2, 3 (59).

In the mean time, the fifty-four members who had been empowered by the freemen to act as an assembly, withdrew from the council and organized a lower house with Thomas Wynne as speaker. They took up the whole question of their rights under the charter, and after long debate and a conference with the council passed an Act of Settlement,[1] legalizing the change just made in the constitution of the legislature. This act was only a temporary arrangement, and Penn asked the assembly whether it would have the old charter or a new one. The assembly said that it would have a new one,[2] and during the ensuing two weeks the governor and the houses were busy draughting the new frame. On April 8, 1683, "the Great Charter of the province was read, signed, sealed, and delivered by the governor to the inhabitants and received by the hands of James Harrison and the speaker, who were ordered to return the old one with the hearty thanks of the whole house."[3] The new government, as was to have been expected, differed from the old only in details. The council was reduced from seventy-two to eighteen, and the powers of the governor were further curtailed.[4] It is important to note that this constitution emanated from the assembly and not from the proprietary.

[1] *Pa. Col. Records* (1838), I., 4 (60); *Votes of Assembly*, I., 7–10; *Laws of the Province of Pa.*, 123–126.
[2] *Pa. Col. Records*, I., 7 (63).   [3] *Ibid.*, 16 (72).
[4] Poore, *Constitutions*, 1527; Shepherd, *Proprietary Government in Pennsylvania*, 251, 252.

An important difficulty had thus been met and safely passed, and the machinery of Penn's Holy Experiment was once more running smoothly. The proprietary, by brotherly love, earnest good-nature, and large sympathies, had won the confidence of the people. When, in May, 1684, the first assembly under the new frame was held, a feeling of loyalty and harmony prevailed and expressions of devotion to the proprietary took form in a law for the preservation of the governor's person not only from attack but also from slander.[1] So long as Penn should remain to soften animosities and check bitterness of feeling there was every reason to expect a harmonious government.

Unfortunately, in August, 1684, the proprietary felt obliged for two reasons to leave the province and return to England. The dispute with Lord Baltimore was now at such a point that the proprietary was absolutely needed in England to defend his cause before the Lords of Trade. At the same time the English Quakers were undergoing such bitter persecution at the hands of the government that Penn believed he ought to be in England to mitigate their sufferings. His long friendship with the king and the duke of York made it more than likely that his intercessions at court would meet with success.

Nor was he mistaken in his belief. In October,

[1] *Pa. Col. Records*, I., 53, 54 (107); *Laws of the Province of Pa.*, chap. clxxi., 173.

1685, he obtained a favorable report from the Committee of Trade and Plantations regarding the lower counties; and after the duke of York became king, in February of the same year, he secured the release of more than twelve hundred members of the Society of Friends, imprisoned as Dissenters. The next year, when for the sake of the revenues the king caused writs of *quo warranto* to be issued against the proprietary and charter colonies, Penn warded off the attack on Pennsylvania and Delaware;[1] and in 1688, when Andros was made governor of the Dominion of New England and New York, and the Jerseys were added, he obtained the exemption of Pennsylvania and Delaware from the new jurisdiction.[2]

But in almost every other respect Penn's absence was injurious both to himself and to his colony. His close connection with James II. and the court, his influence in securing the royal pardon on so many occasions, and his acceptance of the king's declarations of indulgence issued in defiance of law, brought him under suspicion. Before the revolution of 1688 he was charged with being a Jesuit and afterwards with being a Jacobite;[3] he was arrested, threatened with imprisonment, and denounced even by many who should have stood loyally by him.

---

[1] Dixon, *Life of Penn*, 539, 559.

[2] *N. Y. Docs. Rel. to Col. Hist.*, III., 536, 537, 543; *Cal. of State Pap., Col.*, 1685–1688, § 1688.

[3] "The Jacobite party, of which Penn is known to be the head" (*Cal. of State Pap., Col.*, 1689–1692, § 2472).

After 1688, when the accession of William and Mary cost him all his influence at court, he would gladly have returned to his colony, but he could not. He was seriously embarrassed financially, his wife was dangerously ill, and he himself was three times arrested for treason. For thirty months he had to remain in retirement, during which time his enemies sought to ruin him. On March 10, 1692, an order in council was issued authorizing the governor of New York, Fletcher, to take Pennsylvania under his authority during the king's pleasure,[1] thus depriving Penn of his colony. It was a staggering blow to the heavily burdened proprietary, who had been watching the progress of affairs in the colony and knew that he was needed there more than ever, and that a man of Fletcher's type would only make matters worse. The possible failure of his Holy Experiment was a greater sorrow to Penn than his own financial losses at home.

After Penn's departure in 1684 the colony prospered commercially, but was disturbed by political, territorial, and religious disputes. The deputy governor, council, and assembly were unable to agree regarding the proper application of the constitution, for the Frame of Government gave to the council the power to frame bills and to the assembly only the right to accept or reject them. The council, which on Penn's departure was au-

---

[1] *Cal. of State Pap., Col.*, 1689–1692, §§ 2118, 2227; *N. Y. Docs. Rel. to Col. Hist.*, III., 835.

thorized to act as governor,[1] was inclined to play the leading and dominant part, to the resentment of the assembly, which for ten years struggled to obtain the right to initiate legislation. In 1685, and again in 1686, the assembly protested because the council did not issue bills in the name of the governor, council, and assembly, as the charter required;[2] and eventually adjourned in great wrath. This disagreement with the council was accompanied with an unfortunate internal quarrel. The assembly impeached Nicholas Moore, chief-justice of the provincial court, and one of its members, for sending unlawful writs to the sheriffs, for interfering with trial by jury, for denying justice, overawing witnesses, and perpetuating endless and vexatious suits, and it petitioned the council to remove him from office.[3] The council believing, as Penn himself did afterwards, that the charges were the result of personal ill-will, did no more than request Moore to give up his office till the charge should be tried. Eventually the matter was dropped entirely.

Penn was perplexed and angry, both because of the friction in the government of his colony and of the inability of those whom he had left in command to rule wisely. "For the love of God, me, and the poor country," he wrote to James Harrison, one of

[1] *Pa. Col. Records*, I., 66 (119).
[2] *Ibid.*, 82 (133); Frame of Government, § 14.
[3] *Ibid.*, 83–85 (135–137).

the justices, "be not so governmentish, so noisy,
and open in your dissatisfactions."[1]   Unable to
go to Pennsylvania, as he ardently desired,[2] he
determined to change the form of government.
He revoked the executive functions granted to the
council, and appointed as governor five commissioners or councillors (three of whom were to make
a quorum) to watch over the council and assembly
and prevent quarrels and disorder, and to compel
all to do their duty under the charter.[3]   The
new arrangement worked no better than the old.
Finally, in September, 1685, he made another and
more important change: instead of allowing an
elected council or a board of councillors to act as
governor, he selected an appointee of his own, one
Captain Blackwell, a resident of Boston, son-in-law
of Cromwell's associate, Lambert, and formerly
treasurer of Cromwell's army.[4]

Blackwell came to Philadelphia in December,
1685, with a grim determination to organize an
efficient government.   As he was not a Quaker, he
was soon opposed by the leaders of the Quaker
party, chief of whom was Thomas Lloyd, master
of the rolls and keeper of the broad seal.[5]   Un-

[1] Proud, *Hist. of Pennsylvania*, I., 297.

[2] *Pa. Magazine*, IX., 81.

[3] Proud, *Hist. of Pennsylvania*, I., 305–307; Shepherd,
Proprietary Government in Pennsylvania, 261–262.

[4] *Cal. of State Pap., Col.*, 1685–1688, § 824.

[5] *Pa. Col. Records*, I., 186 (194–197), 207 (234–242), 256
(279, 280).

fortunate controversies followed till Lloyd became
so excited that the governor had to adjourn the
council, and Lloyd and his followers remained behind and made so much noise and clamor that
passers-by in the streets stood still to hear.[1]
When Penn heard of this painful incident he wrote
to Lloyd in reproof, saying: "Do not be so litigious
and brutish. . . . O, that some one would stand up
for our good beginnings and bring a savour of
righteousness over that ill savour."[2]

When Blackwell asked for his own recall Penn
yielded too ready a compliance to the wishes of the
opposition. He placed the question of the future
government in the hands of the council, and agreed
that he would accept any governor that they might
select, or he would be content if the council itself
acted as governor. Burdened with his cares in
England, he begged his people to "avoid factions
and parties, whisperings and reportings and all animosities," and to put their "common shoulder to
the public work."[3] The council, assuming the
governorship itself, chose Lloyd as president, and
made one more unsuccessful experiment. New
questions arose: the inhabitants of the lower counties, differing in blood and religion from those of
Pennsylvania proper, began an agitation for separate government that ended ten years later in their

[1] *Pa. Col. Records*, I., 252 (293, 294).
[2] Penn to Lloyd, *Historical Magazine*, 1st series, III., 105.
[3] *Pa. Col. Records*, I., 274 (316).

separating from Pennsylvania and having a legislature of their own.   In 1691, owing to the apostasy
of George Keith, a schism took place among the
Quakers which brought grief to members of the
society everywhere.   The tales of petty informers
in England, who took pleasure in persecuting Penn,
now that he had lost much of his influence at court,
found support in the exaggerated accounts of the
bickerings and quarrels among Penn's colonists
in America.

These quarrels in Philadelphia were to no small
extent responsible for the royal order of William III.,
in 1692, depriving Penn of his proprietorship "by
reason of great neglects and miscarriages in the
government," whereby "the same is fallen into disorder and confusion, the public peace and administration of justice broken and violated," insufficient provision made for "the defence of the
province against" the French, and danger of entire
loss to the crown.   For two years Pennsylvania
was governed as a dependency of New York, until
in 1694 the territory was restored.   In 1696 Penn
himself came over at last for a residence of five
years in his colony.

Though the tale on the political side is largely one
of confusion and discord, yet in other respects the
history of the province is one of steady and sound
progress.   Philadelphia increased rapidly in size,
was deemed large enough for incorporation as a
borough in 1684, and was incorporated with mayor

and aldermen in 1691.[1] The commerce was such that in the West India trade it was rapidly becoming the only rival of New York, and was competing with her for the control of the Indian trade of the Northwest. The position of the province, half-way between New England and Virginia, was a particularly strong one and gave promise of a great future. Despite the unsettled condition of government, the condition of the province in other respects was hopeful and encouraging.

[1] *Pa. Col. Records*, I., 64 (117); *Pa. Magazine*, X., 61–77; XV., 344.

CHAPTER XIII

DEVELOPMENT OF VIRGINIA

(1652–1675)

OF all the colonies on the main-land of America Virginia was the one most loyal to the Stuarts. Berkeley had driven the religious Puritans out of the colony; and those who cherished Puritan ideas of government gave no sign of their presence. The royalists in Virginia increased after 1649, and the colony, though it might well have held out against a siege, surrendered without a struggle to the fleet sent by Parliament in 1651 to effect its reduction. The surrender was the work of that large body of planters and freeholders, parliamentarians and cavaliers alike, who desired peace, trade, and prosperity, and who saw in resistance and possible defeat a further restriction upon their market, and consequent ruin. Though Berkeley "blustered and talked of resistance,"[1] and even raised a force to oppose the parliamentary commissioners, after long and serious debate an agreement was reached.

By the articles of surrender, signed March 12,

[1] Neill, *Virginia Carolorum*, 220, 221.

1652, Virginia acknowledged entire dependence upon the Commonwealth of England. In return, full pardon was promised to all who had acted or spoken against Parliament, land titles were guaranteed, and the people of the colony were granted "free-trade as the people of England do enjoy to all places and with all nations according to the laws of the commonwealth." This clause certainly did not promise absolute free-trade, and was never so construed by the home authorities. Licenses were granted to traders who desired to ship goods to Virginia, and trade with the Dutch was forbidden to the Virginians, as well as to others, by the navigation act of 1651.[1] In 1656 the planters complained that the navigation act, "unless it be a little dispenct withall," would ruin part of the trade it was intended to advance.[2] The Virginian assembly, in an act of 1659, declared that the restriction of trade hindered the "estimation and value of the only commodity — tobacco;"[3] and we know from the instructions to Berkeley in 1662 that trade with the Dutch and other peoples of Europe had to be carried on surreptitiously.[4]

Under the commonwealth and the protectorate the colony seems to have prospered, though no attempt was made on the part of the home au-

[1] *Cal. of State Pap., Col.*, 1574–1660, pp. 403, 420.
[2] Thurloe, *State Papers*, V., 80, 81; *Rawlinson MSS.*, in Bod. Lib., A 38, 703.   [3] Hening, *Statutes*, I., 450.
[4] Hazard, *State Papers*, II., 610, § 5.

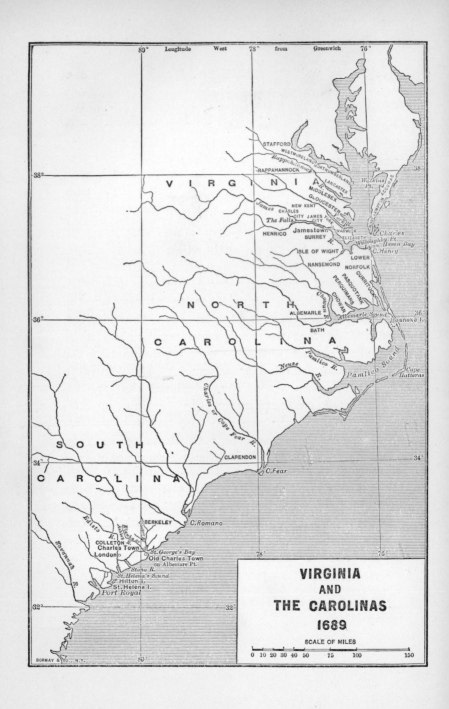

VIRGINIA
AND
THE CAROLINAS
1689

SCALE OF MILES

0 10 20 30 40 50   75   100   150

thorities to give settled form to the government.
No doubt Cromwell fully intended at the earliest
opportunity to issue a commission for a governor,
because in 1653 and again in 1654 he discussed the
matter with his council and expressed his determination to do so.[1] But as nothing was done, the
House of Burgesses in the colony, acting under the
terms of the articles of surrender, assumed full
authority and elected its own governor, first Bennett, and afterwards Mathews. Dissatisfaction soon
arose. Divers merchants, planters, and others closely identified with the colony, sent addresses to the
Protector begging him to consider the distracted
state of the plantation. The committee of the
council to whom the addresses were referred upheld the petitioners, and declared that the government in Virginia was very loose, the public administration very defective, the produce of the
colony debased, and "all the hopeful improvements
designed and begun" received no encouragement.

The committee urged that some fit person be commissioned as governor; and, after conference with
the merchants, proposed Edward Digges as one who
had given "a testimony of his prudence, conduct,
and moderation."[2] While thus the matter was
under consideration at home, a controversy arose
in the colony between Governor Mathews, who

[1] *Cal. of State Pap.*, *Col.*, 1574–1660, pp. 397, 413.
[2] *Ibid.*, 1574–1660, p. 461; *Egerton MSS.*, in British Museum,
2395, f. 147.

evidently believed that his powers should come from England and be the same as those of a regularly appointed governor, and the House of Burgesses, which desired to retain authority in its own hands. Mathews in 1657 dissolved the assembly; the burgesses denying his right to do so, voted that any deputy accepting dissolution should be deemed a traitor "to the trust reposed in him by his countrymen." [1]   In the end the burgesses won the day.   Although the Council of State thrice took the matter of Virginia's government under advisement, it never found time or opportunity to act, and the popular body was left in full control. [2] Mathews yielded the point in dispute, acknowledged the supreme authority of the House of Burgesses, and accepted another election as governor. [3]

After the abdication of Richard Cromwell, in 1659, England was thrown into confusion. The Virginian assembly, forced to rely on its own resources, took matters into its own hands, passed a law declaring that the supreme power was vested in itself, and ordered that all writs should run in its name until "such a command and commission come out of England as shall be by the assembly judged lawful." [4]   In July, 1660, it elected Berkeley as its governor, and authorized him to summon an assembly once in two years, or oftener if necessary,

---

[1] Hening, *Statutes*, I., 499, 500.   [2] *Ibid.*, 509, 511, 512.
[3] *Cal. of State Pap., Col.*, 1574–1660, p.461; Neill, *Virginia Carolorum*, 263.   [4] Hening, *Statutes*, I., 530.

to appoint councillors and a secretary of state with
its approval; and to dissolve the assembly, but only
with its own consent.

In Virginia, as in England at the same time, the
current of popular sympathy was running in the
direction of the old order of things. The new
assembly, which was elected under the liberal
franchise of 1657 and 1658, represented better than
had any previous body the sympathies of the
people at large, who were ready to greet loyally the
old governor, the old church, and the old system.
This assembly elected Berkeley with the same
readiness that an earlier assembly had welcomed
the commissioners and elected Bennett, eight years
before.

In September, 1660, when the official announcement of the restoration of the Stuarts reached the
colony, Berkeley's proclamation of September 20
ordered for the first time that legal writs be issued
in the king's name. Berkeley himself returned to
England in the same year, and there received from
the king definite instructions regarding the government of the colony. He was to see that the Church
of England was established, to have churches built or
repaired, and ministers provided with glebe-lands.
He was to recognize the constitutional standing of
the assembly, and to obtain the passage of laws
suppressing vice, encouraging the building of towns
after the fashion of New England, limiting the
planting of tobacco, and stimulating the production

of other staple commodities.   Above all, he was to observe the acts of trade and to transmit to England yearly reports on the state of the colony.[1] Returning to Virginia in 1662, Berkeley summoned an assembly and presented for its consideration the various commands of the king.[2]

During the fourteen years from 1662 to 1676 conditions prevailed in the government and life of the colony which prepared the way for the great outburst of popular discontent known as Bacon's rebellion.   Berkeley became the ruling spirit, "aspiring to a sole and absolute power and command."[3] He named his own councillors, and gradually gathered about him a party composed of the wealthier planters devoted to his interests and their own.   He secured control of the House of Burgesses by proroguing it from session to session, until it sat almost as long as did the "Cavalier Parliament" in England, thus transforming the assembly into a close corporation legislating in the interest of a small oligarchy.   The assembly in 1669 limited the franchise to freeholders, and so deprived part of the freemen of their right to vote, on the ground that voting in Virginia, as in England, should be the privilege of the wealthier classes, and that the freemen had little interest in the coun-

[1] *Cal. of State Pap., Col.*, 1661–1668, § 368; Hazard, *State Papers*, II., 607–611.
[2] Hening, *Statutes*, I., 172–176.
[3] Complaints from Charles City County, in *Va. Magazine*, III., 134.

try, making "tumults" at the elections and "dis-
turbing" his majesty's peace.[1]

Though the assembly made some noteworthy
efforts to curtail expenses, its policy in the matter
of taxation was neither far-sighted nor just. The
councillors were paid by exemption from taxation,
a practice which was hardly a grievance to others
so long as taxes were small, but became a heavy
burden when taxes increased.[2] Taxes were imposed with little regard for the needs and conditions
of the people at large. Acting under the king's
instructions, the assembly in 1663 levied a tax
of thirty pounds of tobacco per poll wherewith to
encourage the building of towns;[3] but towns never
flourished and the money was wasted. To defend
the colony against the Dutch and the Indians, it
made a number of levies for the erection of forts;
but the Dutch made their attack before a fort
could be built, and for fighting the Indians such
strongholds were of little value.[4] Additional levies
were made to support agents sent to England—"a
necessary but grievous tax considering the general
poverty of the country"—and for local court-houses
that cost three times as much as they were worth.[5]

[1] Hening, *Statutes*, II., 280.

[2] *Ibid.*, II., 32, 84; complaints from Isle of Wight County, in
Va. Magazine, II., 390 (art. 25).

[3] Hening, *Statutes*, II., 172–176 (act xvi.).

[4] *Ibid.*, 220, 259, 291; *Cal. of State Pap., Col.*, 1675 – 1676,
§ 1099; *Va. Magazine*, IV., 120.

[5] "A Review, Breviary, and Conclusion," MS. in Public Record Office, *Colonial Entry-Book*, No. 81, f. 41.

Many of the complaints were undoubtedly exaggerated, but the assembly at best showed little regard for the poverty of the people, and levied some of its heaviest taxes in 1675 and 1676, when signs of distress and discontent were everywhere manifest. Long sessions and frequent meetings of the assembly increased the expenses of the counties for the salaries of burgesses, some of whom drew their stipend without attending, and charged up against their constituents the cost of the liquors they drank.[1] Little wonder that the people became rebellious: government was in the hands of a ring; the assembly was elected by the wealthier classes; councillors were exempted from taxation; salaries were excessive, sessions long, meetings frequent, and the abuse of office a daily practice.

The robbery at headquarters was accompanied with maladministration in local affairs also. The counties, of which in 1666 there were nineteen, were governed by appointed commissioners, one of whom was always made sheriff by the governor. These commissioners had general oversight of county affairs and constituted the court of the county, and to the sheriff was intrusted the collecting and disbursing of levies.[2] Other local officers were the vestrymen; the local collectors of export

[1] *Cal. of State Pap., Col.*, 1675–1676, § 1068; 1677–1680, §§ 45, 82, 1211.

[2] Ludwell's account, *ibid.*, 1661–1668, § 250; *Va. Magazine*, V., 54–59; Hening, *Statutes*, II., 65, 66, 315, 316.

dues, castle and port charges;[1] and the king's
collectors of the penny a pound imposed by the
navigation act of 1672. Against these officials
complaints were frequent and persistent.[2] The
justices were charged with oppression, with levying tobacco on the people for their own accommo-
dation, and with raising other funds in the interest of particular friends. The sheriffs were
charged with buying their offices and remaining in
them longer than was lawful, with exacting excessive fees, harrying poor debtors, and misusing
funds.[3] The colonial collectors were complained
of in half a dozen counties for failure to render
account of their collections and for pocketing the
money.[4]

The burden of bad government might not have
been so heavily felt by the poor classes of Virginia
had it not been for the instability of their staple
commodity—tobacco. Steadily during these years
the price of tobacco declined. Beverley ascribes
this fall in large part to the operation of the navigation acts, which, he says, cut with a double edge,
first reducing tobacco to a very low price, and,
secondly, raising the value of European goods to
whatever the merchants chose to put upon them.
Furthermore, the penny a pound levied after 1672
restricted export and reduced the profits of the

[1] Hening, *Statutes*, I., 534; II., 13.   [2] *Ibid.*, II., 353–355.
[3] *Va. Magazine*, II., 289, 290, 291, 387, 388.
[4] *Ibid.*, II., 166, 169, 170, 386–389; III., 35.

planters.[1]   John Bland, in a famous petition of 1663 against the operation of the act of 1660, declared that France and Holland had begun to grow tobacco of their own, and that the tobacco industry of Virginia was threatened with ruin because the demand was limited to what England needed for her own consumption.[2] This assertion was probably not true; but the Virginia assembly made the same statement in the preamble to one of its acts.[3]

More serious than the navigation acts in its effects upon the economic life of the colony was the overproduction of tobacco. Save for a trade in beaver skins, Virginia had no other commodity for export, and people raised no other crop except the food that they needed. As far back as 1630 the attention of the planters was called to this danger,[4] but no heed was paid to the warnings, and the inevitable result followed. The price of tobacco fell lower and lower. A greater number of pounds than before was required to obtain the English goods upon which the Virginians depended; taxes, heavy at best, became heavier, because more tobacco had to be deducted to meet them; fees,

[1] Beverley, *Hist. of Virginia*, 58, 59, 66; *Va. Magazine*, II., 267, 268.

[2] *Ibid.*, I., 141; *Cal. of State Pap., Col.*, 1675–1676, § 923; Bruce, *Econ. Hist. of Virginia*, I., 360–362.

[3] Hening *Statutes*, II., 141.

[4] *Va. Magazine*, II., 281 (art. 26); VII., 376; IX., 176–178; Keith, *British Plantations in America*, 135.

reckoned in depreciated currency, seemed exorbitant, and the financial depression bore with exceptional weight upon the poor planter. The price of tobacco was not regulated by the demand in the colony, for the great bulk of the crop went to England, and the English merchants, possessing a monopoly of the trade, paid for tobacco pretty much what they pleased.[1] As the people said, "The planters are the merchants' slaves."

Every effort was made to check production and to raise the price. A dozen acts of assembly were passed to encourage the growing of other staple commodities, such as flax, hemp, and silk; as many more acts were passed forbidding the planting of tobacco for a given length of time, so that the supply might be decreased. These measures proved futile. The Virginians refused to turn their attention to other forms of production, and the neighboring colonies, notably Maryland, refused to co-operate in diminishing the supply.

Virginia suffered from other troubles arising outside the colony. The war between England and Holland led to an attack in 1667 by the Dutch upon the shipping in the James River, that reminds one of the contemporary disgrace in England when the Dutch burned the English ships in the Medway. Five Dutch men-of-war attacked the king's frigate lying off Jamestown and carried off eighteen mer-

---

[1] Thurloe, *State Papers*, V., 80; *Tanner MSS.*, in Bod. Lib., 31, ff. 137–139.

chant ships.[1] Six years later, in 1673, the Dutch appeared again, this time with eight ships, and in a fight that lasted four hours burned eleven English vessels.[2]

More serious than these attacks was the great danger that threatened the colony when, in 1672, the very year of the Stop of the Exchequer, Charles II. granted the whole of Virginia for thirty-one years to his friends and advisers, Arlington and Culpeper, and erected it into a proprietary province similar to that of Maryland.[3] The powers of the grantees were to be those of a feudal lord, and many of the political privileges which the colony possessed were in danger of entire destruction. Immediately the colony bestirred itself and sent three agents to England to secure the vacating of the grant, and to obtain a charter which would settle all questions of land titles and forms of government in the future. The agents labored earnestly and with success; they obtained from the grantees a renunciation of the grant, with the exception of the quit-rents and escheats, and were on the eve of securing a liberal charter (November, 1675)[4] when civil war in the colony compelled them to postpone further effort.

[1] *Cal. of State Pap., Col.*, 1661–1668, § 1508; *N. Y. Docs. Rel. to Col. Hist.*, II., 527.
[2] *Cal. of State Pap., Col.*, 1669–1674, § 1123.
[3] *Ibid.*, § 769.
[4] *Ibid.*, 1669–1674, § 770; 1675–1676, §§ 602, 603; Burk, *Hist. of Virginia*, II., App., lv.–lvii.

CHAPTER XIV

BACON'S REBELLION AND ITS RESULTS

(1675–1689)

FOR some years before 1675 there were dangerous symptoms in Virginia. In 1663 "the discontented people of all sorts," chiefly servants, united under the leadership of some Cromwellian soldiers in the "Berkenhead plot" to murder their masters. The difficulty then concerned tobacco; the larger grievances had scarcely come to the front, and the quarrel between the governing oligarchy on one side and the overtaxed, neglected, and angry colonists on the other had not begun.

The immediate cause of the serious outbreak known as Bacon's rebellion was a war between the colonists of Virginia and the Indians. Since 1630 relations with the tribes along the frontiers had been peaceful and the beaver trade brisk. In the summer of 1675 Docg Indians murdered two Virginian planters; and Mason and Brent, who commanded the military forces of Northumberland County, along the Potomac, with ill-judged zeal slew not only the murderers but other Indians also. Soon the frontier was in an uproar and the number of forays increased daily. The frightened colonists appealed to Berkeley for aid, but the old man, broken in health, deaf, very irritable, and influenced it may be by the ring of politicians who controlled the government and made profits out of the Indian trade, brought down upon himself the maledictions of his contemporaries by refusing to have anything to do with the matter.[1]

When the Susquehannocks rose in January, 1676, and murdered thirty-six Englishmen, the situation became desperate, and again Berkeley was called upon to protect the colony. He sent Sir Henry Chicheley with a large force to guard the frontier of the upper Rappahannock and Potomac rivers, but before the militia was fairly under way he revoked the order. Fearing for their lives, sixty planters fled from their homes, but others less fortunate were murdered, among them the overseer of young Nathaniel Bacon, a recent arrival in the province. Even in this emergency Berkeley refused to act until the next assembly, summoned for March.[2]

The assembly at first was active in providing for the military defence of the colony,[3] but in the end it proved as inefficient as the governor. The Indians continued their ravages, and the people, disheartened by the additional taxes which the

[1] Beverley, *Hist. of Virginia*, 58; *Va. Magazine*, I., 57, 59; III., 137–139; IV., 121.

[2] *Va. Magazine*, IV., 118; Mrs. Bacon's letter, *Egerton MSS.*, in British Museum, 2395, f. 550.   [3] Hening, *Statutes*, II., 326–336.

assembly levied for the building of forts, gave up
all hope of relief through their authorized leaders.
Once more they petitioned,[1] with the result that
Berkeley not only refused to listen to them, but
ordered them to send no more petitions to him.
Then the men of Charles City County began to
enlist volunteers and selected Nathaniel Bacon as
their leader. With three hundred men behind him
Bacon marched into the wilderness to seek the
enemy. Berkeley, hearing that Bacon had taken
military command without a commission, promptly
declared all the volunteers a band of rebels and
ordered them to return. All but sixty obeyed the
order and turned back, but the others continued
their march. Berkeley then raised a body of
troops and pursued the "rebels," but without
success.[2] Bacon pushed on, stormed an Indian
palisade, and slew one hundred and fifty Indians.

In the mean time, stirring events were taking
place in Jamestown. During the governor's absence the people "drew into arms" and demanded
the dismantling of the forts, the dissolution of the
old assembly, and the summons of a new body that
should be elected by an open franchise. Berkeley,
fearing "the rage of the people,"[3] agreed to all
that was demanded, and soon after the meeting of
the new assembly, in June, 1676, pardoned Bacon,

---

[1] *Cal. of State Pap., Col.*, 1675–1676, § 921.
[2] " A Review, Breviary, and Conclusion," MS. in Public Record
Office, *Colonial Entry-Book*, No. 81, f. 41.   [3] *Ibid.*, 3.

and restored him to his place in the council, apparently to prevent his entering the assembly to which he had been elected and in which his influence was bound to be felt. According to the Baconians, Berkeley promised Bacon a regular commission as commander-in-chief of the militia. The new assembly, under the guide of competent leaders, became a reforming body and handled many difficult questions with moderation and judgment. It provided for an efficient prosecution of the war against the Indians, and remedied many abuses, notably in local government.[1]

While the assembly was in session a dispute arose between Berkeley and Bacon regarding the commission, the exact merits of which it is not easy to discover. The governor either refused to grant the commission or delayed so long that Bacon, anticipating refusal and perhaps fearing arrest, left Jamestown, and, gathering a body of five hundred followers, determined to obtain the commission, if necessary by force. Berkeley, importuned by both council and House of Burgesses, yielded, and intrusted Bacon with a command against the Indians;[2] but no sooner was Bacon well on his way to the frontier than Berkeley summoned the militia of Gloucester and Middlesex

[1] Hening, *Statutes*, II., 341.
[2] The various accounts agree in these details; Sherwood's letter, *Va. Magazine*, I., 170; *Cal. of State Pap., Col.*, 1675–1676, §§ 964, 965, 969.

counties to take the field against him. The troops
as well as the people refused to support Berkeley,
who, after a second time proclaiming Bacon a
rebel, fled across the bay to Accomack. There he
hoped to find a welcome, because the people of
this county had been peculiarly loyal to Charles II.,
had proclaimed him king in 1649, and had declared
in 1652 that they were "disjointed and sequestered
from the rest of Virginia." But even the people
of "this our kingdom of Accomack" now began
to talk of a redress of grievances and a greater
liberty of trade, and Berkeley soon found himself
deserted by all save a few faithful followers.[1]

With the flight of Berkeley the situation underwent a change. The question of Bacon's commission and the war with the Indians fell into the
background, and the movement took the form of
a struggle between Berkeley and the people for the
control of the government. Bacon, turning back
from his campaign against the Indians, decided
to become a rebel in very fact and to lead his
followers against their legally constituted authorities. That he was actuated by the ambition
of a demagogue we cannot doubt, but we must
also believe that he sincerely desired to alleviate the
prevailing misery and distress.[2] But like others of his
kind, he was headstrong and self-willed, and though

---

[1] *William and Mary Quarterly*, I., 191; Burk, *Hist. of Virginia*,
II., App., iv.
[2] *William and Mary Quarterly*, IV., 133.

possessing force and eloquence, was lacking in foresight and judgment. He was upheld by two-thirds of the people of the colony—employés, apprentices, servants, slaves, small freeholders, and a few planters—the "scum" of the province, Berkeley's adherents most unjustly called them. His lieutenants were not the ignorant, desperate adventurers that the small clique of royalists declared them to be, but were able and intelligent men like the Scotsman, William Drummond, who had been governor of Albemarle in the year 1664.

Bacon's first move was to summon a convention or mass-meeting of leading men, which draughted an oath of allegiance to the new order of things.[1] He then made an appeal to the people of Accomack justifying his conduct,[2] and sent his associates, Bland and Carver, across the bay to capture Berkeley if possible. In the mean time he ordered the assembly to meet on September 4, 1676, and himself started on a new campaign against the Indians. Berkeley, having defeated the expedition led against him by Bland and Carver, took advantage of Bacon's absence, returned to Jamestown at the head of six hundred men, and seized the little town. Bacon, hearing of this turn of affairs while wandering among the woods near the falls of the James, hastened down the river, and surrounding the town prepared

---

[1] *A Narrative*, 16–19; T. M., *Bacon's Rebellion*, 21; "A Review, Breviary, and Conclusion" (cited above), 7.
[2] *Va. Magazine*, I., 61, 62.

for a regular investment. He successfully defended his men from a sally by the governor's party, and, according to the commissioners who investigated the matter afterwards, "got hold of the wives and women relatives of the governor's party and used them on the ramparts to keep the enemy from firing."[1] For a second time Jamestown fell into the hands of Bacon, and for the second time Berkeley fled to Accomack.

On the night of September 19, Bacon set fire to the town and burned church, state-house, and dwellings, in order to prevent all sieges in the future; but while preparing to invade Accomack and to organize an efficient settling of the government, he was stricken with fever contracted "by lying in a very wet season in the trenches before the town,"[2] and he died. After the death of Bacon, October 26, 1676, the rebellion dragged on for two months under Ingram, one of Bacon's lieutenants, but without chance of further success. It gradually degenerated into a scramble for plunder. Ingram was finally persuaded to surrender; the servants and slaves among the followers were sent home to their masters; and the freemen were imprisoned awaiting Berkeley's decision.

Although Charles II. had issued a proclamation promising amnesty to all prisoners, Berkeley on his return from Accomack paid no attention to the king's decree, and, on the ground that too much

[1] *Va. Magazine*, IV., 148; *A Narrative*, 23, 24.
[2] "A Review, Breviary, and Conclusion" (cited above), 11, 12.

leniency would certainly incline the rebels to a new rebellion, wreaked a bitter vengeance and caused thirteen Baconians to be put to death.[1] William Drummond refused to surrender, and was finally captured in January, 1677. "Mr. Drummond, you are welcome," said the old governor, bowing low. "I am more glad to see you than any man in Virginia. Mr. Drummond, you shall be hanged in half an hour." To which Drummond replied "As your honor pleases." And in four hours from that time he was dead.[2] The king did not approve of this summary proceeding, and eventually restored to Drummond's widow the estates which Berkeley had seized and confiscated.

The authorities in England had already taken efficient steps for the suppression of the rebellion, which, during the months from September to November, 1676, loomed up before them as a serious civil war. The king issued letters for Berkeley's recall, appointed Sir Henry Chicheley lieutenant-governor, proclaimed a general amnesty, and considered sending a commission with fleet and troops to Virginia to suppress the revolt and to inquire into the grievances of the colonists. Notwithstanding the advice of Moryson, Virginia's agent, to the contrary,[3] the council, in October, 1676,

---

[1] Hening, *Statutes*, II., 366–371; Force, *Tracts*, I., No. x.
[2] T. M., *Bacon's Rebellion*, 23; *Cal. of State Pap., Col.*, 1675–1676, § 1035 (p. 454), 1677–1680, § 424.
[3] *Rawlinson MSS.*, in Bod. Lib., A. 185, f. 256.

decided to despatch a fleet, under the command of Sir John Berry, and five companies of regulars (one thousand men) and a body of volunteers, under Captain Herbert Jeffreys, of the First Guards, with equipment and supplies for three months. Jeffreys, Berry, and Moryson were constituted a commission with instructions for the pacification of the colony. Jeffreys was appointed governor of Virginia, and a general proclamation was issued against Bacon,[1] October 27, the day after Bacon's death.

January 29, 1677, Berry and Moryson arrived in Virginia, and shortly afterwards Jeffreys came to anchor with the main body of the troops. The first impression of the commissioners was favorable, for Bacon was dead and the rebellion over, and they were inclined to present Berkeley's conduct in a friendly light. They were puzzled, however, to know what to do with their soldiers, and probably failed to appreciate Berkeley's sarcastic comments on their position or the fears of the people at the presence of so many troops.[2] Their favorable impressions gradually altered, and they soon wrote home that they had been mistaken or deceived in Berkeley.

In fact, the old man, either fearing an infringement of his own authority or urged on by others, hindered the work of the commissioners by every means in his power. He refused to recognize

---

[1] *Cal. of State Pap., Col.*, 1675–1676, §§ 1036, 1044, 1045, 1050, 1053–1064, 1132.   [2] *Ibid.*, 1677–1680, § 25.

Jeffreys as governor or to return to England; he paid no attention to the orders of the commissioners; he persuaded the assembly to refuse to show them official papers; and he actually intimidated the people and made it difficult for the commissioners to obtain adequate information. He treated them with mock honor, calling them "Right Honorables," until, as Moryson wrote, "This country will make us all fools and shortly bring us to Cuddy Cuddy." Finally, Berkeley decided to sail for England, and when the commissioners called to take their farewell leave of him capped the climax of indignities by sending them home in his coach with the common hangman as postilion.[1]

The commissioners, thoroughly angry, reported Berkeley's conduct to the authorities in England, and thus prepared a warm reception for the old governor when, in his dotage, irritable and hardly responsible, he came home to die in his native land. The Lords of Trade passed a severe censure upon him and upheld the report of the commissioners. The king, greatly displeased, charged him with disobedience, bad government, and illegal exactions, and refused to see him or to listen to his plea. But in consideration of present infirmities and past service he took no action against him. Berkeley died in July, 1677.[2]

[1] *Cal. of State Pap., Col.*, 1677–1680, §§ 171, 181, 216, 821, 1675–1676, § 173.
[2] *Journal of the Lords of Trade*, II., 176–178; *Cal. of State Pap., Col.*, 1677–1680, §§ 239, 244, 245, 247, 386.

After Berkeley's departure Jeffreys assumed the office of governor and pushed forward rapidly the work of investigation and inquiry. The commissioners obtained from each county a statement of its grievances, negotiated a treaty of peace with the Indians, and relieved the province of a heavy burden by sending back to England most of the troops that for five months had been in camp in Middle Plantation. A hundred men remained to settle in the colony as planters. The commissioners also prepared an elaborate account of the rebellion for transmission to the king and Lords of Trade,[1] and when all had been finished, in the autumn of 1677, Berry and Moryson returned to England.

Bacon's rebellion was at bottom a protest against bad government, and was induced by an unfavorable condition of the industrial life of the colony. Men complained of the way the government was carried on; they objected to the management of affairs by a few men who were exploiting the colony for their own profit; and when the opportunity came, gave vent to their discontent and their misery by supporting a leader whom events had thrust to the front. The favorable results of the rebellion were that the colonists got rid of Berkeley, and obtained through the commissioners an opportunity to state their grievances; and many of the abuses were remedied by the express command of the king.

[1] *Cal. of State Pap., Col.*, 1677–1680, §§ 171, 240, 272, 433.

They also gained peace with the Indians, to the advantage of their fur trade.

Nevertheless, a great and lasting disadvantage of the rebellion was that it checked the negotiations with the king for a charter of privileges, and in the end led to the issue of a document far less liberal than that which the king had originally intended to grant. The draught "Charter" of November, 1675, contained nearly all that the Virginians had asked for; it vested full powers in the assembly, and estopped the king from further interference with the land titles of the colony. But the new "Charter," or grant of privileges,[1] obtained after the rebellion, said nothing about the right of the assembly to control taxation; and on the question of land grants made no promise as to what the king would or would not do in the future.

Notwithstanding the efforts of the commissioners, the colony remained in an excited and overwrought condition. The people complained of Indian ravages, of the quartering of soldiers upon them, and of wide-spread ruin due to pillage and plunder. Jeffreys died in 1678, and was succeeded by Sir Henry Chicheley, whom Baltimore spoke of as "superannuated," and whom a sea-captain called "very old, sickly, and crazy." Chicheley was unable to alleviate the distress. Lord Culpeper, who was appointed governor in 1679 and served till 1684, reached the colony the next year. An

---

[1] Burk, *Hist. of Virginia*, II., App., iv.–lvii., lxi., lxii.

assembly that he summoned to meet in June, 1680, passed an act of indemnity and oblivion to quiet the country, and another ordering that all export, castle, and port dues be devoted to the expenses of the government—a wise and wholesome measure.

Culpeper was an able man, but he was corrupt and pleasure-loving, extravagant and mercenary, and came to Virginia to recoup his fortunes. To this end he persuaded the king to grant him an annual salary of £2000, and £150 for house rent out of the colonial revenue; and during the four months that he was in the colony (May 3–August 30, 1680) he extended perquisites and fees, trans formed gratuities into regular payments, and com- pelled masters of ships or sailing-vessels to give, instead of presents of liquors or provisions, twenty or thirty shillings for every vessel clearing the harbor.[1] Little wonder that Burk, in commenting on Culpeper's withdrawal to England in August, says that he had gone to enjoy "the ample revenues of his office."

In the mean time the colony fell into a sad state of disorder because of the old difficulty—the low price of tobacco. Culpeper comprehended the situation during his short residence in the colony, but saw no other remedy than free-trade.[2] After

---

[1] Cal. of State Pap., Col., 1681–1685, § 319; Hening, Statutes, II., 458, n., 466; Hartwell, Blair, and Chilton, Present State of Virginia, 142; Beverley, Hist. of Virginia, 78, 79.

[2] Cal. of State Pap., Col., 1681–1685, § 156.

Culpeper's return to England, Chicheley, as deputy governor, summoned the assembly, which sought to quiet popular agitation by passing a law limiting the number of ports where merchandise could be landed and tobacco shipped. The measure proved of no avail, and in the attempts made to enforce it many vessels sailed away without a cargo, and the situation became worse rather than better.[1]

Another assembly was called in the spring of 1682, and Chicheley wrote without effect to Baltimore, hoping that the two colonies might agree on a limitation of tobacco-planting for a year.[2] Then numbers of the people, disappointed that no limiting-law had been passed, took the matter into their own hands. Beginning in Gloucester County, bands of men advanced from plantation to plantation cutting down the tobacco plants and destroying "in an hour's time as much tobacco as twenty men could bring to perfection in a summer." The rioting spread into New Kent and Middlesex counties, and for a time the militia was unable to control it. The plant - cutters at first acted openly during the day, but afterwards did their work at night, and were aided not only by the servants, but by the planters themselves. When the men were arrested the women took up the work, and com-

---

[1] Hening, *Statutes*, 471–478, 561; *Cal. of State Pap., Col.*, 1681–1685, § 424.

[2] Bruce, *Econ. Hist. of Virginia*, I., 405, *n.; Cal. of State Pap., Col.*, 1681–1685, § 232.

mitted serious damage before they were checked.[1]
These ravages went on until August, 1682, when,
after large amounts of tobacco had been destroyed,
the energy of the rioters flagged and the movement
came to an end.

In November, 1682, at the express command of
the king, Culpeper came back; and though he had
been unwilling to return to the colony, he showed
himself on the whole a prudent and energetic governor. After the arrest of several of the tobacco-
cutters, the colony became peaceful, the price of
tobacco rose, fears of the Indians decreased; and
though rumors of pirates were frequent, no serious
trouble appears to have been caused by them at
this time. Still, Culpeper could not long maintain
an energetic rule, and could not forget his own
doctrine that no colonial governorship was worth
while in which there was no profit. Therefore, in
1684 he returned to England and was immediately
deprived of his governorship for having left the
colony without permission. Even after his return
he petitioned the treasury to aid him in suing the
colony for money that he claimed as his own.[2]

The people, still poor and in many ways thrift-
less, seemed to have exhausted their energies in
the late troubles. Nevertheless, the next governor,
Lord Howard of Effingham, got into constant

---

[1] *Cal. of State Pap., Col.*, 1681–1685, §§ 494, 495, 524.
[2] *Treasury, In Letters, Indexes, Reference-Book*, III., 314–316,
in Public Record Office.

difficulties with the deputies, who refused to pass measures recommended by the governor until some grievances should be redressed.[1]   A prolonged deadlock ensued.   In truth, Lord Howard was not fit for his place: he badgered and bullied the assembly, and, when it opposed him, complained to the king of its "peevish obstinacy."   James II. upheld his servant, approved of his actions, and reproved the burgesses, whom he charged with holding irregular and tumultuous meetings.

The colony seemed on the eve of another revolt, and when the news came of the revolution in England, in the winter of 1688–1689, rumors of all kinds spread among the people.   Roman Catholics were believed to be concerting with the Indians to murder the Protestants; and people in various parts of the colony took up arms to protect themselves. Men feared that French war-ships were about to attack the province, and in Virginia, as in Maryland at this same time, it was believed that there was neither king nor government in England.   Finally, in April, 1689, fears were quieted by orders received from England to proclaim the new sovereigns; and with "unfeigned joy and exultation" William and Mary were declared sovereigns of England and her dominions.

Virginia suffered during the years that followed Bacon's rebellion from the character of the men

---

[1] Hartwell, Blair, and Chilton, *Present State of Virginia*, 137–142.

whom the Stuart kings selected to rule over her.
The colony was kept in a constant state of agitation,
for the people were prone to tumult and the assembly to opposition; and the governors did little to
quiet the discontent. The settlers were pushing
into the back countries, establishing homes on the
upper waters of the Potomac, Rappahannock, York,
and other rivers, where they were suffering dangers
from the Indians incident to frontier and wilderness
life, and complaints of Indian raids from the northwest were frequent. Great distances made government throughout the colony difficult; councillors
lived widely scattered, on the eastern shore, in low-
land necks, and in the up-country; wind and weather
made rapid movement impossible; and, in winter,
days and even weeks passed before all the members
of the council could be assembled. With the burgesses the difficulties were even greater. Nevertheless, the colony prospered, and when Nicholson came
in 1691 as lieutenant-governor under Lord Howard,
a new and more peaceful era began.

CHAPTER XV

DEVELOPMENT OF MARYLAND

(1649–1686)

MARYLAND reproduced more than Virginia the religious and political conditions that prevailed in the mother-country. The proprietary, Lord Baltimore, possessed powers that were little less than royal; and the people, sharing in legislation, yet prevented from controlling the government, because of the prerogatives vested in the proprietary by the charter, were divided into religious as well as political factions, that were more uncompromising in their hostility for each other than were any of the parties that upheld or opposed the policy of Berkeley. The first sixty years in the history of the colony were contemporary with the era of revolution in England, and there is scarcely a phase of the home conflict, from 1640 to 1688, that does not find its counterpart in the struggle in Maryland.

The revolutionary changes in England during these years often placed Baltimore in the awkward position of standing between two fires. His charter, granted by Charles I. in 1632, was annulled in 1645

232

by the Long Parliament because of the Roman
Catholic character of his colony;[1] and the republic
established in England after 1649 was hostile because Baltimore's acting governor, Thomas Greene,
a Roman Catholic, very indiscreetly proclaimed
Prince Charles as king of England.[2] On the other
hand, Baltimore, to whom toleration was a matter
quite as much of business as of conscience, gave a
welcome to all Protestants, in order to prevent the
establishment of a Jesuit régime in Maryland; and
permitted a large body of them to settle half-way up
the Chesapeake on the Severn River. This admit-
tance of Dissenters cost him the favor of the Stuarts;
and Charles II., then in France, annulled his charter,
and appointed Davenant, the dramatist, as governor
of Maryland.[3]

The anomalous position occupied by the proprietary imperilled his authority in the province,
and the Puritans even planned to separate from
his government and set up a state for themselves. This pressing danger of secession within
the province was soon lost sight of, however, in
the presence of a greater danger which threatened
the proprietary from abroad. On March 29, 1652,
the commissioners whom Parliament had sent to
America to effect the reduction of Virginia and

---

[1] *Md. Archives*, III., 164, 165.
[2] Bozman, *Hist. of Md.*, II., 670.
[3] Langford, *A Clere and Sensible Refutation of Babylon's Fall*
(1655), quoted, *ibid.*, 672.

"all the plantations within the Chesapeake," appeared at St. Mary's, and obtained the submission of the colony to the "authority of the keepers of the Liberties of England."

Baltimore, whose legal title was in no way impaired by this event, refused to allow his authority in the province to go by default. He asserted his right to hold his province under Parliament as formerly he had held it under the king, and demanded that the people of Maryland recognize without limitation his full title under the charter. He bade Governor Stone, whom he had appointed in 1647 to succeed his brother, to issue a proclamation declaring that all land patents should be renewed and all writs issued in the name of the proprietary, and ordering the inhabitants to take an oath of fidelity on penalty of the loss of their lands.[1]

The Puritans refused to submit, and sent a petition to the commissioners, stating that the oath which Baltimore required was not agreeable to their idea of liberty of conscience. They said that it compelled them to swear "absolute subjection to a government, where the ministers of state are bound by oath to countenance and defend the Roman popish religion, which we apprehend to be contrary to the fundamental laws of England, the covenant taken in the three kingdoms, and the consciences of true English subjects, and doth carry on an

[1] *Md. Archives*, III., 298–300.

arbitrary power, so as whatever is done by the people at great costs in assemblies, for the good of the
people, is liable to be made null by the negative
voice of his lordship." [1]

Here in a nutshell is the issue frankly stated.
Lord Baltimore was a Roman Catholic, a royalist,
an upholder of toleration for Roman Catholics as
well as Dissenters, the proprietor of all lands under
the charter, and the possessor of prerogatives that
no parliamentarian could acknowledge. The Puritans were Dissenters and parliamentarians, intoler-
ant in religion as were their fellows in England and
New England, hating all Roman Catholics, hostile
to the Stuart doctrine of government, and restless
under any other control than that of God and
themselves.

The commissioners in replying to the petition
protested against Stone's proclamation, but bade
the Puritans remain peaceful. When in 1654 Cromwell became Lord Protector, Baltimore greeted his
elevation with satisfaction, believing that the master-
ful man who had just put an end to the rule of the
Rump Parliament and had suppressed Leveller up-
risings by force of arms, would give him support.
He bade Stone issue another proclamation recognizing the protectorate and declaring that Maryland was "subordinate unto and dependent upon
the aforesaid government of the Commonwealth." [2]

---

[1] "Baltimore's Case Answered" (Force, *Tracts*, II., No. ix.),
29–31.   [2] *Md. Archives*, III., 304.

The commissioners, aroused by this defiant act, at once returned to Maryland, and, when Stone refused to withdraw the proclamation, placed themselves at the head of the Puritans of Patuxent and the Severn, marched against St. Mary's, and compelled him to submit.[1]

The next step was to depose Stone from the governorship and place in his stead, in the name of the Lord Protector of England, a Puritan, Captain William Fuller. They remodelled the government after that then existing in England and erected a council of ten men, the majority of whom were Puritans. October 20, 1654, an assembly was called at Patuxent, which bears unmistakable marks of its Puritan character. By its votes, Roman Catholics were disfranchised and practically outlawed; and acts were passed touching drunkenness, swearing, and keeping of the Sabbath, and regulating administrative affairs. All was done in the name of the Lord Protector; and even Baltimore's title to the lands of the province was ignored.[2]

Stone wrote a full account of these events to Lord Baltimore, who took immediate steps to recover his province. On appeal to Cromwell, the Protector wrote to Bennett, bidding him avoid further trouble and in all probability recommending the colonists of Maryland, as he had done those of Virginia, to pursue "peace, love, and the great

---

[1] Account of the Commissioners, *Md. Archives*, III., 311, 312.
[2] *Ibid.*, 339–356.

interests of religion."[1]   Baltimore at the same time
wrote to Stone, enclosing a new set of instructions
and reproving him for his tame submission.[2]   Stung
by this rebuke, Stone, according to Bennett's report
to Thurloe, "forced his highnesses' subjects to take
arms one against another, seized the records of the
province, armed Papists and others, plundered, dis-
armed, and imprisoned all those who refused to join
with him, . . . railing at and reviling the people,
calling them Roundheads, rogues, dogs, etc., setting
up Lord Baltimore's colors against the colors of the
commonwealth."[3]

In the presence of these threatening actions the
Puritans prepared for war.   Stone sailed from St.
Mary's, March 24, 1655, with a flotilla bearing between one and two hundred men,[4] prepared for
making an attack on the Puritan settlement on the
Severn.   There he was confronted by a force under
Fuller, numbering one hundred and seventy, drawn
up on shore to resist him.   The day was won by
the Puritans, aided by a New England trading
vessel, under a Puritan master named Heamans,
which happened to be lying in the harbor.   The
victory was stained by the unwarranted execution
of three of the defeated party and by the disposition
of the Puritans to carry their vengeance further.

[1] *Cal. of State Pap., Col.*, 1574–1660, § 413.
[2] Bozman, *Hist. of Md.*, I., 694, 695; Thurloe, *State Papers*,
V., 485.   [3] *Ibid.*, 485.
[4] The accounts differ, one giving 137, another 200.

Only the intercession of the women and of some of the soldiers themselves saved the lives of others of the proprietary party.

The Puritans, who were now in full control, made immediate use of their power. They sequestered Stone's estate, kept Stone and many of his followers prisoners, and put others under bonds for their good behavior. However, they do not appear to have abused their opportunity, for they demanded no heavier punishment than the imposition of fines upon thirty-six of the St. Mary's men, "to cover losses made by the late march." [1]

When Baltimore heard of the defeat and capture of his governor he despatched to the colony new instructions, appointing Josias Fendall, one of Stone's party, governor in Stone's place, and naming five others as his council. Thus two governments existed for the province: one at St. Mary's, under Fendall; the other at Providence, under Fuller. Of the two, the Puritan government was the stronger, and there is reason to believe that the Puritans were planning to separate themselves entirely from the remainder of the province and to set up an independent government of their own.

Baltimore was by no means at the end of his resources. With characteristic astuteness he bowed to the rising sun, and presented to the Protector a statement in which he emphasized in exaggerated terms his devotion to the commonwealth. [2] Com-

[1] *Md. Archives*, X., 412–430.   [2] *Ibid.*,. III., 280, 281.

missioner Bennett, at this time also governor of Virginia, endeavoring to meet what he called Baltimore's "specious pretences," also drew up a document, in 1656, and attempted to show how false was Baltimore's claim of loyalty to the existing government in England.[1] Yet Baltimore obtained a reference of the case to the committee of trade.[2] There the matter was discussed and a report prepared, probably recommending some modification of Baltimore's powers; but the Protector was too much distracted by public business in England to settle the government of Maryland.

The delay worked to Baltimore's advantage, for in 1657 and 1658 indications in England were pointing to the failure of the Puritan commonwealth.[3] Without waiting for a decision from Cromwell, Bennett and Mathews, his colleague, made overtures for a settlement, and reached an agreement with Baltimore. Acting for the Puritan party, they conceded the chief point at issue—recognition of the proprietary's prerogative—and gave up the struggle. The people of Maryland promised to return to their allegiance if the proprietary would preserve all land titles and maintain in force the toleration act of 1649. On November 30, 1657, the agreement was finally signed.[4]

[1] Thurloe, *State Papers*, V., 483.
[2] *Cal. of State Pap., Col.*, 1574–1660, pp. 435, 436, 447.
[3] Thurloe, *State Papers*, V., 482.
[4] *Md. Archives*, III., 332–334.

Thus Baltimore won the victory over enemies who had twice defeated his authorized deputy, Governor Stone, and twice deprived him of his proprietary rights. Though his success was due to skilful diplomacy and to a shrewd regard for the main chance, he might have had too little influence with the committee of trade, or even with Cromwell himself, but that religious interests were giving way to those that were political and economic. Merchants who were members of the colonial and trade committees in England were anxious for a cessation of hostilities in order that the colonies might be restored to a normal condition of prosperity. Baltimore's claims were entirely just from the legal point of view, and there was no other solution of the problem than to give back the colony to its legitimate proprietary; but the English merchants, to whom the tobacco trade was a means of livelihood, threw themselves into the balance on the same side. At this time the influence of the merchant and trading classes in shaping the policy of the government at home was a factor of great and growing importance.

Lord Baltimore, though victorious over the Puritans, had one more crisis to face before he could enter upon the full possession of his propriety. Notwithstanding a long dispute with Virginia over the possession of Kent Island and the proper location of the boundary-line between the two colonies on the eastern side of the bay, Mary-

land was always more or less influenced political-
ly by her powerful neighbor. In March, 1660, the
Maryland assembly attempted to follow the example of Virginia; and, despite the fact that Baltimore
was the legal and accepted head of the government,
the House of Delegates declared itself "a lawful
assembly, without dependence on any other power
in the province," and took to itself the authority
of the "highest court of judicature." [1]

Fendall, whom Baltimore had appointed governor in 1657, came out boldly against the proprietary, and said that in the charter the king
had originally intended to grant the freemen full
power to make and enact laws, which, when published in the proprietary's name, were to have
force without the proprietary's consent. [2] He
carried the council, against the remonstrance of
Philip Calvert, who held his brother's commission
as secretary. Emboldened by this support, the
delegates proposed to abolish the upper house or
council altogether, and Fendall resigned his commission as governor, to become speaker of the
lower house—an act implying a complete denial of
the rights of the proprietary.

The attempt was too late to be successful. Before
the news of this action reached England, Charles
II. was on the throne. Lord Baltimore acted
with efficiency and despatch. He appointed Philip
Carteret governor, and obtained from the king

[1] *Md. Archives*, I., 388.   [2] *Ibid.*, 389.

a proclamation denouncing Fendall's sedition and commanding the people to yield obedience to the proprietary. In November, 1660, Calvert, acting on his brother's instructions, proclaimed a general amnesty to all who would acknowledge Baltimore's jurisdiction. Some of the members of the assembly were pardoned, others were deprived of their civil rights, and Fendall was allowed to leave the province. The conspiracy is significant as an early phase of the struggle between the assembly and the feudal executive, that was to mark the history of all the provincial colonies in later times.

The factional quarrel between the proprietary and the Puritans checked the economic prosperity of the province. Maryland was not wealthy, and the colonists could hardly be called thrifty. The settlements lay along the shores of the Chesapeake, from St. Mary's north to the mouth of the Susquehanna, and south on the eastern shore from Hermann's plantation, called Bohemia, to Watkins Point. The coast-line was broken by frequent rivers and bays, about which were swamps and morasses that made communication other than by water almost impossible. Though the uplands, where tobacco was cultivated, were fertile, inducements to thrift and economy were few; and, in the main, farms were mean and small, and the taxes, even when moderate, were felt to be a burden.

Alsop's description of the province in 1666, and Hammond's statements in his *Leah and Rachel*, are probably too favorable, and give a picture of comfort and ease that is not borne out by other observers or the evidence of the laws. The main body of the settlers lived isolated, often primitive, lives, subsisting on wholesome but coarse food, including little milk or butter, and drinking frequently and heavily in those portions of the colony where lands were low and the climate damp.[1] For planters and farmers alike the sole industry was tobacco planting, and so rich was the soil that, according to contemporary report, tobacco could be raised for thirty years on the same piece of land. Labor was performed by servants and negroes, whose life, as seen by Dankers and Sluyter, was wretched in the extreme.[2] Yet the Maryland people, though inclined to be unprogressive and indolent, were comfortable and in the main contented.

The colonists paid their quit-rents, taxes, and fees in tobacco; and whatever touched the price of this staple touched the welfare of the colony. There was almost no coin in circulation, and the demand made in Maryland by Lord Baltimore and in Virginia by Governor Berkeley, that quit-rents be paid in money, raised a great outcry. As tobacco fell steadily in price after 1660, long and earnest inquiry was made into the cause, and the assembly

---

[1] Dankers and Sluyter, *Journal*, 216–219; Cook, *Sot-Weed Factor*, 4, 5.

[2] Dankers and Sluyter, *Journal*, 191, 192, 217; *Md. Archives*, XIII., 451–457.

tried hard to effect an arrangement with Virginia, whereby tobacco planting might be stinted; but all plans for this purpose were vetoed by the proprietary.[1]   Baltimore did not believe that overproduction was the greatest obstacle to the progress of the colony, and he frankly told the Lords of Trade that in his mind the navigation acts held first place.   Nevertheless, he made honest efforts to carry out the acts,[2] and pointed to the customs receipts in England to show how valuable Maryland was to the crown.   The colony had no shipping of its own, and was dependent on others to do her carrying-trade.   The irregular manner in which the New - Englanders disposed of Maryland tobacco can hardly be charged against the proprietary, so long as he saw to the taking out of bonds or the payment of the penny a pound demanded by the act of 1672.

In 1661 Charles Calvert was sent over as governor, and on the death of Lord Baltimore in 1675 became himself the proprietary.   Except for an absence in 1676, he remained in Maryland until 1684 and personally directed the government of the province. He had little of his father's tact, and made few efforts to conciliate those who opposed him, or to compromise with the dominant party in the colony. He had his father's strength of will without his sense of humor, and he saw no remedy for Mary-

[1] *Md. Archives*, III., 457, 476, 504, 547, 550, 558.
[2] *Ibid.*, 446, 454, 459, 484; V., 24, 25, 31, 47, 123, 124.

land's troubles except in manipulating government in such a way as to maintain his authority. He was always at the head of a minority. He ruled arbitrarily, saw but one side of a difficulty, and employed men that were not always trustworthy and means that were not always creditable. Nevertheless, he was interested in the colony, and studied to improve its condition, winning his adherents rather by adding to their prosperity than by heeding their political demands.

Though life in the colony from 1661 to 1675 was peaceful, the old discontent was not quieted. Complaints were frequent, quarrels between the council and the lower house were of common occurrence, and government was in the hands of a few and controlled by the proprietary's relatives. The governor and the council were accused of levying excessive taxation, of placing Roman Catholic members of the governor's family in offices of state, of favoritism in subordinate appointments, and of interference in the elections. Many of the charges were true, others were but the shreds and patches of truth.

It is true that Calvert manipulated government so that he might control it. He formed a political ring made up of his relatives;[1] he followed the example of Virginia in restricting the suffrage;[2] and he summoned, as Virginia had done, but half

[1] Sparks, *Causes of the Revolution of 1689*, pp. 64, 65.
[2] *Md. Archives*, V., 77, 78.

the deputies elected, in order to save the counties half the expense of their members. By limiting the suffrage he disfranchised the poorer classes; and by refusing to summon all the delegates, he kept out of the assembly men of influence who opposed him.

In 1676 Calvert, now Lord Baltimore, went to England, and left Notley as governor in his place. The discontent already prevalent in the colony was increased by rumors of an Indian invasion, which many of the Protestants declared was incited by the Roman Catholics of Maryland, acting in collusion with the French, for establishing a "Jesuitical" government in Maryland.[1] The excitement was increased by the reports that came from Virginia of Bacon's uprising; and scarcely were the rumors of an Indian war shown to be baseless when a number of colonists—Davis, Pate, and others— "malcontents, but otherwise of laudable characters"[2]—drew up a "seditious" paper, and gathered together sixty men for the purpose of overawing the governor and the assembly (1676). Notley acted with commendable speed, and arrested and hanged Davis and Pate. This summary proceeding, followed by the death of Bacon in Virginia, brought the premature and ill-advised uprising to

---

[1] See remonstrance of 1676 in *Md. Archives*, V., 134–149; Doyle, *English in America*, I., 317; *Cal. of State Pap., Col.*, 1661–1668, § 404 (wrongly dated).

[2] T. M., *Bacon's Rebellion* (Force, *Tracts*, I., No. viii.), 21.

an end.[1] Like Bacon's rebellion, this revolt against the authority of the proprietary in Maryland had its origin in poverty, ignorance, and political discontent.

During the next four years, the rival powers of governor and assembly came frequently into conflict in the legislature of the colony, the popular body seeking to limit the authority of the executive. Also after 1678 Lord Baltimore was confronted with additional difficulties, the most unfortunate of which was the dispute with William Penn. The merits of this boundary case can never be satisfactorily determined: the technical right lay with Baltimore, and we cannot admire Penn's inclination to ignore it; nevertheless, sympathy is bound to lie with Penn in his desire to save his capital and to obtain a commercial outlet for his colony.[2] In an age of confused and conflicting land grants, when scarcely one of the colonies was able to retain without dispute the boundaries originally assigned, we can hardly accept a plea based on nothing else than a literal interpretation of the terms of a charter. Were such a plea admitted as final, every colony would be more or less under indictment.

For both proprietaries the results were most disastrous. Baltimore and Penn went to England in 1684, each to present his own view of the case,

[1] *Md. Archives*, V., 153.
[2] *Cal. of State Pap., Col.*, 1681–1685, §§ 468, 469.

and each, though eager to return, was detained there at a time when his presence was greatly needed in his colony to uphold his prerogatives. Baltimore's presence in England was needed because he was already out of favor with the Lords of Trade on account of his quarrel with the royal collector. Until 1676 Calvert acted as his own collector of customs, but in that year he recommended the appointment of Christopher Rousby, with whom and with Badcock, the king's surveyor of customs, he was soon in controversy. Rousby appealed to the Lords of Trade. Badcock accused Baltimore of interfering with him in the performance of his duty. The Lords of Trade in 1681 decided in favor of the officers; reprehended Lord Baltimore; bade him refund £2500, of which they claimed he had defrauded the customs by his interference; and threatened him with the loss of his charter if he did not obey the acts of trade.[1]

Rousby returned to Maryland, and, while Baltimore was in England, became involved in a quarrel with George Talbot, Baltimore's hot-headed relative and head of the council, and was murdered. This unfortunate incident led to the issue of a writ of *quo warranto* against the charter, and though the writ was never executed, Baltimore's standing in the eyes of the home authorities was very much impaired.

If the trouble with Rousby pointed to the proprietary's neglect of the acts of trade, a new trouble

---

[1] *Journal of the Lords of Trade*, III., 319, 320.

with Fendall, who for twenty years had been a
leader among the Protestant enemies of the proprietary, seemed to indicate unrest and discontent
within the province that Baltimore was unable to
control. In 1681, taking advantage of the quarrel
in England between Charles II. and the parliament
of that year, Fendall endeavored to stir up the people
of Charles and St. Mary's counties, and to tamper
with some of the proprietary's officers. With a
fellow-agitator, John Coode, he planned the overthrow of Baltimore's government and the expul-
sion of all Roman Catholics from Maryland.[1] But
with Coode and another malcontent, Godfrey, he
was arrested and imprisoned; and in November,
1681, was tried for "mutinous and seditious speeches,
practices, and attempts" against the proprietary,
"to the subversion of the state and government
of the province." Coode was acquitted, Fendall
fined 40,000 pounds of tobacco and banished, and
Godfrey sentenced to be hanged, though the penalty
in the latter's case was afterwards remitted.[2] The
evidence brought forward at the trial discloses an
unsettled condition of public opinion in the province,
and shows how ready were the enemies of Baltimore
and the Roman Catholics to take advantage of
every changing fortune in English affairs to effect
their overthrow.

[1] *Cal. of State Pap., Col.*, 1681–1685, § 351.
[2] *Md. Archives*, V., 313–328; *Cal. of State Pap., Col.*, 1681–
1685, § 391.

Baltimore planned to return to Maryland in September, 1686, but was compelled to remain in order to thwart Penn's attempt to obtain the disputed territory below the fortieth parallel and to meet the king's attack on the charter; he therefore sent over William Joseph as his deputy. News of the birth of a son to King James in 1688 led to excessive demonstrations of loyalty in Maryland that did not serve to allay popular fears regarding the Roman Catholic and monarchical tendencies of the government.[1] But the governor's speeches and the proclamations regarding the young prince, ridiculous though the phrases were in which they were couched, did not arouse any special excitement at the time; and a list of grievances which the assembly handed in to the governor shortly afterwards was so moderate in character as to show that certainly the deputies, and probably the greater part of the people, had no thought of revolution.

When contrasted with Virginia, Maryland shows no such combination of circumstances leading to revolution as prevailed below the Potomac at the time of Bacon's rebellion. Indian difficulties were less acute; the policy of the proprietary party, though similar in character to that of the ring in Virginia, was less offensive and less burdensome than in that colony; the people at large, widely scattered and divided by a broad expanse of water into two parts, were less competent to act efficiently

[1] *Md. Archives*, VIII., 15; XIII., 184, 185, 210.

against the proprietor even had they been inclined;
while there were present no leaders on either side
in Maryland like Berkeley with his spleen and
Bacon with his commanding personal magnetism.
The revolution that finally took place in Maryland
was, as the sequel will show, not a popular movement nor one which would have succeeded independently of influences from England. It was
but a phase of the general uprising in the colonies
which followed the revolution of 1688 in England.

CHAPTER XVI

DIFFICULTIES IN NEW ENGLAND
(1675–1686)

WHAT was going on in New England during these years of turmoil in the south? For a long time after 1668, the enemies of Massachusetts waited their time. The early complaints sent in to the Lords of Trade were largely personal in character, affecting individuals and not the crown. These complaints and the report of the commissioners, who had so unfortunate an experience in 1665 in Boston, gave the colony a bad name in England, where she was charged with the possession of a peevish and touchy humor; but they did not offer a sufficient basis for an attack on the charter. When, however, new complaints began to come in, showing that the king's revenue and the king's prerogatives were threatened by the colony, the Lords of Trade began to consider in earnest a policy of coercion.[1]

In 1675, when Massachusetts was involved in King Philip's War, her enemies renewed the attack;

[1] Evelyn, *Diary*, II., 66; *Cal. of State Pap., Col.*, 1669–1674, § 1059; *Hutchinson Papers*, II., 174, 175, 204.

and in 1676 London merchants came to their aid by declaring that New-Englanders were accustomed to avoid customs dues by trading directly with the Continent, and to get all the trade into their own hands by underbidding competitors.[1] In the eyes of the council, New England was guilty of carrying silk and wool to France and tobacco to Holland, Spain, Portugal, and the islands; and of bringing back European goods from the Continent and wines and brandies from the islands, and so making New England, and not old England, the mart and staple, prejudicing the navigation of the kingdom, impairing the king's revenue, lessening the price of home and foreign commodities, decreasing trade, and impoverishing the king's subjects. It did not matter that the charges were exaggerated; the Lords of Trade took them seriously.

For Massachusetts the time was critical. The rapid growth of population hastened the inevitable struggle between the white man and the Indian for the possession of territory that had hitherto been large enough for both. As long as Massasoit, chief of the Wampanoags, and Canonicus, chief of the Narragansetts, lived, the relations were eminently friendly. With the death of the former in 1660, and of his son, Alexander, in 1662, conditions changed, and under Meatocom, or Philip, as the English called him, the Wampanoags were aroused to war against the English.

[1] *Cal. of State Pap., Col.*, 1675–1676, § 787.

The first attack was made on Rhode Island, at this time under the control of the peace-loving Quakers: and the first blood was shed at Swansea, June 24, 1675. Soon all central and southeastern New England was ablaze. Efforts made by Connecticut and Massachusetts to control the Nipmucks failed; and in August that tribe joined Philip and began a career of murder and pillage that chilled the heart of the bravest of the colonists. Deerfield, Northfield, Springfield, and Hatfield were attacked, houses ravaged and burned, settlers slain and scalped, women and children carried into captivity.

Fearing that the Narragansetts were preparing to join the murderous fray, Massachusetts, Plymouth, and Connecticut attacked their swamp fort on December 19, 1675; and after a fierce and bloody fight, in which sixty-eight Englishmen were killed and one hundred and fifty wounded, captured the stronghold and dispersed the surviving members of the tribe. The defeated Indians, hot with desire for revenge, joined Philip and initiated a second period of massacre. In Rhode Island the men of the main-land fled to the island, leaving their homes to be pillaged and burned; Captain Pierce, of Plymouth, was cut off and killed with a small contingent of men; towns along the Massachusetts frontier were sacked with wanton waste and then destroyed.

For four months the horrors continued, but

gradually the strength of the Indians gave way. Canonchet, of the Narragansetts, was taken and shot in April, 1676; in May one hundred and thirty warriors were cut down on the Connecticut; and others suffering from want of food began to weaken in their loyalty to their leader. Philip's confederacy of Wampanoags, Nipmucks, and Narragansetts broke up. On August 12, Philip himself was run down and slain by a doughty Indian fighter, Colonel Benjamin Church, at the Indian stronghold, Mount Hope; and the last serious attempt of the Indians to check the triumph of the English in New England was brought to an end.

The war had wrought great devastation and ruin. Houses and towns on the frontiers were in ashes. During the campaign Indians had often penetrated into the heart of the colony, and, as in the case of Plymouth, had destroyed the growing crops, which were at the fulness of their ripening. So serious was the famine threatening some parts of New England that the colonists sent to Virginia for food, and bought such quantities of all sorts that the Virginia assembly promulgated a law forbidding the exportation of provisions from that colony. More serious for the prosperity of New England than the loss of the harvest was the injury done to the beaver trade, which was almost entirely destroyed; to the fishing industry, which was badly crippled; and to the whole exporting business to Barbadoes, whereby the New-Englanders obtained

wine, liquors, and money, and, by exchange with the
Virginia planters, tobacco and other commodities.
Governor Berkeley, writing before the war was over,
said that, as it was, the New England colonists
would not "recover these twenty years what they
have lost"; and that if the war continued for a year
longer they would be "the poorest, miserablest people of all the English plantations in America."[1]

While in this plight Massachusetts was called
upon to face a renewal of the attack on her charter.
As early as August, 1671, it was suggested that a
commissioner be sent to Massachusetts. The complaints regarding trade touched king and lords in
a tender spot, and effected that which Quakers,
Anglicans, and other individual complainants had
not been able to accomplish. Two months before the
death of Philip (June, 1676), Edward Randolph, one
of the most remarkable characters in New England
history and an arch-defender of the Stuart cause
and policy, landed at Boston to begin an inquiry
into the condition and conduct of the colony. Randolph henceforth was the chief complainant against
Massachusetts. Looking into every part of the
colonial government, and criticising every detail
with a prejudiced eye, he concluded as early as
July, 1677, that a *quo warranto* ought to be issued
against the colony. From this time forward he
had but one object in view—to bring the colony
into a closer dependence upon the crown, and thus

[1] *Cal. of State Pap., Col.,* 1675–1676, § 859.

to make it more useful to the kingdom. To this extent he was, in fact, the "subverter of Massachusetts liberties."

All the old charges and complaints now rose up to discomfort the colony: Massachusetts authorities had failed to capture the regicides; had treated insolently the commissioners of 1664; had evaded the king's command to broaden the suffrage, even while pretending to obey it;[1] had disregarded the Mason and Gorges claims in extending jurisdiction over York County and the Merrimac territory; had oppressed weaker neighbors, as in the boundary disputes with Plymouth, Connecticut, and Rhode Island; had established a mint and coined money; had levied taxes on non-freemen as well as on freemen; had denied the right of appeal to England from the courts of the colony; and in general had passed laws and exercised powers not warranted by the charter.

Notwithstanding the gravity of these accusations, Massachusetts might have escaped but for other charges, general rather than individual in character, touching the interests of the king and the kingdom: first, the independence affected by the colony; secondly, the colony's neglect of the king's express commands and its apparent indifference to the king's authority; and thirdly, its evasion of the navigation acts, whereby the royal revenues were curtailed.

[1] *Hutchinson Papers*, II., 146, 147.

The first of these charges was not new. The commissioners of 1664 commented on the refractoriness of the colony; and when they were recalled, many people in England believed that Massachusetts would separate from England and set up for herself.[1] The council declared that the Massachusetts oath of fidelity ought to be abolished because it placed allegiance to the colony before allegiance to the king.[2] The colony, while mollifying the royal anger by letters of adulation and offers to take the oath of allegiance, reaffirmed the oath of fidelity more strongly than before,[3] and took the definite ground that, as regards the orders of the king and the laws of Parliament, it was protected by its charter; and that no act, of navigation or other, had any validity in the colony unless it had been passed by the colonial assembly.[4]

These somewhat abstract complaints did not, however, irritate and provoke wrath as did the colony's impolitic disregard of the royal commands. Massachusetts, while clinging to her prerogatives with all the tenacity of a Stuart, seemed to go out of her way to flaunt her claims in the face of the home authorities. In 1665, when ordered to send

[1] *Hutchinson Papers*, II., 140–153; Toppan, *Edward Randolph*, I., 41, *n.*, 103; Evelyn, *Diary*, II., 66.
[2] *Cal. of State Pap., Col.*, 1677–1680, § 668.
[3] *Mass. Col. Records*, V., 153, 154, 191–193.
[4] Randolph's Answers to Queries (*Hutchinson Papers*, II., 232).

over agents, she delayed until the Lords of Trade could charge her with deliberate refusal,[1]

This policy was repeated ten years later, when the agents arrived nearly two years after the colony had been instructed to send them; and in each case the agents were found to be so limited in powers as to give the impression that the colony hoped to tire out the home government by a policy of delay. When for the third time the colony neglected the king's order in this matter, and in others also, the Lords of Trade became angry; charged Massachusetts with sending "frivolous, insufficient excuses" and "insufficient pretences"; and in October, 1681, wrote that if she did not despatch her agents within three months they would order the vacation of the charter. Strange as it may seem, the colony delayed sending agents for four months, and then instructed them, in case the charter were called in question, to say that they had no instructions on that point.[2]

Behind all else lay the charge that the colony undermined the royal revenues. During 1676 and 1677, complaints regarding illegal trade increased, and an important petition from the mercers and silk-weavers of London charged New England with depriving the king of £60,000 a year. Immediately an embargo was placed on New England

---

[1] *Cal. of State Pap., Col.*, 1681–1685, § 266.
[2] *Ibid.*, 1675–1676, §§ 755, 1070, 1186, 1677–1680, §§ 351, 1028, 1681–1685, §§ 266, 416.

trade, and Massachusetts, in her alarm, passed a law, October 10, 1677, enforcing the navigation acts.[1]

With the appointment of Randolph as collector, surveyor, and searcher of the king's customs, a new cause of irritation was created, and the colonists did not hesitate to abuse Randolph himself and to obstruct his business. How little they loved him may be inferred from the doggerel verse written in January, 1679, to greet him after a month's absence in New Hampshire:

> " Welcome, Sr, welcome from ye easterne shore
> With a commission stronger than before
>   To play the horse-leach; robb us of our ffleeces,
>   To rend our land, and teare it all to pieces:
> Welcome now back againe." [2]

Randolph, in his turn, had no sympathy with the colonists, and was determined to do his duty. as he saw it. The colonists hated him and determined "to entertain him not with joy but grief." He hated the colonists, and as a connection of the Mason family, which had fought for twenty years the claim of Massachusetts to New Hampshire, he was prejudiced against them beforehand. Furthermore, he was dependent for his salary and position on the good-will of those in office at home. He was

---

[1] *Cal. of State Pap., Col.*, 1675–1676, §§ 880, 881, 898, 1677–1680, § 41; Toppan, *Edward Randolph*, I., 77; *Mass. Col. Records*, V., 155.

[2] Farmer and Moore, *Historical Collections*, III., 30–32.

called upon to justify his employment both to the Masons and to the Lords of Trade, and the pity of it is that Massachusetts gave him many opportunities to prove his usefulness.

In the three years after Randolph's return to New England, in 1680, his complaints numbered at least twenty - nine. Of these, twenty - three deal with nothing except breaches of the navigation acts— all other questions seemed to him of less consequence. The Mason and Gorges difficulty was settled in 1679, when, by a decision of the Lords Chief-Justices of the King's Bench and Common Pleas and by a commission under the great seal, New Hampshire was made a crown colony.[1] Maine, which Massachusetts had purchased of the heirs of Gorges in 1678, without the king's consent, was, by decision of the same judges, restored to its proprietary; but as there was some doubt regarding the legal assignment of the government, Charles II., in June, 1679, took the province into his own hands, promising to pay Massachusetts the amount of the purchase money whenever her agents surrendered the title-deeds to the crown. Needless to say, this condition was never fulfilled.[2]

Randolph's charges on trade may be divided into three groups: (1) He complained that the mer-

---

[1] Mass. Hist. Soc., *Collections*, 3d series, VIII., 238–242.
[2] *Cal. of State Pap., Col.*, 1677–1680, § 1028; *Journal of the Lords of Trade*, III., 21; *Rawlinson MSS.*, in Bod. Lib., A 321, f. 148.

chants and shippers of New England carried on a
constant and direct trade with foreign countries
and exported thither forbidden commodities, neither
giving bonds nor taking oaths; (2) he asserted
that the magistrates and people connived at this
illicit trade, making it impossible for the collector
to get justice in the courts, where the juries always
decided against the king; (3) and he charged that
the colony, maintaining that it was not bound by
the navigation acts of England, had usurped control
of the business by erecting a naval office in 1681,
which practically neutralized his own authority by
keeping all fines and forfeitures for contraband
goods, instead of dividing them between the informer and the king.

The lords believed what Randolph told them,
the more so as Culpeper, of Virginia, and Cranfield,
of New Hampshire, supported him. The committee reported to the king that the government of
Massachusetts was conducted without the slight-
est regard for the authority or the revenue of the
crown,[1] a charge which, in the eyes of the mer-
cantilists, was a sufficient warrant for annulling
the charter.

The colony was threatened with the writ of *quo
warranto* in 1681, and for two years Randolph continued to urge its issue on every possible occasion.
In 1682 the Massachusetts government was willing

[1] *Cal. of State Pap., Col.,* 1681–1685, §§ 147, 200, 264, 266,
954, 1129.

to submit on nearly every point in dispute. But in the mean time the Lords of Trade stiffened their demands and determined that, even though Massachusetts should submit, her charter should be modified. Therefore, they warned the agents that if the colony would not instruct them to accept such modifications the king would "cause a *quo warranto* to be brought against the governor and company for the abuse of their charter."[1] The time was critical. Charles II. was threatening municipal and other corporations in England, and the agents, discouraged by the prospect, wrote to the colony that many of the English corporations had submitted and they feared that the colony would have to yield.[2]

On June 12, 1683, judgment was filed against the charter of London; and on the next day the Privy Council ordered the attorney-general to bring a writ against the Massachusetts company,[3] a writ which Randolph (in England at the time) was instructed to serve upon the colony. Again time and distance saved the day. Randolph delivered the writ, but, delayed by accident and by the tactics of the obstructionist party in the colony, he was

---

[1] *Cal. of State Pap., Col.*, 1681–1685, § 559. See instructions to agents, *Journal of the Lords of Trade*, IV., 57–59 (omitted in the *Calendar*).

[2] Mass. Hist. Soc., *Collections*, 4th series, VIII., 499.

[3] *Mass. Col. Records*, V., 421, 422; *Journal of the Lords of Trade*, IV., 173–176; *Cal. of State Pap., Col.*, 1681–1685, §1159.

unable to reach England again before the writ expired.[1]

A second writ was issued but not sent. The council finally decided to bring a suit in the court of chancery upon a writ of *scire facias*, which, being against the corporation and not against the individual members, would require no delivery in the colony, and so not be affected by time and distance. On October 23, 1684, the court adjudged the patent forfeited,[2] and Massachusetts stood deprived of her charter.

With the annulling of the charter of Massachusetts the lords were confronted with a new problem. What form of government was "fittest for the king's service in these parts?"[3] They had already made up their minds that no more proprietary colonies should be created; for when, in 1682, Robert Barclay asked for a grant of East New Jersey, and the earl of Doncaster for a grant of Florida, they refused, saying "that it was not convenient for his Majesty to constitute any new proprieties in America or to grant any further powers which may render the plantations less dependent on the crown."[4]

Although they had already declared in 1684 that

---

[1] *Cal. of State Pap., Col.*, 1681–1685, §§ 1159, 1541, 1566, 1567.

[2] Toppan, *Edward Randolph*, I., 243, 244; Mass. Hist. Soc., *Collections*, 4th series, II., 246–278.

[3] *Journal of the Lords of Trade*, V., 21, 22.

[4] *Ibid.*, IV., 64.

the charters of Connecticut and Rhode Island de-
barred them from adding those colonies to Massachusetts, they went deliberately to work to obtain evidence whereon to base new writs of *quo
warranto*. Edward Randolph easily obtained sufficient information for them, and with almost no
debate the decision was reached to annul the charters of these colonies, and to add them, as well as
New York, the Jerseys, and Delaware, to the proposed "dominion" of New England. The plan for
a governor-general of New England had been under
consideration for at least eight years,[1] and was
urged by Randolph and by various governors of
New York. The Lords of Trade came to believe
that it was prejudicial to the king's interest to
have so many independent governments maintained
"without a more immediate dependence on the
crown."[2]

To carry out the new policy, Colonel Percy Kirke
was already selected to be lieutenant and governor-
general of the new dominion of New England. He
had recently come back from Tangier, where his experiences had hardly prepared him for the government of a liberty-loving people like the stubborn
inhabitants of Massachusetts. Randolph had wit
enough to know that Kirke was not the proper man,
and repeatedly said so in his appeals to the Lords

[1] Nowell to Bull, September 26, 1676 (Mass. Hist. Soc., *Collections*, 4th series, VIII., 573).
[2] *Journal of the Lords of Trade*, V., 163.

of Trade and others;[1] but Kirke was supported by Charles II., and his commission was actually drawn up when Charles died. James had other work for Kirke to do, and in his place selected Sir Edmund Andros, who was nominated governor of New England, May 16, 1686.[2]

During the interval a temporary government had been put in force in Massachusetts, with Joseph Dudley as president and Randolph as secretary, and many members of the new council were taken from the old government. The new system differed in one striking particular from that established under the charter: the colony no longer possessed a representative assembly, and a clause authorizing such an assembly was purposely struck out of Kirke's commission, probably at the instigation of the duke of York. Even though the attorney-general declared that the colonists had the right "to consent to such laws and taxes as should be made or imposed on them," notwithstanding the forfeiture of the charter, James II. struck a similar clause out of Dudley's commission. An admiralty system was established in Massachusetts, and Dudley wrote in June, 1686, that he was preparing to carry out the navigation acts. More serious still was the proposal to demand new patents

---

[1] Toppan, *Edward Randolph*, I., 247, 248, 259, 261; *N. E. Historical and Genealogical Register*, XXXVII., 269.

[2] Mass. Hist. Soc., *Collections*, 5th series, IX., 145 – 152; *Cal. of State Pap., Col.*, 1685–1688, § 680.

of land and to impose quit - rents upon grants of unoccupied territory,[1] June 15, 1686, for the first time an Episcopal church was established in Boston.[2]

The government thus erected did not include Connecticut and Rhode Island. The Lords of Trade were far from sure whether charges against them could be obtained sufficient "to ground such a process on."[3] Nothing can be more censurable than the deliberate way in which the duke of York for his own advantage went to work to destroy the independence of these colonies. Whatever the provocation from Massachusetts, Connecticut and Rhode Island had given none. James, whether as duke or king, had no appreciation of the term "liberties of Englishmen," and he endeavored to destroy the corporations in New England, in the interest of his revenues, with the same indifference he showed in manipulating corporations in England in the interest of a Tory majority in Parliament.

Hence, Randolph had no difficulty in finding "articles of high misdemeanor" against several colonies, and without discussion or delay the writs were issued. The stated reason was that the duke and the Lords of Trade had become con-

[1] *Cal. of State Pap., Col.*, 1681–1685, §§ 1928, 1953, 1685–1688, § 357; for the attorney-general's report, see *Journal of the Lords of Trade*, V., 193; Toppan, *Edward Randolph*, I., 30; IV., 81, 114, 115.

[2] Foote, *Annals of King's Chapel*, I., 44.

[3] Toppan, *Edward Randolph*, I., 244; *Journal of the Lords of Trade*, V., 22; *N. Y. Docs. Rel. to Col. Hist.*, III., 340, 341.

vinced that it was to the great and growing prejudice of the king's affairs in the plantation and
to his customs revenue in England that such independent government should continue to exist.[1]
Randolph went to America with five writs in his
pocket—against Rhode Island, Connecticut, the two
Jerseys, and Delaware. The first two he delivered
soon after his arrival, recommending to the colonies
immediate submission. Although the writs had
expired before they were delivered, both colonies
gave Randolph the impression that they would be
willing to surrender their charters.[2]

In the mean time matters did not run smoothly
in Massachusetts under the temporary government.
Dudley and Randolph did not work well together,
the latter thinking the president too considerate
of the "independent faction."[3] At the same time
an opposition began to gather strength among the
people. Ipswich, Rowley, and Woburn refused to
obey the orders of the government, individuals ut-
tered seditious words and were arrested and imprisoned, hatred of Randolph became everywhere manifest, and every possible obstacle was placed in his
path. So serious had the situation become that

[1] *Cal. of State Pap., Col.*, 1685–1688, § 279; Toppan, *Edward Randolph*, I., 257, 258; *N. Y. Docs. Rel. to Col. Hist.*, III., 362.
[2] *Ibid.*, 368, 386, 387; *Conn. Col. Records*, III., 352, 356; *R. I. Col. Records*, III., 190; *Cal. of State Pap., Col.*, 1685–1688, § 794.
[3] Toppan, *Edward Randolph*, IV., 161, 162; Hutchinson, *Hist. of Massachusetts Bay*, I., 350, 351.

Randolph was glad enough when, on December 20, 1686, Andros finally reached Boston and took charge of the government as governor - general of the dominion of New England.

The administration of Andros lasted from December, 1686, to April, 1689, a period of two years and a half. During that time his efforts were directed to the one great task of erecting a firm, centralized government for his large territory, besides cultivating friendship with the Indians, securing his frontiers, and settling the internal organization according to his instructions. In this difficult and practically impossible undertaking he displayed the same qualities he had shown as governor of New York; but he had a far more difficult people to deal with, and was himself much more out of touch with the principles and ideas that they represented than he had been with those of the majority of the New-Yorkers.

The administration of Andros was throughout an attempt to unite and consolidate a number of self-governing colonies under the rule of a single man, and to govern them according to a system diametrically opposed to that previously in force. He had a better appreciation of the difficulties of the task than had his master, James II.; but as a soldier and subject it was his business not to use his own judgment but implicitly to obey the orders that had been given him. Hence, soon after his arrival he organized his government, quieted the disturbed people by friendly promises to uphold their interests, and took measures to strengthen the fortifications around Boston.

The next step was to write to Plymouth, Rhode Island, and Connecticut, bidding them surrender and accept annexation. Plymouth and Rhode Island submitted, and sent representatives to sit in Andros's council in December.[1] On January 12, 1687, Andros dissolved the Rhode Island government, broke the seal of the colony, changed the administration to that of an English county, and admitted seven of the inhabitants to his legislative council.[2] The Connecticut authorities, upon whom Randolph had served a second writ, December 28, 1686, replied that they had sent a letter to the king begging to be allowed to remain as they were. This letter, which was ambiguously worded, left the impression upon the minds of the Lords of Trade that the colony was ready to surrender if the king insisted; and consequently they recommended to the king that Andros be instructed to signify "his Majesty's good liking and acceptance of their dutiful submission" and to take them under his government.[3]

The king's order to this effect, signed at Windsor,

---

[1] Toppan, in Amer. Antiq. Soc., *Proceedings*, October, 1899, p. 242.

[2] *R. I. Col. Records.*, III., 219.

[3] Mass. Hist. Soc., *Collections*, 4th series, II., 297; *Journal of the Lords of Trade*, VI., 69; *Cal. of State Pap., Col.*, 1685–1688, §§ 1321, 1534; *Conn. Col. Records*, III., 377, 378.

June 27, 1687, did not reach Andros until October 18. Soon after its receipt the governor, who had held off because he knew perfectly well that the colony had not submitted,[1] wrote to Governor Treat announcing his purpose of visiting Hartford. October 26, he left Boston, met the Connecticut court called in special session on November 1, and read his own commission and the king's special order.[2] He dissolved the government, erected a county organization, appointed judicial and military officers, and admitted Connecticut representatives into his council. The colony was thus annexed to the dominion of New England, but it never surrendered its charter, tradition having it that the instrument was spirited away and hidden in an oak-tree,[3] and that the colony was never deprived of it by any legal process.

The enlargement of the dominion of New England by the annexation of Connecticut and Rhode Island was but preliminary to a larger union of all the colonies from Delaware Bay to Nova Scotia. Such a plan had been decided on as early as March, 1686, on the ground that for defence against the French and Indians one government was better

[1] *R. I. Col. Records*, III., 224.

[2] Bulkeley, *Will and Doom* (Conn. Hist. Soc., *Collections*, III., 137–142); Toppan, *Edward Randolph*, II., 45, 46; Sewall, *Diary*, I., 193.

[3] Trumbull, *Hist. of Conn.*, I., 390; Bates, in *Encyclopædia Americana*, art. "Charter Oak"; Hoadly, in Acorn Club, *Publications*, No. 2, 1900.

than ten;[1] but not until July 3, 1688, was the commission to Andros issued which constituted him captain-general and governor-in-chief of all that tract of land from forty degrees north latitude to the St. Croix and St. Lawrence rivers and westward to the South Sea, Pennsylvania and Delaware only excepted.[2] August 11, Andros visited the newly annexed territory of New York and received from Dongan the seals of office. He published his authority in the Jerseys, visited Albany and the Five Nations, and solemnized the birth of the prince of Wales, news of which event he received from Boston.[3] Having appointed Francis Nicholson deputy governor of New York, he returned to Boston, and soon after journeyed to Pemaquid, where he made careful inquiry into the conditions of his frontiers.[4]

[1] Toppan, *Edward Randolph*, IV., 216.

[2] *Journal of the Lords of Trade*, VI., 142; *N. Y. Docs. Rel. to Col. Hist.*, III., 537.

[3] *Cal. of State Pap., Col.*, 1685–1688, §§ 1877, 1895, 1901; *N. Y. Docs. Rel. to Col. Hist.*, III., 550–554; *N. J. Archives*, II., 26.

[4] Toppan, *Edward Randolph*, IV., 239–243.

CHAPTER XVII

THE REVOLUTION IN AMERICA

(1687–1691)

WHILE James II. was thus consolidating the royal power in America he was destroying it in England. A long course of arbitrary acts culminated in the attempt to "dispense" with the effect of acts of Parliament in April, 1688. A body of nobles wanted William of Orange, nephew and son-in-law of James, to take the throne; he landed in England November 5; James quitted the kingdom December 22; and in February, 1689, Parliament offered the crown to William and his wife Mary, daughter of James. This revolution did much more than to overturn James II.: it set aside the doctrine of the divine right of kings and substituted the authority of Parliament for the royal prerogative; it demonstrated the right of the people to resist the claims and demands of their rulers, when these demands went counter to the needs and the constitutional privileges of their subjects; and it marked the close of a long period of constitutional reorganization which had begun with the reforms of the Long Parliament in 1641.

The English revolution, even in its widest aspect, was not the cause of the movements in America, but it often gave shape to the action of the colonists and direction to their efforts. Local causes were always operative: fears of the French and Indians, rumors of Roman Catholic conspiracies, and tales of governmental plots spread with remarkable rapidity; they seized upon the imaginations of the colonists, and provoked action long before the news that William of Orange had landed reached any of the colonies. The earliest, the boldest, and the completest of these local revolutions was in Massachusetts.

In 1687 Andros undertook to establish his new dominion at his seat of government, Boston. The system as defined in his commission was strictly feudal and autocratic. As governor he was commander-in-chief, vice-admiral, and dispenser of pardons; and with the advice and consent of his council he could make laws and impose taxes, erect courts, administer justice, grant lands, and collect quit-rents. These were royal powers which in the hands even of a tactful and conciliatory man would have aroused opposition in democratic New England. In the hands of Andros, who was a soldier and disciplinarian, a man faithful to duty and accustomed to command, an obedient subject who considered the orders of the king of more importance than the wishes of the people, they led to revolution.

The men of Massachusetts, needing to justify

their action, and failing to realize that the revolution was a conflict between two irreconcilable systems of government, held Andros guilty of injustice, tyranny, and abuse.   They charged him with having governed arbitrarily and in excess of his powers. They said that he demanded new patents of land and imposed quit-rents payable to the king; that he deprived the people of their liberties in making laws and imposing taxes without their consent; that he allowed a faction to control the government, knowing that it would oppress the colony; that he authorized tyrannical and illegal laws; that his administration of justice was oppressive and unjust; that he and his friends made themselves rich by illegal exactions, fines, and fees; that he endeavored to deprive the colony of religious liberty and was a conspirator in a "popish plot," and that his acts as vice-admiral brought misery upon the province and stifled trade.[1]

A critical study of the acts of Andros in the light of his instructions shows that these adversaries grossly exaggerated the burdens of the government, and that Andros gave to Massachusetts a better administration than that of Maryland or Virginia.   Andros did not go beyond his orders.   Bluff, impatient, and hot-tempered he often was, but he was neither brutal nor oppressive nor beyond the law.

Indeed, there is not one of these charges that may

[1] Whitmore, *Andros Tracts*, I., passim.

not be disproved altogether or shown to be based
on a legitimate attempt of the governor to carry out,
unwisely it may be, the orders of the king. For
example, the allegations that the writs were oppressive is vague and unsubstantial and will not stand
the test of comparison with the facts. The claim
that the colonists were illegally deprived of the
privileges of the Habeas Corpus act is not justified,
inasmuch as the act had no application to the
colonies;[1] the belief that Andros was engaged in
a Roman Catholic conspiracy was part of that
general suspicion prevalent throughout all the colonies, notably in New York, Maryland, and Virginia,
that the royal and proprietary governors were
planning to call in the French and Indians to overthrow the Protestants;[2] and a reflection from the
corresponding fear in England that was aroused by
the tales of Titus Oates.

What bore most heavily upon the colonists was
not the enforcement of the navigation acts, as Randolph would have us believe, but the loss of a representative assembly. As early as August, 1687,
Ipswich and Topsfield refused to pay taxes levied
without their consent, and later Andover did the
same. Individuals who declared that the existing
situation was one of slavery were called to account
for seditious utterances.[3]   Others, objecting to a

[1] Carpenter, in *Amer. Hist. Review*, VIII., 21.
[2] Toppan, *Edward Randolph*, IV., 264, 265.
[3] *Cal. of State Pap., Col.*, 1685–1688, §§ 1447, 1534, iv., v.

government deprived of the representative principle, and to all laws of whatever character that were
not made by the people, petitioned the king for an
assembly, but without result.[1]

With the issue of the new commission in 1688,
the news of the birth of the prince of Wales, and
the rumor in the spring of 1689 that James II.
had taken flight, the excitement in Boston steadily
increased. Since Andros had proclaimed widely the
news of the prince's birth, he roused suspicion by
endeavoring to suppress the declaration of the
prince of Orange.[2] The agitation spread. "The
general buzzing among the people," of which Andros wrote to Brockholls, soon grew into a revolt.
April 18, 1689, the inhabitants of Boston rose
against the government, seized the fort, castle, and
king's frigate, imprisoned Andros, and sent Randolph to the common jail. "We have been quiet,
hitherto," was their declaration, "but now [that]
the Lord has prospered the undertaking of the
prince of Orange, we think we should follow such
an example. We, therefore, seize the vile persons
who oppressed us."[3]

The insurgents established a council, with Bradstreet, the former governor, as its president; and
on May 24, following the example of the English

[1] Hutchinson, *Hist. of Massachusetts Bay*, I., 362, *n.*
[2] *Andros Tracts*, I., 75–79, II., 194; Toppan, *Edward Randolph*, V., 57.
[3] Toppan, *Edward Randolph*, IV., 271–281; *Cal. of State
Pap., Col.*, 1689–1692, §§ 152, 196, 261.

revolutionists, they summoned a convention, and re-established the government according to the old charter. With the arrival of a vessel from England on May 26, bearing orders for the proclamation of William and Mary, all danger was over. The joy of the people was intense, for the revolution had been bloodless, as had been that in England.

Connecticut and Rhode Island, on hearing of the revolution in England, resumed their charter governments and restored their organization as it had been before the arrival of Andros. This act was upheld by legal opinion in England on the ground that the charters, having never been surrendered, remained good and valid in law; and that the corporations, notwithstanding their submission to the authority of Andros,[1] had a perfect right to execute again the powers and privileges that had originally been granted them. None of the many attempts made afterwards to invalidate their charters proved successful.

Massachusetts was, however, to suffer for her former stubbornness and excessive caution. Even while Andros was in power, the agent of the colony, Increase Mather, tried to persuade King James to restore the charter. The king replied with fair words, promising a "Magna Charta of Liberty";

---

[1] *Conn. Col. Records*, III., 250–253; *R. I. Col. Records*, III., 257; Mass. Hist. Soc., *Collections*, 5th series, IX., 175; Hutchinson, *Hist. of Massachusetts Bay*, I., 406, 407; *Cal. of State Pap., Col.*, 1689–1692, § 746.

but nothing further was done.   From time to time
rumors came to the colony that the old charter was
to be restored; and the attorney-general, Sir Thomas
Powys, a very fair-minded man, raised hopes by
stating that the charter had been illegally vacated.[1]
Yet, notwithstanding every effort of Massachusetts,
William III. took the ground that the government
under the old charter had been insubordinate; and
when in 1691 a revised charter was granted, it created
a government of the type of New York or New Jersey, instead of the old, popular government.

In Maryland the beginning of the storm came
in the autumn and winter of 1688, when reports
of an Indian attack became current; and many began to believe once more that the Jesuits were in
league with the French and Indians to massacre
the Protestants.   For a time excitement ran high,
notably on the Eastern Shore; and it was only
after strenuous efforts by those who knew the false-
ness of the rumors that the terrors were allayed.[2]
Scarcely was this crisis passed, when new reports
spread regarding the policy of the proprietary.   In
December came the flight of James II., and in February, 1689, William and Mary became sovereigns
of England.

After the receipt of the news in the colony,
weeks passed before any proclamation of the new

---

[1] *Cal. of State Pap., Col.*, 1689 – 1692, § 152; Hutchinson,
Hist. of Massachusetts Bay, I., 373; *Andros Tracts*, III., 130.
[2] Henry Darnell's narrative (*Md. Archives*, VIII., 156).

king and queen was made in Maryland. Baltimore, it seems, had sent the necessary instructions, but the orders never reached the province.[1] The delay, for which Baltimore was in no way responsible, gave strength to the rumor that he did not intend to proclaim the new sovereigns, but was planning to make Maryland a Roman Catholic colony by force. The people believed that Governor Joseph, who did not dare act without authority, was concealing his orders for purposes of his own; and so great was the excitement that Colonel Spencer, of Virginia, wrote to William Blathwayt, secretary of the Privy Council and auditor general, prophesying an uprising of the people and the proclamation of William and Mary "to the entire disorganization of the government."[2]

Such was the situation in the spring and summer of 1689: the proprietary was absent, irritating conflicts were taking place in the assembly, and a plot was brewing against the government. The revolution in England, which drove a Roman Catholic from the throne, gave to the hostile Protestant faction in Maryland a precedent and an example for revolutionary action.

In April, 1689, an association was formed, with John Coode at its head, for the purpose of defending the Protestant religion and asserting the right of

---

[1] The messenger died at Plymouth. See *Md. Archives*, XIII., 113, 114.

[2] *Ibid.*, 112; *Cal. of State Pap., Col.*, 1689–1692, § 92.

William and Mary to the province of Maryland.
Coode began to raise an armed force on the Potomac,[1] and was joined by Jowles, colonel of the
militia, Blakiston, collector of customs, and Chesel-
dyne, speaker of the assembly. The rebels having seized St. Mary's and captured the records on
July 27, issued a proclamation in which they defended their course and presented a large number
of grievances framed for revolutionary purposes.[2]
August 1, Coode attacked and took Mattapany fort,
Lord Baltimore's residence, where lay the leaders
of the proprietary party, and with this capture
of the headquarters came into possession of the
government. The leaders at once despatched an
address to William and Mary, couched in terms of
fulsome flattery, laying the province at their feet;
they issued summons for the election of an assembly,
and on September 10 proclaimed the new sovereigns.
The Maryland revolution was complete.

Baltimore made zealous efforts to recover his
province, but was entirely unsuccessful. The new
Lords of Trade were determined to adopt the policy
of their predecessors, and in the interest of trade
and military defence to bring all the colonies into a
closer dependence upon the crown.[3] The Lords
having no special reason to favor Baltimore, they

---

[1] Henry Darnell's narrative (*Md. Archives*, VIII., 156).

[2] *Ibid.*, 101-107; Steiner, *Revolution of 1689*, 299-302;
Sparks, 102-107.

[3] *Cal. of State Pap., Col.*, 1689-1692, §§ 102, 124.

listened with patience to the presentation of both sides of the case; and King William, desiring a settled government in the colonies as well as at home, was naturally friendly to the Protestants.

Just at this point the situation was rendered worse for Baltimore by the murder of John Payne, collector of customs and a prominent member of the association in Maryland, by the sailors of Sewall, Baltimore's step-son. The king and his council had every reason to think that Baltimore's party was the aggressor, and this belief gave weight to the list of grievances that the association sent to be laid before the king.[1]

Though no legal proceedings were instituted against Baltimore's charter; and though Baltimore himself was never formally deprived of his province, the result for the time being was the practical loss of the charter. The king, reserving to Baltimore his revenue and land titles unimpaired, took the government into his own hands, and sent over Copley as governor, with orders to investigate the situation and to report to the Lords of Trade. Copley arrived in Maryland, and on April 9, 1692, opened the first assembly under the royal government. He made no investigation of the rights of the case and sent no report. The question was not again brought up for discussion by the English

---

[1] *Md. Archives*, VIII., 163, 219–220, 241–262, 307–312; *Cal. of State Pap.*, *Col.*, 1689–1692, § 1206.

authorities, but for a quarter of a century Maryland remained a royal province.

In New York the effect of the English revolution was even more picturesque and dramatic than in Maryland. Though no democratic institutions had been recognized by the royal proprietary, the prevailing discontent was so active as to render it certain that the English colonists in the city and adjacent counties would take an early advantage of every dilemma in which the king might find himself.

For a few months after the appointment of Nicholson, in 1688, matters went smoothly, and negotiations with the Indians formed the most important part of the duties of the deputy governor. Then came rumors of the revolution in England; in April, 1689, the report that Andros had been seized and imprisoned in Boston. Finally word was brought that Louis XIV. had declared war on England, and that the French were preparing a new invasion of colonial territory. New York and the adjoining towns at once revealed their latent dislike of the royal government. The towns of eastern Long Island, and likewise those of Queens and Westchester counties, drove out the king's officers and set up others of their own.[1] Eastern Long Island demanded that the forts should be placed in the hands of such men as they could trust, and the militia of New York drew up a loyal ad-

[1] *N. Y. Docs. Rel. to Col. Hist.*, III., 575.

dress to the new sovereigns. Nicholson, in lack
of official orders to proclaim William and Mary,
hesitated, and contented himself with summoning
the council, city magistrates, and officers of the
militia to consult "how best to allay the uproar
and rebellion." [1]

Tactful and conciliatory measures at this juncture
might have calmed the people, but Nicholson lost
his temper and gave utterance to words that stirred
the people to wrath.[2]   In May, 1689, the rumor
spread that he was going to burn the city and that
the inhabitants were to be "sold, betrayed, and
murdered." Led by a German merchant, Jacob
Leisler, a man of energy and ability, but rash in
action and careless of the means employed, a faction
of the people seized the fort and refused to obey
their legally constituted authorities. The uprising
in New York, like that in Maryland, was directed,
ostensibly, at least, against the "papists"; and
there is reason to think the Maryland movement
served as an incentive to the New-Yorkers.[3]   On
June 10, Nicholson foolishly deserted his post, took
ship for England, and left the government in the
hands of three of the council—Phillips, Cortlandt,
and Bayard. Leisler, disregarding their authority,
summoned a convention composed of delegates from

[1] N. Y. Docs. Rel. to Col. Hist., III., 587, 591.
[2] Cortlandt to Andros, ibid., 594; Cal. of State Pap., Col.,
1689–1692, § 190.
[3] Doc. Hist. of New York (octavo ed.), II., 25, 31, 42,
181–183.

seven of the counties, which in its turn appointed him captain of the fort and commander-in-chief of the province with almost dictatorial powers.[1]

Notwithstanding this commission Leisler desired a more legal warrant for his position, and an opportunity to obtain one soon came: for on December 11, 1689, orders arrived from King William, authorizing Nicholson, or in his absence "such as for the time being take care for preserving the peace," to assume the full governorship of the province; Leisler seized the document and claimed that it applied to him. With this order as his commission he established a government for the city, appointed justices, sheriffs, clerks, collectors, and officers of the militia. He beat down all opposition, and though upheld by only a minority of the people, was able to overawe the remainder. Albany at first refused to recognize his authority, but finally yielded, in March, 1690, because of Indian troubles.[2]

The English government received early information of the rebellion, but the Lords of Trade were involved in a multitude of vexatious problems connected with the colonies, and had in their hands the appointment of at least six new colonial governors. Yet they acted promptly and with wisdom, and in August, 1689, recommended that a governor

---

[1] *Doc. Hist. of New York* (octavo ed.), II., 11, 23.

[2] *N. Y. Docs. Rel. to Col. Hist.*, III., 606; *Doc. Hist. of New York*, II., 45, 51, 53, 56, 65, 66, 77–79, 97–99, 108, 117, 120, 121, 127, 128, 145, 148, 150–154, 179–182, 291, 347–354, 389, 430.

be selected at once, and that troops be sent to overthrow the rebellion.   In September the king commissioned Henry Sloughter as governor, and authorized the raising of two companies of troops. Partly because of confusions in the admiralty office and partly because of deliberate intention (so Sloughter believed), the expedition was delayed month after month till November 12, 1690, while the Lords of Trade and the enemies of Leisler continually urged the importance of speedy departure. Though the troops reached the city in February, Leisler refused to yield to Ingolsby, their captain, and Sloughter did not arrive in New York till March 16, 1691.[1]

On his arrival, however, Leisler surrendered, and in May was tried, and, with his son-in-law, Milborne, was sentenced to be hanged. Sloughter, to his shame be it said, signed the death-warrant, and the sentence was carried out.[2] Leisler was no traitor; he was loyal to his sovereigns; and though he had been the chief actor in a rebellion, he had done so believing that he was upholding a righteous cause. His methods were tyrannical and his government was often unnecessarily harsh, but he was no more deserving of death than were his compatriots in Massachusetts and Maryland.

[1] *Cal. of State Pap., Col.*, 1689–1692, §§ 395, 399, 451, 887, 891, 892, 897, 939, 1013, 1020, 1040, 1076, p. 429, 1465; *N. Y. Docs. Rel. to Col. Hist.*, III., 761.
[2] *Doc. Hist. of New York*, II., 372–382, 386, 433, 434.

After Leisler's rebellion and the change of sovereigns in England, a continuance of arbitrary government in New York was impossible. By his commission, Sloughter was instructed to summon an assembly of the freeholders, who were to join with governor and council in the making of laws.[1] April 9, 1691, the first assembly under the new commission met, and on May 13 passed an act "declaring what are the rights and privileges of their Majesties' subjects in New York." This act was practically a duplicate of the charter of 1683, except that it called for annual instead of triennial elections, defined a freeholder as one possessing forty shillings a year in freehold, and disfranchised Roman Catholics. Strangely enough, this statute, less liberal than that which the duke of York had approved, was annulled by the Protestant William on the ground that it granted "too great and unreasonable privileges."[2] Though from this time forward New York possessed representative government, the rights and privileges of the people in their assemblies remained undefined, and the struggle for free press and free speech continued for a quarter of a century longer.

[1] N. Y. Docs. Rel. to Col. Hist., III., 624; Colonial Laws of New York, I., 221.
[2] Colonial Laws of New York, I., 244–248; N. Y. Docs. Rel. to Col. Hist., IV., 263, 264.

CHAPTER XVIII

SOCIAL AND RELIGIOUS LIFE IN THE COLONIES
(1652–1689)

THE number of the colonists in 1689 may be estimated at from two hundred thousand to two hundred and fifty thousand, variously distributed: New Hampshire contained about five thousand inhabitants; Massachusetts, including Plymouth and Maine, fifty thousand; Rhode Island, four thousand; Connecticut, between seventeen and twenty thousand; New York, between eighteen and twenty thousand; East New Jersey, somewhat fewer than ten thousand; West New Jersey, four thousand; Pennsylvania and Delaware, twelve thousand; Maryland, thirty thousand; Virginia, between fifty and sixty thousand; North Carolina, between two and three thousand; and South Carolina not more than three thousand.

The territory thus occupied extended for about a thousand miles from Pemaquid to Charles Town, for the colonists passed but short distances back from the ocean, and then chiefly along the navigable rivers. Between adjoining colonies, even in 1689, boundaries were largely undefined, and, except where rivers determined the line of division, were destined to be a source of perplexity and trouble, in some instances for a century to come. Territorial claims growing out of conflicting royal grants continued to offer to the colonists difficult and vexatious problems that could be solved only by compromise and agreement; and unfortunately in some cases the mutual good will essential to such a solution was wanting.

In the main the settlers were of English stock. New England was ethnically almost homogeneous, though a few French Huguenots, Scots-Irish, and Jews were found scattered among her people. In New York more than half the inhabitants were Dutch, the remainder English and French, the former largely predominating, and a sufficient number of Jews to warrant the building of a synagogue.[1] New Jersey was largely English, though there were many Scots, Dutch, and French living here and there in the towns and plantations. West New Jersey contained many Swedes and Dutch as well as English; and Pennsylvania was a composite of Finns, Swedes, Dutch, Germans, Scots, Welsh, and English. Maryland, Virginia, and North Carolina were settled by Englishmen only; South Carolina, on the other hand, a colony of one city, had already begun to show diversity of stocks, and though in large part settled by Englishmen, included French-

---

[1] Miller, *Description of New York*, 31, 37; Lodwick, " Account of New York," *Sloane MSS.*, in British Museum, 3339, f. 252.

men and Scots among its inhabitants. Not until the next century, however, did the immigration of Swiss, Scots-Irish, and German palatines into South Carolina begin in earnest.

This population was made up of free settlers, bond servants, and slaves, though bondage and slavery played a very small part in New England, where the economic conditions were unfavorable to such labor. Still, Randolph could report two hundred slaves there in 1676,[1] and we know that, notwithstanding the Quaker protest against the slave - trade in Rhode Island, Newport was the receiving and disbursing centre for most of the negroes who were brought from Guinea and Madagascar.[2] In New York slaves were used chiefly as body - servants and for domestic purposes, and Coxe mentions four in West New Jersey in 1687.

Even in the South the economic importance of slavery was as yet hardly recognized, and though there were many slaves in Maryland, Virginia, and South Carolina, they did not form the indispensable laboring class that they afterwards became. Berkeley, writing in 1671, said that there were forty thousand persons in Virginia, of whom two thousand were "black slaves" and six thousand "Christian servants"; and that in the preceding seven years but two or three ships of negroes had come to the

[1] *Hutchinson Papers*, II., 219.
[2] Amer. Antiq. Soc., *Proceedings*, October, 1887, p. 111.

colony.[1] Yet the numbers increased rapidly, and
towards the end of the century a planter, stocking
a new plantation, was able to draw his supply
from the colony itself.[2]

During the seventeenth century in the south,
white servants were preferred to the negroes as
laborers, and Berkeley could say that fifteen hundred
came every year to Virginia. Many were Irish and
Scottish, but the great mass of the servants was
English. They came to America under the indenture or redemption system, according to which
servants bound themselves to work for a certain
number of years, generally from four to six, on the
lands or in the houses of the masters who advanced
money to pay the shipmasters for their passage.
This practice became one of the most efficient
aids to colonization in the seventeenth century,
and thousands of settlers came to America under
this obligation to labor. The New-Englanders had
few servants, except on hired wages,[3] but they
experimented with Indians, who proved very inefficient as laborers and servants, being not only
inapt but unwilling.

Writers differ somewhat in their estimates of the
servant's life in America. Dankers and Sluyter,
the Labadist missionaries, strongly prejudiced

[1] Berkeley's Answers to Queries, in Public Record Office,
Colonial Papers, XXVI., No. 77, i.
[2] Bruce, Econ. Hist. of Virginia, II., 87, 88.
[3] Hutchinson Papers, II., 219.

against the practice, spoke in terms of severe condemnation of the "planter's avarice, which must be fed and sustained by the bloody sweat of their poor slaves."[1]   But other accounts are more favorable. Alsop, himself an indentured servant, believed that the position was less grievous than that of the ordinary apprentice in England.[2]   Hammond says that servants were not put to "so hard or continuous labor as husbandmen and handicraftsmen were obliged to perform in England. . . . Little or nothing is done," he adds, "in winter time, none ever work before sunrising or after sunset.   In the summer they rest, sleep, or exercise themselves five hours in the heat of the day; Saturday afternoon is always their own, the old holidays are observed, and the Sabbath spent in good exercise."[3]   G. L., writing from West New Jersey, confirms this account when he says that "servants work here, not so much by a third as they do in England, and I think feed much better, for they have beef, pork, bacon, pudding, milk, butter, fish, and fruit more plentiful than in England, and good beer and syder."[4]

However hard the servant's life may have been, there was always the expectation of serving their time and becoming hired laborers at two shillings or two shillings and sixpence a day.   Some of the

---

[1] Dankers and Sluyter, *Journal*, 191, 192.
[2] Alsop, *Character of the Province of Maryland*, chap. iii.
[3] Hammond, *Leah and Rachel*, 12.
[4] "Quaker's Account of New Jersey," *Rawlinson MSS.*, in Bod. Lib., D 810, f. 55.

best of the later colonists, particularly in the south,
traced their descent to industrious indentured servants who "crept" out of their condition, got good
estates of cattle, houses, and servants of their own,
and became husbandmen and freeholders.[1]

During the period from 1650 to 1690 the colonists
gained steadily in the conveniences and comforts
of living. Food and shelter were easily obtainable,
and in the large towns even luxury prevailed to a
small extent. There was sometimes serious suffering
from the miseries of Indian attacks, the frequency
of serious sickness, and in the north the inclemency
of the winter. In South Carolina many of the new-
comers complained of the miseries of chills and
fever—"seasoning" they called it; and in Maryland and Virginia there was a good deal of poverty owing to the fluctuations of the tobacco crop.
Moryson, speaking for Virginia in 1676, said that the
"better sort" lived on poultry, hogs, and what deer
and fowl their servants could kill for them. They
drank, though "this not common," beer and ale.[2]

Thomas Newe, in 1682, found the people of Charles
Town drinking molasses and water, and learned
that no malt up to that time had been made in
the colony.[3] In the Jerseys beer was a common

[1] "Quaker's Account of New Jersey," *Rawlinson MSS.*, in
Bod. Lib., D 810, f. 55; Hammond, *Leah and Rachel*, 14; Wilson, *Account of Carolina* (Carroll, *Hist. Collections*, II., 24).

[2] Moryson's "Answers," *Rawlinson MSS.*, in Bod. Lib., A
185, f. 256.

[3] Newe to his father, May 17, 1682, *ibid.*, D 810, f. 53.

drink, and we hear occasionally of brew-houses, and meet with requests sent to England for brewers. Cider was used chiefly in the middle and northern colonies, and occasionally brandy and wines were obtainable, when vessels from the West Indies and Canaries came to the colonies.

The "ordinary sort" of people in Virginia, Maryland, and Delaware lived on Indian corn, "a grain of general use to man and beast." "They beat it in a mortar," says a traveller, "and get the husks from it, and then boyle it with a piece of beef or salted pork with some kidney-beans, which is much like to pork and pease at sea, but they call it hommony." The people ate also bread made of the same corn, ground by hand, for grist-mills, common in New England, were scarce in the southern colonies; and raised a few vegetables, often of the coarsest kind.[1] Cook describes the planter's home in Maryland in words that may well be based on experience:

> " So after hearty Entertainment,
> Of Drink and victuals without Payment;
> For Planters' Tables, you must know,
> Are free for all that come and go.
> While Pon and Milk, with Mush well stoar'd,
> In wooden Dishes grac'd the Board;
> With Homine and Syder-pap,
> (Which scarce a hungry Dog wou'd lap)
> Well stuff'd with Fat, from Bacon fry'd,
> Or with *Molassus* dulcify'd." [2]

[1] Moryson's "Answers," *Rawlinson MSS.*, in Bod. Lib., A 185, f. 256; Dankers and Sluyter, *Journal*, 217, 218; *Sloane MSS.*, in British Museum, 2291, f. 1.

[2] Cook, *Sot-Weed Factor* (Md. Hist. Soc., *Fund Publications* No. 36), 4.

In South Carolina the conditions were better, and Wilson assures us that while those living near the marshes were subject to ague, settlers on the higher ground did very well. He says that the soil was fertile and produced good corn, excellent pasture, wheat, rye, barley, oats, pease, and garden vegetables in large variety; that cattle, sheep, horses, and other animals were easily raised, while negroes thrived better than in the north and required fewer clothes, which, as he naïvely remarks, "is a great charge saved." [1] Thomas Newe's letters to his father give a favorable view of the colony, and are especially valuable as the unbiased impressions of a new-comer. "The soil," he writes, "is generally very light, but apt to produce whatever is put into it. There are already all sorts of English fruit and garden herbs, besides many others I never saw in England." He thinks that the colony is in very good condition, considering the fact that most of the first settlers were "tradesmen, poor and wholly ignorant of husbandry, and till of late but very few in number, so that their whole business was to clear a little ground to get bread for their families, few of them having wherewithal to purchase a cow."

As for prices, Newe thought things dear in Charles Town: milk, 2d. a quart; beef, 4d. a pound; pork, 3d. a pound, "but far better than our English"; and he attributes these prices to the fact that

[1] Wilson, in Carroll, *Hist. Collections*, II., 26, 27.

"cattle sold so well to new-comers that the planters
saved none for killing," being furnished by the
Indians with fowl, fish, and venison "for a trifle."[1]
G. L. shows that prices were a little lower in West
New Jersey, and quotes pork at 2½d. a pound,
beef and venison 1d. a pound, a fat buck 5s. or 6s.,
Indian corn at 2s. 6d. a bushel, oats 2s., and barley
2s.[2] By witness of all, money was very scarce,
payment being made in natural products, or occasionally in Spanish coin, receivable in England
at four or five shillings less in the pound than in
the colonies.

In Pennsylvania, New York, and New England
the standard of living was higher than in Maryland
and Virginia, for the attention of the colonists was
not absorbed in the cultivation of tobacco to the
neglect of other staple products of the soil. Many
fruits and vegetables were raised, and others were
found growing in the woods; cows, sheep, goats, hogs,
as well as geese and chickens, were easily cared for;
and in the large cities of the north, and of the south
as well, colonial products, such as cloves, pepper,
and other spices, could be found, brought from
England or the West Indies. In many of the colonies, notably South Carolina, Maryland, and the
Jerseys, oysters were obtainable in large quantities from the river mouths and inlets, and every-

---

[1] Newe to his father, *Rawlinson MSS.*, in Bod. Lib., D 810,
ff. 53, 54.
[2] "Quaker's Account of New Jersey," *ibid.*, f. 55.

where fish was plentiful, and venison was easily procured.

Houses were at first of logs; later frame buildings, clapboarded and shingled, were erected. In West New Jersey, says G. L., "the poorer sort set up a house of two or three rooms themselves in this manner. Their walls are cloven timber about three inches broad, like planks, set upon end in the ground, the other [end] nailed to the raising, which they plaster warm, and they build a barn after the same manner."[1] Dankers and Sluyter mention similar houses in East New Jersey, "rude in structure but comfortable, constructed of trees split and stood on end and shingled."[2] The great majority of houses everywhere were built of wood, often larger than those just mentioned, having two or three rooms to a floor, and in New England a second floor, an attic, and generally a lean-to. A few of the southern plantations boasted elaborate wooden houses.

In the cities some brick buildings existed. In 1660 Boston was a great town, with two churches, a state-house, market-place, and good shops;[3] in 1679 it was described as "a large city on a fine bay, with three churches, the houses covered with thin cedar shingles nailed against frames and then filled

[1] "Quaker's Account of New Jersey," *Rawlinson MSS.*, in Bod. Lib., D 810, f. 55.

[2] Dankers and Sluyter, *Journal*, 173, 175.

[3] Maverick, *Description of New England* (*N. E. Historical and Genealogical Register*, XXXIX., 43).

with bricks and other stuff." [1] Maverick describes Plymouth and New Haven as poor towns, the latter not as glorious as it once was; Hartford as a gallant town with many rich men in it.[2] Albany had about two hundred houses, mostly of stone and brick, and a fort fifteen feet high, made of logs. New York had eight hundred houses built of the same materials, and a fort, with four bastions and thirty-nine guns, well maintained and garrisoned with a large body of soldiers. It faced the harbor, in which Governor Dongan thought a thousand ships might ride safe from wind and weather. Its chaplain, Wolley, was not very favorably impressed with the appearance of the city, but Denton thought it exceedingly pleasing with its houses covered with red tiles.[3]

Across the river were the towns of East New Jersey, small and unpretentious, though Elizabeth had a court-house, a prison, and six hundred inhabitants, and was the largest and most important in the region. Perth Amboy was well situated at the head of a spacious harbor, into which, says G. L., a ship of three hundred tons burden could "safely come and ride close to the shore within a plank's length just before the houses of the town. . . . The land there," continues the same writer,

----

[1] Dankers and Sluyter, *Journal*, 394, 395.

[2] Maverick, *Description*, 45, 47.

[3] Wolley, *Two Years' Journal*, 55; Denton, *Brief Description of New York*, 2; Dongan's Answers to Queries (1687), *Cal. of State Pap., Col.*, 1685–1688, § 327.

"is not low, swampy, marsh ground, but pretty high ground, rising thirty, in some places forty, foot high, and yet hath many conveniences for landing goods."[1]   The whole region from the Hudson to the Delaware, according to the testimony of many witnesses, was healthful and fertile, and many of the correspondents of this period think a man better off in New Jersey and Pennsylvania than in England.[2]

From East New Jersey to West New Jersey and Philadelphia one stepped into a different social atmosphere.   There were large places like Burlington, Salem, and Gloucester, centres of commerce and trade, and readily accessible "in boats from a small canoe to vessels of thirty, forty, fifty, and in some places of a hundred tons."[3]   Gabriel Thomas describes Burlington as a famous town, with many stately brick houses, a great market-house, with markets and fairs to which the people from the country round were wont to gather; while outside the town were country-houses for the gentry, gardens and orchards, bridges and ferries over the rivers.[4]   Wherry boats plied across the Delaware to Philadelphia, already a large and commodious town, with wharves and timber-yards, ship-yards

[1] "Quaker's Account of New Jersey," *Rawlinson MSS.*, in Bod. Lib., D 810, f. 55.

[2] Whitehead, *East Jersey under the Proprietors*, App., passim.

[3] "Quaker's Account of New Jersey," *Rawlinson MSS.*, in Bod. Lib., D 810, f. 55.

[4] Thomas, *Description of West New Jersey*, 15, 19.

and rope-walks. Near by were four market towns
—Chester, Germantown, New Castle, and Lewiston
—among which watermen plied their wherries.
Farther back in the country were villages—Haver-
ford, Merioneth, and Radnor—whose names betray
their Welsh origin.

Passing from the Delaware to the Chesapeake, a
traveller entered still another environment, and,
as he pushed down the eastern shore, journeyed
generally on foot or by boats from plantation to
plantation, crossing many creeks and rivers, and
lengthening his course by circuitous routes around
marshy places and impassable morasses. On the
high ground lived the planters, rich and poor, with
their servants and slaves. Nowhere in Maryland
were there compact settlements such as we find
in New England, nor yet were the conditions exactly the same as those in Virginia. The Puritan
settlement, Annapolis, was a town, and the names
of Oxford Town, Calvert Town, Charles Town, and
Battle Town bear witness to the efforts of the
proprietary to erect centres of population in his
province. His best endeavors were never very successful; even St. Mary's City, the seat of government, was without social or economic unity, for its
inhabitants lived for thirty miles along the bay.
Virginia, on the other hand, had not a semblance of
a town. As contemporary writers put it, "there
were neither towns, markets, nor money,"[1] only

---

[1] Hartwell, Blair, and Chilton, *Present State of Virginia.*

scattered plantations along the rivers, each with its
wharf and landing - place, an independent, self-
sufficing community. In North Carolina, if we
may judge from the account given by George Fox
in his journal, the inhabitants lived as widely
separated from one another as in Virginia, com-
municating with difficulty and at rare intervals.
South Carolina had one city, Charles Town, situated
on low ground at the junction of the Ashley and
Cooper rivers. Founded as a village of a few
houses in 1680, it had risen by 1682 to be a town of
one hundred structures, all built of wood, though
there appears to have been good material for
brick in the neighborhood. The city faced an excellent harbor, was capable of strong defence, and
was readily approached by small vessels and (with
the aid of a pilot) by ships of many tons burden.
In the immediate neighborhood were a few plantation settlements, but up to 1689 no attempts were
made to push back the frontier and explore the
interior.

Among the colonies, as a whole, communication
was infrequent. Coasting vessels ran from New
England to New York, the Delaware, Virginia, and
Carolina, and larger ships occasionally put in from
England or the West Indies. Transportation was
almost entirely by water; horses were used at times
for cross-country travel, but they were expensive,
and the colonists bred them rather for export than
for use. Land travel was generally on foot, and

consequently the mass of the people journeyed very little.

Habits and modes of life throughout all the colonies were of the very simplest sort. Very few houses were elaborately furnished, and, except in the commercial centres, few fabrics or furniture of English or foreign manufacture were seen. It is extraordinarily rare to find a settler, like Giles Brent of Maryland, boasting of three estates, well stocked, large quantities of gold and silver plate, many precious stones, including "one great diamond" worth £200, tapestry wrought with gold and silk, linen, pewter, and brass sufficient to furnish two large houses, and "a fair library of books" worth £140.[1] One can but wonder if Brent had friends among the buccaneers.

Daily intercourse was devoid of ceremonial, and, in New England especially, social standards, though often rigid and even aristocratic, were free from the strict class distinctions of English society. In New York, among the officials of the city and the soldiers of the garrison, and in the southern colonies among councillors, governors, and proprietaries, English practices and ceremonies prevailed.

An example of stateliness was the funeral of William Lovelace. The room in which the deceased lay was heavily draped with mourning and adorned with the escutcheons of the family. At

[1] Copley c. Ingle, *Admiralty Court*, *Libels*, Public Record Office, 107, No. 265.

the head of the body was a pall of death's-heads,
and above and about the hearse was a canopy
richly embroidered, from the centre of which hung
a garland and an hour-glass. At the foot was a
gilded coat of arms, four feet square, and near by
were candles and fumes which were kept continually burning. At one side was placed a cup-
board containing plate to the value of £200. The
funeral procession was led by the captain of the
company to which the deceased had belonged,
followed by the "preaching minister," two others of
the clergy, and a squire bearing the shield. Before
the body, which was borne by six "gentlemen
bachelors," walked two maidens in white silk,
wearing gloves and "cyprus scarves," and behind
were six others similarly attired, bearing the pall.
After the maidens came the uncle of the deceased,
Governor Francis Lovelace, and his councillors, and
four halberts wearing coats richly embroidered
with crests. Then, preceded by the mace, came the
mayor of the city, the aldermen, and a long line of
ship - captains, burghers, and others, Dutch and
English, walking two and two. The procession
wended its way to the fort, where amid salvos of
musketry the body was lowered into the grave.
Until ten o'clock at night wines, sweetmeats, and
biscuits were served to the mourners.[1]

[1] "Funeral Solemnities at the Interment of Mr. William Lovelace at New York, 1671" (*Ashmolean MSS.*, in Bod. Lib.,
846, f. 54).

Such elaborate and expensive ceremonies were elsewhere unknown to the colonists; usually the commemorations of births, marriages, and deaths were exceedingly unpretentious.   Money was scarce, and while a few governors, like Berkeley in Virginia, kept a coach and pair, and could have diamond-shaped panes in the windows of their houses, even the royal appointees at this time made but little attempt at ostentatious display.   Exhibitions of wealth and of family arms and crests were hardly in keeping with the temper of the colonists; and though there were families of rank in New England as well as in Virginia, there was little opportunity, and less desire, to exercise the prerogatives of rank.

Outside New England, religious and intellectual life was as yet undeveloped.   The Church of England was to all intents and purposes the established church of South Carolina, as it was of Virginia, and there are few traces of other denominations, though Nonconformists had aided in settling the colony.   Virginia in 1671 had forty-eight parishes, and presumably as many ministers, though that does not necessarily follow.   Berkeley spoke of the ministers as well paid, but wished that they would pray oftener and preach less, and said that no ministers of ability had come to Virginia since "the persecution in Cromwell's tyranny drew divers worthy men hither." [1]

[1] Berkeley's Answers to Queries (MSS. in Public Record Office, *Colonial Papers*, XXVI., No. 77, i.).

Maryland has been considered the strongest Anglican colony; but the strength of the church in Maryland has been exaggerated. Three-quarters of the colonists were Dissenters, and of the remainder a considerable number were Roman Catholics. In 1676, John Yeo reported only three ministers of the Church of England in Maryland, though he spoke of others who pretended to be such "that never had a legal ordination." In 1677, even Baltimore could mention only four ministers with plantations of their own.[1] Contemporary evidence shows clearly that in many ways the condition of the church in Maryland was deplorable. Yeo, writing from Pawtuxent to the archbishop of Canterbury in 1676, bewails the state of the province, calling it a Sodom of uncleanness and a pest-house of iniquity. Dankers and Sluyter speak of the religious life there as stagnant, the people as godless and profane, listening neither to God nor to His commandments, and having neither church nor cloister.[2] This statement may be deemed a prejudiced one, as the narrators were Labadists, seeking a home for their sect in America; nevertheless it is borne out by the petition of Mary and Michael Tany of Calvert Town, who about 1685 prayed king, archbishop, and all the bishops of England to send over a minister to a suffering community, where the people were too poor, on account of the navigation

---

[1] *Cal. of State Pap., Col.*, 1675–1676, § 1005, 1677–1680, § 348.
[2] Dankers and Sluyter, *Journal*, 218.

acts, to maintain church or clergy. They recalled the fact that as a result of a former petition Charles II. had sent over "a minister and a parcel of Bibles and other church-books of considerable value," but that now they were without church or settled ministry of any kind.[1] Cook, in his *Sot-Weed Factor*, agrees with these views.[2]

The Labadists were hardly more complimentary to New York, where an Anglican church had been established at the conquest in 1664. Though the duke of York appointed a chaplain to the garrison at New York as early as 1674, no clergyman appeared until Wolley came over in 1680, as chaplain of the fort. Miller in his description is very scornful of the religious life of New York, deeming all Dissenters only "pretended ministers" and charging them with leading ungodly lives.[3] In New Jersey the first Anglican church was at Elizabeth, where the services were conducted by a lay reader; and in Philadelphia the first Episcopal church was not built until 1695.

Though by express command of the king Episcopacy was tolerated in Massachusetts after 1660, the authorities there were wholly averse to the discipline of the Church of England, and resisted every attempt to organize a congregation. Mason, of New

---

[1] Petitions of Mary and Michael Tany, *Tanner MSS.*, in Bod. Lib., 31, f. 137–139.
[2] Md. Hist. Soc., *Fund Publications* No. 36, p. 5.
[3] Miller, *Description of New York*, chap. iii.

Hampshire fame, brought over Books of Common Prayer sent by the bishop of London before 1682,[1] but an Episcopal church was not established in Boston until 1686. The colonists were fearful lest the Stuarts should force Episcopacy upon New England; but the fear was unfounded, and Episcopacy made no progress in the Puritan colonies during the seventeenth century. Even Maine, which had begun as an Anglican settlement, was Congregationalized before 1692.

At first all the Anglican churches in the colonies were under the charge of the archbishop of Canterbury; and a very important part of Clarendon's policy after 1660 was his plan of making a bishopric of Virginia, and consolidating all the colonial churches under the authority, inspection, and jurisdiction of Archbishop Sheldon and his successors. About 1666 a patent was drawn up constituting Virginia a bishopric and a diocese, and declaring all the churches in the Bahamas, Bermudas, Jamaica, and the other island and continental colonies except New England—to be parts and members of the diocese of Virginia.[2] Though this patent does not appear to have been acted on, the appointment of Alexander Murray, former companion of King Charles in his wanderings, and at this time in-

---

[1] Letter from Boston (unsigned), December 11, 1682, *Tanner MSS.*, in Bod. Lib., 35, f. 110.

[2] Patent for the erection of Virginia into a bishopric, *ibid.*, 447, ff. 69–76.

cumbent of Ware parish in Virginia, to be bishop of that colony was seriously considered in 1673.[1]

Jurisdiction over the colonial churches was soon after vested in the bishop of London, who, as a member of the Lords of Trade and Plantations, took frequent occasion to impress upon the committee the needs of the church in America. But for many years to come the Episcopal jurisdiction amounted to little, and did not include the licensing of marriages, probation of wills, or induction of ministers. In Virginia, a commissary, representing the bishop, was sent over in 1689, but inasmuch as his authority was too limited to be of importance, he became little more than a special correspondent who sent letters to the bishop regarding the religious condition of the colony.

In the north, Congregationalism, not Episcopacy, was established. Every town in New England had its Congregational church supported by taxation, and the larger communities and townships had two or more ecclesiastical societies. Connecticut had chiefly "large" Congregationalists, who accepted the Half-way Covenant, and a few "strict" Congregationalists, Presbyterians, and Quakers.[2] Rhode Island had no state church, recognizing to the utmost the right of "soul liberty" and inviting all denominations to share its territory. Quakers and Baptists, however, predominated over other denominations.

---

[1] *Harleian MSS.*, in British Museum, 3790, ff. 1-4.
[2] *Conn. Col. Records*, III., 297; Allen, *History of Enfield*.

From New York to Pennsylvania a mixture of religious faiths appears. In the former, besides the Anglicans, were the Dutch Lutherans and Calvinists, Congregationalists, Presbyterians, and Jews.[1] In Albany all the colonists were Dutch Calvinists, in Long Island the majority were Congregationalists. There were many French Huguenots on Staten Island, but they had no church.[2] In New Jersey there were mainly Congregationalists, Lutherans, and Quakers. In West New Jersey there were several Quaker meetings and some Presbyterians and Baptists. In Philadelphia the Quakers, who were divided into two bodies by the apostasy of George Keith, controlled the government; but the city contained also congregations of Swedish Lutherans, English Baptists, and Presbyterians.

In the southern colonies were many Nonconformists — Presbyterians, Baptists, Roman Catholics, Labadists (about a hundred, in Maryland), and Quakers. In North Carolina the Anglicans had done nothing to establish Episcopacy, and the colony was in control of the Quakers. Thus, in the main, the Church of England was the established church of the south, and Congregationalism was the established religious system of the north; while in the middle colonies there existed a mixture of religious

---

[1] Miller, *Description of New York*, 37; *N. Y. Docs. Rel. to Col. Hist.*, III., 262.
[2] Dankers and Sluyter, *Journal*, 142; Lodwick's *Description*.

bodies, no one of which could claim superiority to the others in numbers or influence.

The educational and intellectual life of the colonies was low. Public schools were common in New England, where the people, coming from the towns of old England, had high ideals of the value of education. Massachusetts and Connecticut provided schools for nearly every township. Plymouth and Rhode Island were more backward, and education made little progress in those colonies until the next century.

In New York there seem to have been no schools at all—at least, no contemporary speaks of them, and Andros in his reply to the queries of the Lords of Trade says nothing of education. New Jersey had no schools until 1693,[1] and Budd in his account of New Jersey and Pennsylvania urges the establishment of schools, and proposes that white men and Indians alike shall be educated, not only in liberal arts, but in manual training also.[2] Ten years later Gabriel Thomas reported several good schools of learning in Pennsylvania, and we know that William Bradford introduced a printing-press there in 1685.

Apparently Maryland had no schools of any kind. Berkeley's famous reply to the queries of 1671 indicates the condition of Virginia at that date. "But I thank God," he says, "there are no free schools nor printing, and I hope we shall not have

---

[1] Whitehead, *East Jersey*, 159–174.
[2] Budd, *Account of New Jersey and Pennyslvania*, 43, 44.

these hundred years, for learning has brought disobedience and heresy and sects into the world and
printing has divulged [them] and libels against the
best government. God keep us from both." [1] A
few years later provision was made for schools
and school - masters and for a system of licensing whereby the standard of teaching might be
raised. The greater part of the colony, however,
retained the old customs, in accordance with which
every man instructed his children according to his
ability.

The only institution for higher education in
1689 was Harvard College, founded in 1636 and
incorporated in 1650. It was quartered in "a fair
and comely edifice, having in it a spacious hall, and
a large library with some books in it." [2] "Every
scholar that on proofe is found able to read the
Originals of the Old and New Testament into the
Latin tongue, and to resolve them Logically, withall
being of godly life and conversation; and at any
publick Act hath the Approbation of the Overseers
and Master of the Colledge, is fit to be dignified
with his first degree." [3] Higher qualifications of
a similar character admitted the student to the
second degree. Mather, writing in 1691, said that
the degree of master of arts was won after "seven

---

[1] Berkeley's Answers to Queries, MSS. in Public Record Office,
Colonial Papers, XXVI., No. 77, i. (query 23). But cf. Tyler,
England in America, chap. vi.

[1] Dankers and Sluyter, *Journal*, 385.

[2] *New England's First Fruits* (1643), 16.

years standing, as 'tis in Oxford and Cambridge. . . .
We never," he adds, " (more's pity) had any Drs." [1]

Those who watched the college at its birth, who
draughted the "Rules and Precepts that are observed in the Colledge," and who drew up the "Times
and Order of their Studies," with "Chaldee at the 9th
houre" and "Syriack at the 10th houre," might
have been scandalized had they read the account
of Dankers and Sluyter, written after visiting the
college in 1679. These men declared that they saw
only ten students sitting around, smoking tobacco
in a room which smelt like a tavern; that they
tested these students in speaking Latin, with sad
results; and that the library contained nothing
in particular. The authorities of Harvard might
have been equally scandalized had they known
of the later career of Sir George Downing, who as
Georgius Downingus, in 1642, fulfilled in part the
requirements of the first degree by defending
successfully such ethical theses as these: *Justitia
mater omnium virtutum, Mentiri non potest qui
verum dicit; Juveni modestia summum ornamentum.*

Except for theological writings in New England,
and a few journals and descriptions of country and
travel, the colonies developed little literature before
1689. There were very few physicians and scarcely
any lawyers, a strong prejudice against the latter
existing everywhere. Letchford, in Massachustts,

---

[1] Increase Mather to Anthony á Wood (*Tanner MSS.*, in
Bod. Lib., 26, f. 48).

had not been allowed to practise his profession and took his revenge by writing in his *Plaine Dealing* a scathing criticism of the colony's method of doing justice. Lawyers seem to have been allowed in East New Jersey;[1] but the Quakers in Pennsylvania were bitterly opposed to law-suits in every form. Gabriel Thomas rejoiced that Pennsylvania did not need either the tongue of the lawyer nor the pen of the physician, both, he says, being "equally destructive of men's estates and lives."[2] Alsop, in Maryland, said that if the lawyer there had "nothing else to maintain him but his bawling, he might button up his chops and burn his buckram bag"; and Cook shows his opinion of lawyers when he speaks of them as breaking the peace and wrangling for plaintiff and defendant. The hostility for this class of professional men became in Virginia so marked as to lead to legislation against the practice of law.[3] A few years later Colonel Byrd said that while there were a few men in the colony who called themselves doctors they were "generally discarded." As for North Carolina, a resident of Albemarle County wrote to his father in England that "those who profess themselves doctors and attorneys are scandalous to their profession, impudence and notorious impertinence making up their character."

[1] Whitehead, *East Jersey*, 166.

[2] Thomas, *Account of the Province of Pensilvania*, 32.

[3] Alsop, *Character of the Province of Maryland*, 47; Cook, *Sot-Weed Factor*, 12, 19; Hening, *Statutes*, I., 495, II., 71; *Sloane MSS.*, in British Museum, 748, f. 12, 4040, f. 151.

CHAPTER XIX

COMMERCIAL AND ECONOMIC CONDITIONS IN THE COLONIES

(1652–1689)

THOUGH education and religion were neglected, and the colonists were content with home-made remedies for disease and home-made methods of settling disputes, their material needs had to be provided for. During the first seventy years, life in the colonies was largely agricultural, and the settlers busied themselves with cutting down the forests and extending the cultivable area. It was not an easy matter for them to discover at once the natural staples of the country, though as early as 1616 Virginia appreciated the merits of the tobacco industry and by 1640 Maryland made tobacco her leading product. South Carolina, though experimenting with rice and indigo at an early date in her history, did not realize till after 1700 that either was especially adapted to her climate and soil.[1] In fact, the colonists, often urged on by those pecuniarily interested at home, were continually

---

[1] Rivers, *South Carolina*, 172, *n.*; McCrady, *Hist. of South Carolina*, I., 349.

trying experiments to make the new country more profitable and to supply England with materials that she herself could not produce.

To the men of the seventeenth century the New World was a kind of Eldorado, capable of supplying not only herbs, drugs, and fruits unknown to Europeans, but also an infinite variety of valuable products for which Englishmen were dependent on other and rival countries. For this reason many of the descriptions that have come down to us of the proprietary colonies must be taken at something less than their face value.

During the first twenty years of its career as a settled colony South Carolina developed very slowly, owing to the small number of the colonists and to their inexperience as agriculturists and farmers. As elsewhere, the finer grains, such as English wheat and barley, though successfully cultivated in Carolina, were generally disregarded owing to the greater profitableness of Indian-corn, which was not only easy to raise but was also more useful as food. In addition, each family had its stock of pigs and cows, with the increase of which it was able to build up a small export trade. Planters who lived on larger estates outside the town, notably on the southern side of the Ashley River, devoted themselves to raising cattle and corn; while others, nearer the pine belts, prepared tar and pitch and made clapboards. After supplying their own needs the settlers were able to furnish vessels,

privateers and others, which came into the harbor
for victualling; and often on this account the colonists were charged with harboring pirates, of whom
there were many along the coast. They also sent
cattle, corn, pork, pitch, tar, and clapboards to
Barbadoes more cheaply than the other plantations,
because of their nearness to the West Indies. In return they received sugar, rum, molasses, and ginger,
the greater part of which was sent to England and
exchanged for manufactured goods. We are told
that in 1680 "sixteen sail of vessels, some upwards
of two hundred tons, came from divers parts of the
king's kingdom to trade at Charles Town."

The colony had, however, little trade with England in staples of its own, for fur and cedar wood
were the only articles available for that purpose,
and there is reason to believe that none of the latter commodity had actually been exported at this
time. In truth, South Carolina was still more
closely connected with the island plantations than
with those of the main-land. Its isolation, south-
erly location, and the character of its economic
life during the seventeenth century, place it apart
from the northern colonies, in a group with the
English plantations in the West Indies.[1]

After 1616 the shipping of tobacco to England
from Virginia became regular, and though Indian-

[1] Wilson, *Account of Carolina;* Ashe, *Carolina*, in Carroll,
Historical Collections, II., 19–35; *Rawlinson MSS.*, in Bod. Lib.,
D 810, ff. 53–55.

corn and some English wheat were grown, they were kept in the colony for home consumption. A few other things were exported;[1] but as tobacco was the superior commodity, and the most lucrative, various attempts to cultivate flax, rice, and cotton failed utterly. Tobacco became the chief source of Virginia's wealth, the staple product that contributed most largely to her material prosperity, inasmuch as in colonial days it was the only product that could be exchanged with the mother-country for manufactured goods at a reasonable profit.

Virginia could not be roused to take an interest in domestic manufactures except so far as they aided agriculture. Many attempts were made to bring over mechanics and artisans, but their employment was always uncertain, and in some instances they succumbed to the seductive influence of tobacco and became agriculturists.[2] Ship-building was confined to small craft used for local transportation; and other industries, such as glass-making, were undertaken with but little success. Attempts at mining and smelting iron and the plan of exporting linen made of flax spun in the colony came to nothing. Cotton was spun and woven on the plantations, and clothing from both cotton and wool was made, but only for domestic

[1] Brown, *Genesis of the United States*, I., 783; *Cal. of State Pap., Col.*, 1574–1660, 17; Tyler, *England in America*, chap. v.
[2] Bruce, *Econ. Hist. of Virginia*, II., 413.

purposes. Other trades and crafts were pursued only for the purpose of promoting the interests of a dominant agricultural class.

Much the same conditions prevailed in Maryland, where tobacco was the currency and the leading staple. It was easy to raise, and its cultivation brought abundant returns. We may not doubt that tobacco planting encouraged indolence and thriftlessness; and we have seen that overproduction in both Virginia and Maryland created a panic among the poorer colonists and brought distress and poverty upon them. Maryland having no shipping of her own was obliged to export her produce in vessels furnished by Virginia and New England and in Dutch freight-boats and merchantmen; though the latter, after 1665, were forbidden to carry colonial commodities. The New-Englanders brought wines and sugars and took off tobacco and furs, though, as Alsop blandly remarks, they would rather have got fat pork for their goods than tobacco and furs.[1] Vessels from England also came, bringing silks, linen and woollen manufactures, and household goods, which were exchanged for tobacco.

Towards the end of the century there appears to have been an increase in the sowing of corn and wheat, and the colony did what it could to encourage the building of grist-mills. Very few planters, however, made use of these mills, for, inasmuch as

[1] Alsop, *Character of the Province of Maryland*, 68, 69.

wheat flour was used only by the rich, and was therefore not a staple, most of the planters preferred to do their own grinding on their own estates by hand-mills, which were needed for grinding the corn and beating the hominy used by the negroes.[1] Almost nothing was manufactured save what was needed for domestic purposes, so that the colonists, despite the efforts of the government to promote the manufacture of linen and woollen cloth,[2] did not pass out of the agricultural stage during the seventeenth century.

In that wide stretch of country between the Chesapeake and the Hudson, the Swedes, Finns, and Dutch, in what has been wittily called the pre-Pennian era, led a flourishing agricultural and trading life. The Swedes built churches and houses of residence, cultivated their gardens, orchards, and farms, and raised goats, cattle, and swine. They did a good business in tobacco and furs, and continued their agricultural and trading life even after the subjection of the region by the Dutch.[3] D'Hinojossa brought the colony to a high state of efficiency,[4] and before New Netherland fell into the hands of the English, had made provision for extending the fur trade with the Indians and the tobacco trade with Maryland.

---

[1] Tyson, in Md. Hist. Soc., *Fund Publications*, No. 4, 11; Dankers and Sluyter, *Journal*, 216, 217.

[2] *Md. Archives*, II., 324.

[3] *Pa. Magazine*, VII., 271 – 281; Acrelius, *Hist. of New Sweden*, 36.   [4] *N. Y. Docs. Rel. to Col. Hist.*, II., 210.

The impulse thus given to farming and trade continued after the region came under the control of Penn. He found within his colony at least a thousand colonists on the right bank of the Delaware, who owned well-managed and well-equipped plantations. The lower counties became a supply field for the commodities that Pennsylvania exported, and large quantities of produce and tobacco were sent up the Delaware in little boats built at Fort Christina (Wilmington) and New Castle. The governments of West New Jersey and Pennsylvania established fairs, where the farmers exchanged their garden stuff for manufactured articles. Before the end of the century the lower counties had become what they continued to be throughout their colonial history—a farming region having its market at Philadelphia.[1]

Penn, on his arrival, encouraged industrial activity of every kind and endeavored to promote trade with the Indians in furs and skins. From the beginning of his undertaking he intended to make his colony a centre of commerce and industry as well as of agriculture. The words of the charter itself have a commercial ring,[2] and disclose some of the innermost of Penn's thoughts. In his various proposals to adventurers, Penn lays stress upon the "capacity of the place for further im-

---

[1] Holm, in Pa. Hist. Soc., *Memoirs*, III., 90; Scharf, *Hist. of Delaware*, I., 155–170.

[2] See charter, §§ xi., xii., xiii.

provements in order to trade and commerce." [1]
He incorporated the unfortunately unsuccessful
Free Society of Traders for the "better improvement of trade," [2] on the ground that "honest and
industrious traffic has been the usage and praise of
many nations"; and that "union of traffic prevents
emulation," since "every one is interested in every
one's prosperity and the profit must be greater and
surer."

Ship - building began early in the north, and
commerce, both by land and sea, sprang up between
New England, New York, Philadelphia, Maryland,
Virginia, Carolina, and Jamaica, Barbadoes, and
other West Indian islands. In the first account of
his province (1683) Penn said, "More being produced and imported than we can use here, we
export it to other countries in Europe, which
brings in money or the growth of those countries,
which is the same thing, and this is to the advantage of English merchants and seamen." [3] The
forest trees were suitable for ships, some of them
being "stately oaks fifty to sixty feet long and
clear from knots, being straight and well grained";
and the harbor was "safe and commodious, with
numerous docks where quite large ships could lie."
In 1685 a "fair key three hundred feet square" was

[1] Penn's first proposals, in Hazard, *Annals*, 505–513; "A Further Account of the Province," *Pa. Magazine*, IX., 64.

[2] Hazard, *Annals*, 541–550; *Pa. Magazine*, V., 37–50.

[3] Hazard, *Register*, I., 306; *Annals*, 507.

built, and also a rope-walk for the making of cordage.[1]   From these beginnings the commerce of Philadelphia grew rapidly and the city became the entrepôt for the trade of the surrounding country. A great variety of commodities was carried to Europe and the other colonies, to the West Indies and Central America, for the trade was practically free.

Among these exported articles were no manufactured goods whatever;[2] commerce overshadowed every other economic interest.   With money obtained from the West Indies, with sugar obtained from the French sugar islands, and with such exchangeable commodities as they and their neighbors produced, the Pennsylvanians secured all that they wished in the way of manufactured goods from England.   Hemp and flax were spun and woven into cloth for coarse varieties of clothing, and flax and wool were used for druggets, linsey-woolsey, and the like; but the better sort of goods, for men as well as women, were imported directly or made from imported materials.   Philadelphia was against homespun and in favor of goods of foreign manufacture.

West New Jersey stood in much the same relation to Philadelphia as did Delaware.   Economically, it belonged to the group of which Philadelphia was the

---

[1] *Pa. Magazine*, IX., 66; Thomas, *Account of West Jersey and Pensilvania*, 38, 39; Proud, *Hist. of Pennsylvania*, 204.

[2] Macpherson, *Annals of Commerce*, III., 164.

centre and market, and was, therefore, distinct from East New Jersey, which both in staple products and economic connections was attached to New York. At first Burlington promised to be an independent commercial centre. A letter written in 1680 spoke of the town as likely to become "a place of trade quickly." Business was done with Barbadoes, and there was every reason to believe that a good trade with the West Indies might be built up.[1] But as Philadelphia rose, Burlington declined. With its wharves and timber - yards, it was an important centre, and was inhabited by artisans who made cotton and woollen goods, and held fairs for the exchange of produce and wares.[2]

Gabriel Thomas sums up the situation in West New Jersey when he says that in Burlington County the staples for home consumption and for export were peltage and beaver skins, otter, mink, muskrat, raccoon, wildcat, martin, and deer; in Gloucester County, pitch, tar, rosin, grain, and fruit; in Salem County, rice and cranberries, "which in picle might be brought to Europe; and in Cape May County, oil and whalebones.[3] By the beginning of the seventeenth century West New Jersey had given up its trade in furs and was confining its attention to agriculture. Outside of the cities of Burlington, Gloucester, and Salem compact settlement did not exist. The country was filled with wide-stretching

[1] Smith, *Hist. of N. J.*, 113, 114.
[2] Thomas, *Account of West New Jersey*, 15.   [3] *Ibid.*, 32, 33.

plantations, on which corn and other commodities were raised for the Philadelphia and home markets.

In passing northward to the settlements on the west side of the Hudson River, we enter a different economic world. The settlers came mainly from Long Island and New England and brought with them many of the habits and practices common to the agricultural life of New England. About the Raritan and Passaic rivers they built up a miniature New England, in which settlement was by towns and outlying plantations. Lands in Elizabeth, Newark, Woodbridge, Piscataway, and other towns were held in small parcels, while the outlying districts, which in the course of time became separate towns and villages, were occupied by farmers, and were known as out-plantations or quarters. At first the staple products were garden stuffs; later, fish, nuts, and fruits were added. A farmer of this district, writing in 1676, says, "This is a rare place for any poor man, and I am satisfied that people may live better here than they do in old England." [1]

The proprietaries were not content that East New Jersey should remain simply an agricultural Arcadia. They wished to foster a spirit of trade and to stimulate the production of articles suitable for export. In 1676 Governor Carteret made an effort to clear a ship at Elizabeth, but was pre-

[1] *A Further Account of New Jersey* (1676), 2, 3.

vented by Andros, in New York.[1]   Three years later
Carteret made another attempt, declaring Perth
Amboy a free port and stating that all vessels
desiring to come and trade with East New Jersey
might do so freely.[2]   Thereupon ensued a long
and bitter struggle on the part of the province to
obtain the right of independent trade, which the
authorities in New York resolutely refused to grant,
on the ground that a port of entry in East New
Jersey would ruin the trade of New York. The
duties imposed by Pennsylvania and New Jersey
were irregular and temporary in character, while
those imposed by New York were permanent and
onerous, consisting of a two-per-cent. duty on all
excepting certain specified goods, which paid ten
per cent.[3]   The duke of York, desiring profit from
his province, continued the Dutch duties, which had
originated in the monopoly of the Dutch West
India Company, and expected that New Jersey
should contribute to his revenues.

Soon after the arrival of Dongan, in 1682, William
Dyer was appointed collector at Perth Amboy,
and refused to permit any vessel to enter that
port unless it had first gone to New York and paid
the customs duties there. The New Jersey people,
who hated Dyer because he interfered with their
freedom, made his official life a burden by ob-
structing his efforts to prevent illegal trade. Dyer

[1] *N. J. Archives*, I., 231.   [2] *Ibid.*, 232.
[3] *Cal. of State Pap., Col.*, 1685–1688, §§ 330–331.

complained that the juries brought in verdicts against him and that he could not uphold the laws. Finally, he was himself charged with the costs of a case, deprived of his horse in part payment, and shut up in prison in default of the remainder.[1]

This episode seemed a high misdemeanor to the Lords of Trade, and helped to provoke the issue of a *quo warranto* against the proprietaries, and the annexation of East New Jersey to the dominion of New England. The proprietaries endeavored to defend their rights in the matter, while the New York governors asserted that the colony was a nest of illegal traders, and that New York was in danger of ruin if a free port were allowed to exist so near at hand. The Lords of Trade finally compromised, and in 1687 consented that Perth Amboy should be a separate port of entry, provided the same customs were paid as in New York. The revolution of 1689 gave the question a temporary rest, and in 1694 New Jersey erected a customhouse at Perth Amboy and passed an act to encourage trade.[2]

Bellomont, then governor of New York, took up the controversy, and, after long negotiation and many heart-burnings, the port question was finally carried to Westminster Hall, a trial at bar was obtained, and the case was decided in favor of

---

[1] *Cal. of State Pap., Col.*, 1685–1688, § 261

[2] *Ibid.*, §§ 1014, 1160; *N. J. Archives*, I., 540, 543; Whitehead, *East Jersey*, 102.

New Jersey (1700).   It may be an open question
how far East New Jersey would ever have developed
a trade of its own, but it is certain that the struggle
over the port checked its progress at a critical
time and that the favorable decision came too late
to be of service.   Lord Cornbury could report in
1708 that East New Jersey had no export trade;[1]
and during the remainder of the colonial period it
was in large part only a supply territory, receiving
its European goods through New York, just as West
New Jersey received its goods through Philadelphia.

New York was slow in building up its trade, and
during the seventeenth century was more backward
than Philadelphia.   During the early history of the
colony the Dutch were concerned chiefly with the
fur trade, and not until 1638 did they give much
thought to the raising of grain.   The monopoly
of the company was abolished in that year and
the cultivation of the soil was thrown open to all.
Farms were sown with corn, cattle and horses were
imported, and during Stuyvesant's administration
flour, oats, pease, beans, pipe-staves, and lumber began to be exported.   But Stuyvesant was hampered
by the heavy export and import duties, and the
enforcement of the navigation act of 1651 encouraged illegal trade in tobacco with Maryland
and Virginia.

With the transfer of New Netherland to the Eng-

[1] *N. Y. Docs. Rel. to Col. Hist.*, IV., 719., V., 59; *N. J.
Archives*, III., 333.

lish the internal development of the colony became rapid. Settlements were established farther inland, the fur trade increased, and the city grew. But its growth was not in proportion to its age, and very naturally, for New York, after the loss of East New Jersey, controlled but a small area of supply for her shipping; the free-trade of adjoining colonies attracted many of her settlers, and the towns of Long Island, the most densely settled portion of the province, produced but little for export. Within the colony the struggle for political rights, the jealousy of the country districts for the city, of the farmers and producers for the burghers and merchants,[1] the want of an efficient encouragement of trade, the prevalence of a large amount of smuggling, due to the heavy duties and the operation of the navigation acts—all these conditions affected the prosperity of the colony.

Gradually, however, the city rose to prominence. It became a centre for the produce of the adjoining regions, its harbor attracted shipping, a small ship-building industry came into existence, and ketches and other coasting vessels were made. The merchants sent flour, biscuit, beef, pork, bacon, and train-oil to the English colonies in the West Indies, and similar commodities to Surinam, Curaçoa, and St. Thomas. In return they received sub-tropical products of many varieties, liquors, and Spanish coin. The majority of these commodities, except

[1] Dankers and Sluyter, *Journal*, 353–355.

the coin, together with furs, pitch, tar, and rosin, were shipped to England in exchange for manufactured goods. On all these articles duties were paid, but the accounts of the revenues from 1690 to 1696 show striking fluctuations that may be due to decay of trade or to smuggling.[1] Not until Bellomont's administration did trade become steady and prosperous.

In New England, as in the other colonies, the earliest phase of life was agricultural. Although the winters were severe, the summers were favorable to agriculture, and in all the colonies first attention was devoted to the turning of new ground and the cultivation of a supply of food. There were no large plantations and no large yield of any single commodity; but on the acres assigned to each inhabitant a plentiful supply of corn, pease, and other garden vegetables could be raised. "The people make a good shift for victuals," reported Bradstreet to the Lords of Trade, "owing to the free allotment of lands at their first coming hither."[2] The largest single staple was Indian-corn, but English wheat was successfully raised, and hay was prepared for the cattle. The meadows, which were divided into unfenced lots and thrown open in the autumn to the cattle of the proprietors, were a feature of all New England towns. Besides cattle and garden

[1] N. Y. Docs. Rel. to Col. Hist., III., 389–417, IV., 173, 599, 600, 756, 1150, V. 57.
[2] Cal. of State Pap., Col., 1677–1680, § 529.

produce, pipe-staves, clapboards, and lumber were exported to the West Indies, and fish and peltries were sent to New Amsterdam and England.[1] Nearly all the colonies established frontier trading-posts, and, until the fisheries became prominent, furs were a leading staple.

Fishing, not only off the banks of Newfoundland, but off many portions of the New England coast, was recognized early as an industry destined to add to the wealth and prosperity of the colonies. Cod and mackerel were caught, dried, and salted in large quantities and sent to Portugal, Spain, and Italy. From New York and New England sloops went with provisions and rum to Newfoundland and brought back fish, which in turn were exchanged in Europe for manufactured goods. It was estimated that in 1709 three hundred vessels of a hundred tons each, from New England, Nova Scotia, and Newfoundland, were engaged in the industry; and that of all the fishermen those from New England ports took the largest share of the fish from the banks. Mackerel, which were sent to the West Indies, could never compete with codfish, which were in great demand in European countries. Though the fishing industry was seriously affected by King Philip's War, it speedily recovered and remained a prominent feature of New England's economic life to the end of the colonial period.[2]

[1] Weeden, Econ. and Social Hist. of New England, I., 180, 181.
[2] Ibid., 133–136, 139, 371–373.

Thus the mainstay of New England's commerce was the trade in furs and fish. From the beginning the instincts of exchange led to export, while necessity and mechanical ingenuity prompted the building of ships; and there is no more interesting feature of New England history than the way in which nearly every town on sea-coast or navigable river became a builder of vessels, and the ease with which every colonist became a sailor. From 1631, when the *Blessing of the Bay* was launched at Mystic, ship-building became a part of the life of New England. Writers have ascribed this activity to the influence of the navigation acts, but there were many ships in New England before 1651. Six are mentioned in 1635, and also ship-carpenters, who were competent to build vessels of any burden.[1]

After 1640 Boston, Salem, Scituate, Dorchester, Gloucester, Plymouth, Newport, New London, and New Haven were all building vessels and sending them, loaded with produce and lumber, to adjacent colonies, Barbadoes, and England.[2] The vessels were generally small, designed for the coasting trade, though *The Trial* was of three hundred tons burden; and the quality and workmanship so good that the vessels found ready market whenever the owners desired to sell, as they frequently did, not only the cargo, but the vessel also.

---

[1] *Cal. of State Pap., Col.*, 1574–1660, §§ 158, 212.
[2] Weeden, *Econ. and Social Hist. of New England*, I., 143, 151, 162, 163.

During the ensuing half-century ship-building increased, but commercial activity began to centre in a few places adapted for trade and export, such as Boston, Salem, Newport, and New London. Other towns, such as Wethersfield, kept up a small shipping industry, but one that became inconspicuous as the years passed. The larger towns became the seats of exports and imports, receiving supplies from the country round about and furnishing the people with English goods. In 1676 Randolph reported that seven hundred and thirty ships had been built in Massachusetts, but no "ships of burthen," as far as he knew, in either Plymouth or Connecticut. Two years later Andros said practically the same thing; and in 1689 Dongan said that Connecticut had only a ketch or two and a few sloops, and had a small trade with Boston, New York, and the West Indies.[1]

These statements were not strictly accurate, but in the main they were true, and show that trade, partly from natural causes and partly from the necessities of the customs service, was confining itself to a smaller number of ports of entry. Plymouth could say very definitely in 1680 that she imported nothing directly and had as vessels "but scallops and fishing ketches"; and in the same year Connecticut said that most of her com-

---

[1] *Hutchinson Papers*, II., 232; *Cal. of State Pap., Col.*, 1675–1676, §1067; 1685–1688, § 329; *N. Y. Docs. Rel. to Col. Hist.*, III., 263.

modities were transported to Boston and there
bartered for clothing, though a little direct trade
was had with the West Indies, Madeira, and Fayal.[1]
Rhode Island did a considerable export business,
and in 1680 reported forty-nine vessels of all kinds.

Massachusetts Bay was the leading commercial
colony, and at this time Boston was the chief commercial city. Massachusetts was also the birth-
place of American manufactures, which in the
beginning, as in all the other colonies, took the
form of homespun work for domestic purposes.
Grist - mills, saw - mills, and tanneries were to be
found everywhere; and salt works, brick - yards,
glass works, pottery works, and cobblers' shops all
existed, as auxiliaries to farming. Much the same
conditions prevailed in Connecticut to the middle
of the next century; but Massachusetts at a rather
early date turned her hand to more elaborate
manufacturing. Cotton from Barbadoes, wool from
the backs of domestic sheep, as well as from
Bilbao and Malaga, furnished the material. Iron
works were started at Saugus and Weymouth
in 1640, and a man named Jenks was granted a
patent in 1646 for making scythes at Lynn. There
is reason to believe that edged tools of other varieties
also were made.[2]

[1] Cal. of State Pap., Col., 1677–1680, §§ 522, 577.
[2] Mass. Col. Records, II., 105, III., 298; Cal. of State Pap.,
Col., 1661–1668, § 75; Weeden, Econ. and Social Hist. of New
England, I., 183, 184.

Later these industries expanded until the greater part of the New England colonists were wearing articles of their own making, and were using in their daily work utensils hammered out at their own forges. Every New-Englander was a born mechanic and craftsman, and if unable to obtain supplies elsewhere, either because of distance or poverty, knew how to provide for himself. He was not manufacturing for export, he was only trying to live and to work. But the home government, urged on by the manufacturers in England, who desired a market for their products, viewed even the homespun industry with suspicion, fearful lest it might curtail the colonial demand for English goods. No restrictions were imposed during the period under discussion, but during the last decade of the seventeenth century, induced by the complaints of agents in America and urged on by interested parties at home, the English government began to adopt measures designed to prevent the increase of manufacturing in New England and New York.

Thus we see that from the point of view of industry and staple products the colonies fall into certain defined groups. South Carolina was an agricultural colony, carrying on a meagre commerce with the West Indies and closely allied to the West Indian group. Virginia and Maryland, absorbed in the production of tobacco, were wholly agricultural. The middle colonies, areas of agricultural activity, made up two groups with centres in Philadelphia and New York, to which they sent their surplus products for transmission to foreign countries, the West Indies, or neighboring colonies. Delaware, Pennsylvania (outside of Philadelphia), and New Jersey had no independent economic life, being self-sufficing agricultural regions, and reaching the outside world only through the adjacent commercial cities to which, economically, they were attached. Before 1689 no one of the southern or middle colonies had developed an independent manufacturing life or had carried domestic industry to such a point as to arouse the suspicions of the home government. In the south, manufacturing was subordinate to agriculture, and in Philadelphia to commerce. In New York, partly because of a growing mining industry in the hills across the Hudson, manufacturing tended to become a matter of importance; but even there it remained for the most part of little consequence in the seventeenth century.

In New England manufacturing in mills was carried on only in the tidewater regions, an area exceedingly small as compared with the agricultural district behind it, in which manufacturing was subordinate to agriculture, lumbering, and commerce. The instinct to manufacture was an ingrained characteristic of the New-Englander, and it is not surprising to find that manufacturing permeated the New England colonies as it did none of the others. But at best it did not pass out of the domestic stage: people made their own clothes, hammered out their own nails, and provided a thousand and one other necessary conveniences for comfortable living.

At no time in their colonial history did English merchants have any special reason to fear colonial competitions, and though the restrictive policy of England may have succeeded in holding the colonies in check, it is an open question how far the colonists would have manufactured for export had they been let alone. England furnished New England and all the colonies with her own manufactures as well as with those of other countries; but she failed signally in making the colonies in all particulars a vent for her own commodities. All the colonies provided themselves to a certain extent with what they needed, and in New England two-thirds of the people dressed in cloths of their own making.

The mercantilist theory, like others of a similar character but of later date, took no account of the colonist as he actually was. Statesmen of the day created an ideal colonist, and from a vantage-point three thousand miles away endeavored to apply a system of colonial management which they believed to be best adapted to the interest of all. But the mercantilist as well as the Stuart had no comprehension of the difficulties of the problem.

CHAPTER XX

CRITICAL ESSAY ON AUTHORITIES

BIBLIOGRAPHICAL AIDS

FOR general reader and student alike the great bibliographical aid on colonial history is Justin Winsor, *Narrative and Critical History of America* (8 vols., 1888–1889): the field of colonial affairs from 1650 to 1689 is covered by parts of vols. III., IV., and V.; the bibliographical chapters and notes are abundant but not very discriminating. Channing and Hart, *Guide to the Study of American History* (1896), contains lists of secondary authorities on state and local history (§ 23), and a list of colonial records classified by colonies and including local records (§ 29); §§ 98–108, 120–128, are topical lists in the field of this volume. The *Guide* now needs bringing up to date. J. N. Larned, *Literature of American History, a Bibliographical Guide* (1902), contains descriptive and critical notes on the principal authorities on colonial history.

GENERAL SECONDARY WORKS

The period from 1652 to 1689 has been liberally dealt with by writers on colonial history. George Bancroft, *History of the United States* (last revision, 6 vols., 1883–1885), has devoted three-quarters of a volume to the subject; but his version shows strong hostility to the policy of the English government and is marred by unnecessary digressions. Richard Hildreth, *History of the United States* (6 vols., 1849–1852), passes over many phases of the subject with little appreciation of the issues.

Bryant and Gay, *Popular History of the United States* (5 vols., 1896), contains much information, but the treatment is strictly popular. John Fiske's various volumes are of the same character, but of a higher order of thought and scholarship; though written with great charm of style, they vary considerably in value, and often neglect some of the most significant aspects of colonial life. While apparently philosophical in treatment, most of Fiske's writing runs along on the surface and does not penetrate deeply into the causes and conditions of colonial history. Justin Winsor, *Narrative and Critical History of America* (8 vols., 1888–1889), contains in vol. III. excellent chapters on the period; but they are unduly condensed, and the narrative has been sacrificed to the critical apparatus. J. A. Doyle, *English Colonies in America* (3 vols., 1882–1887), as yet incomplete, is the most pretentious work on the period, and the most important; it shows insight and scholarship, but is badly arranged, and is often based on inadequate information. George Chalmers, *Political Annals of the American Colonies* (issued in quarto, 1780), consists of one volume and closes with 1688. The same author's *Introduction to the Revolt of the American Colonies* (reprinted in two volumes in 1845 with a valuable preface) carries the subject from 1606 to 1760. Chalmers's writings are of very great importance, and bring out as no other work has done the unity of colonial history.

GENERAL COLLECTIONS OF SOURCES

The only collection of documentary materials that covers the entire period and subject of this volume is the *Calendars of State Papers, Colonial Series, America and West Indies,* 1574–1696 (9 vols., 1860–1903). The publication of this indispensable work marks an era in the writing of American colonial history. The calendaring has been admirably done, but no abridgment can take the place of the complete documents, to which the student should go if possible. Fortunately many of the documents have been printed in full in America; and manuscript copies of the volumes known as *Proprieties* and *Plantations General* are in the library of the Pennsylvania Historical Society.

Among the collections of documents and extracts which facilitate the work of students and readers are: Peter Force, *Tracts Relative to the Colonies* (4 vols., 1836–1846); Albert Bushnell Hart, *American History Told by Contemporaries* (4 vols., 1898–1902; most of vol. I. treats of English colonization). Lists of specific references to smaller collections will be found in the New England History Teachers' Association, *Report on Historical Sources in Schools* (1901). The colonial charters appear in full in Ben Perley Poore, *Federal and State Constitutions* (2 vols., 1877), and reprints of some in William MacDonald, *Select Charters* (1899). The three great series, *Documents Relative to the Colonial History of New York* (14 vols. and index, 1856–1883), *Documents Relating to the Colonial History of New Jersey* (22 vols., 1880–1900), and *Colonial Records of North Carolina* (10 vols., 1886–1890), contain much general material.

RELATIONS WITH THE MOTHER-COUNTRY

ENGLAND'S COLONIAL POLICY. Little has yet been written upon England's colonial system and policy. The subject may best be approached through William Cunningham, *Growth of English Industry and Commerce* (3d ed., vol. I., 1902; vol. II., two parts, 1903); H. E. Egerton, *Short History of British Colonial Policy* (1897); and G. L. Beer, *Commercial Policy of England toward the American Colonies* (1893). On mercantilism, the best sketch is by Gustav Schmoller, *The Mercantile System* (W. J. Ashley's *Economic Classics*, 1896); the chief contemporary treatises are Thomas Mun, *England's Treasure by Forraign Trade* (1664); Sir Josiah Child, *Discourse on Trade* (1665); and Joshua Gee, *Trade and Navigation of Great Britain Considered* (1727).

NAVIGATION ACTS.—No adequate study of the navigation

acts has been made. Edward Channing's article, "The Navigation Acts" (American Antiquarian Society, *Proceedings*, 1889), does not go behind the letter of the statutes. A useful study is G. L. Beer, "Cromwell's Economic Policy" (*Political Science Quarterly*, XVI., 582–611, XVII., 46–70). Some information regarding the circumstances under which the acts were passed may be obtained from Clarendon, *History of the Rebellion* (1888); Cobbett, *Parliamentary History of England*, 1066–1803 (London, 1808); *Journals of the House of Commons* (127 vols., 1547–1872); such contemporary writings as Edmund Ludlow's *Memoirs* (new ed., 1902), Samuel Pepys' *Diary* (1659–1669); and such biographies as W. D. Christie, *Life of Shaftesbury* (1871), and T. H. Lister, *Life of Clarendon* (1838). Texts of the navigation acts in full appear in *Statutes of the Realm*, to 1813 (12 vols., London, 1810–1838); V. Pickering, *Statutes at Large* (109 vols. and index, London, 1762). There are significant extracts in William MacDonald, *Select Charters* (1899); *American History Leaflets;* and elsewhere.

ADMINISTRATIVE ORGANS.—The organization and policy of the various councils and committees of trade can be studied only in their records. Of first importance is the official *Journal* (1 vol., 1660–1663; 6 vols., 1675–1692). A copy of the entire journal after 1675 is in the library of the Pennsylvania Historical Society. The abbreviated minutes, reports, and recommendations of the committees, and other papers given in the *Calendars*, are often unsatisfactory, and the original, if possible, should be used. Many of these documents are printed in full in the various printed colonial archives. Almost nothing has been written on the administration of the navigation acts in the colonies, except two very brief articles by W. J. Ashley, in *Studies, Economic and Political* (1899).

SOCIAL AND ECONOMIC CONDITIONS

SOCIAL LIFE.—Little has been done in the way of a comprehensive study of the social conditions prevailing in the colonies during the seventeenth century. W. B. Weeden, *Economic and Social History of New England* (2 vols., 1891), contains many facts regarding costumes, furnishings, and habits of life. The writings of Mrs. Alice Morse Earle are excellent, and abound in illustrations from contemporary material. Culture history can best be examined in the journals, descriptions, letters, and diaries of the time. Samuel Maverick, *Description of New England, 1660* (*New England Historical and Genealogical Register*, XXXIX., 33), is important. John Dunton, *Letters from New England*, 1686 (Prince Society, *Publications*, 1867), was written by "an impartial and trustworthy observer." Samuel Sewall, *Diary*, 1674–1729 (Massachusetts Historical Society, *Collections*, 5th series, V. – VII.), is a standard authority for Massachusetts; and Thomas Minor, *Diary*, 1653–1684 (1899), throws a little light on Rhode Island and Connecticut history.

Daniel Denton, *Brief Description of New York* (1670, Gowans' *Bibliotheca Americana*, 1845, reprinted 1903); John Miller, *Description of the Province and City of New York* (1695, Gowans' *Bibliotheca Americana*, 1862, reprinted 1903); and Charles Wolley, *Two Years' Journal* (1701, Gowans' *Bibliotheca Americana*, 1860, reprinted 1902), give us an account of that province. Dankers and Sluyter, *Journal*, 1679–1680 (Long Island Historical Society, *Memoirs*, I.), contains some account of several of the colonies. Many unprinted documents are referred to in the foot-notes above.

For the Jerseys there are many pamphlets and letters contained in W. A. Whitehead, *East Jersey under the Proprietary Governments* (with "Miscellaneous Topics" and Appendix, 1875); in Samuel Smith, *History of New Jersey* (1765); and referred to in Whitehead's article in Winsor, *Narrative and Critical History of America*, III., 421.

For West New Jersey and Pennsylvania we have Coxe's *Account* and *A Quaker's Account* (referred to in the foot-notes above); Gabriel Thomas, *Historical and Geo-*

graphical Account of West New Jersey and Pensilvania
(1698, reprinted 1903); Thomas Budd, *Good Order established in Pennsylvania and New Jersey* (1685, Gowans'
Bibliotheca Americana, 1865, reprinted 1902); the many
letters of Penn (see references in foot-notes above); and
James Claypoole's *Letter-Book*, extracts from which are
printed in *Pennsylvania Magazine*, X., 188, 267, 401.

For Maryland we have George Alsop, *Character of the
Province of Maryland* (1666, Gowans' *Bibliotheca Americana*,
1869; Maryland Historical Society, *Fund Publication* No.
15, reprinted 1903); Lord Baltimore, *Answers to Queries of
Lords of Trade*, 1678 (*Maryland Archives*, V., 264–269);
Hammond, *Leah and Rachel, or the Two Fruitful Sisters,
Virginia and Maryland* (1656); and E. Cook, *Sot-Weed
Factor* and other poems, in B. C. Steiner, *Early Maryland
Poetry* (edited for the Maryland Historical Society, *Fund
Publication* No. 36).

For Virginia we have Hartwell, Blair, and Chilton,
Present State of Virginia (Massachusetts Historical Society,
Collections, 1st series, V.); Berkeley's and Moryson's answers to queries (see references in foot-notes above); many
papers dealing with Bacon's rebellion and the tobacco-
cutting riots; and John Clayton, *Virginia* (Force, *Tracts*,
III., No. 12).

For North Carolina there is little contemporary evidence
except that contained in George Fox, *Journal*, and the
papers in the *Calendars* dealing with the uprising there in
1677.   For South Carolina we have the letters from Thomas
Newe to his father, noted in the text.   Other excellent
books are Samuel Wilson, *Account of the Province of
Carolina*; and Thomas Ashe, *Carolina, or a Description of
the Present State of the Country* (both in B. R. Carroll,
Historical Collections, II., 19–35, 59–84).

RELIGIOUS LIFE.—The standard authority on the Church
of England in the colonies is J. S. M. Anderson, *History of
the Church of England in the Colonies* (2d ed., 3 vols., 1856);
of greater completeness and scientific value is Arthur L.
Cross, *The Anglican Episcopate and the American Colonies*

(*Harvard Historical Studies*, IX., 1902), dealing chiefly with the conditions of the eighteenth century. Of importance are S. E. Baldwin, "Jurisdiction of the Bishop of London" (American Antiquarian Society, *Proceedings*, October, 1899); W. S. Perry, *History of the American Episcopal Church* (2 vols., 1885); F. L. Hawks, *Contributions to the Ecclesiastical History of the United States* (2 vols., 1836–1839); I. Backus, *History of New England, with Particular Reference to the Denomination of Christians called Baptists* (1777–1796, 2d ed. 1871); and the volumes of the American Church History Series with the accompanying bibliographies. W. Meade, *Old Churches, Ministers, and Families of Virginia* (2 vols., 1857), is full of interest for the church in that colony. Special monographs in the *Johns Hopkins University Studies in History and Political Science* are P. E. Lauer, *Church and State in New England;* George Petrie, *Church and State in Maryland;* S. B. Weeks, *Church and State in North Carolina.*

ECONOMIC CONDITIONS.—On the economic history of the colonies only two comprehensive works of value have been written: W. B. Weeden, *Economic and Social History of New England* (2 vols., 1896), and P. A. Bruce, *Economic History of Virginia.* The general and state histories, so far as they deal with this subject, are commonly inadequate.

LABOR SYSTEM AND SLAVERY.—On slavery and the industrial servant system, see Waltershausen, *Die Arbeitsverfassung der Englischen Kolonien in Nord Amerika,* a study based largely on secondary authorities. Other papers (all in the *Johns Hopkins University Studies*) are: J. H. Johnson, *Old Maryland Manors;* Edward Ingle, *Virginia Local Institutions;* J. C. Ballagh, *White Servitude in the Colony of Virginia;* B. C. Steiner, *History of Slavery in Connecticut;* H. S. Cooley, *Study of Slavery in New Jersey;* J. S. Bassett, *History of Slavery in North Carolina.* Still others are: Edward Bettle, *Notices on Negro Slavery in Pennsylvania* (Pennsylvania Historical Society, *Memoirs*); W. B. Weeden, *Early African Slave - Trade in New England* (American

Antiquarian Society, *Proceedings*, October, 1887) ; A. J. Northrup, *Slavery in New York* (State Library, *Bulletin History*, No. 4, 1900).

RELATIONS WITH THE INDIANS

The account of King Philip's War in the text is based on the following: *Old Indian Chronicle* (2d ed., 1836); Thomas Church, *Narrative* (Dexter's ed., 2 vols., 1865); William Hubbard, *History of the Indian Wars* (Drake's ed., 2 vols., 1865); Increase Mather, *Relation of Troubles with the Indians* (1671); John Easton, *Relation* (Palfrey, III., 180); G. M. Bodge, "Soldiers in King Philip's War" (*New England Historical and Genealogical Register*, 31 parts, January, 1883 – October, 1890); Edward Randolph's report (*Hutchinson Papers*, II., 226–230).

MASSACHUSETTS

For the history of the Massachusetts Bay Colony the standard authorities are: Thomas Hutchinson, *History of the Colony of Massachusetts Bay*, 1628–1774 (3 vols., 1764–1828); John G. Palfrey, *History of New England During the Stuart Dynasty*, 1620–1689 (3 vols., 1858–1864).   Palfrey's work is indispensable, but it is a long and one-sided defence of Massachusetts, very deficient on the economic and social sides.   J. S. Barry, *History of Massachusetts* (3 vols., 1855–1857), is an excellent work, clear and readable, but devoid of originality.   Justin Winsor, *Memorial History of Boston* (4 vols., 1880–1882), has a good chapter (vol. I., chap. x.) on the loss of the charter.

The leading collections of documents for Massachusetts and Plymouth are: *Records of Massachusetts Bay*, 1628–1686 (5 vols. in 6, 1853–1854); *Records of Plymouth* (12 vols., 1885–1887), of which vols. IX. and X. contain the records of the United Colonies.   For council proceedings we have John Noble, *Records of the Court of Assistants*, 1673–1692 (1901); R. N. Toppan, "Andros Records" (American Antiquarian Society, *Proceedings*, October,

1899); and, more complete, the minutes calendared in the *Calendars of State Papers, Colonial Series*, 1685–1688.

For the general history of the period, three publications of the Prince Society are of first rank and importance, finely planned and ably edited: *Hutchinson Papers* (2 vols., 1865); W. H. Whitmore, *Andros Tracts* (3 vols., 1868); and R. N. Toppan, *Edward Randolph* (5 vols., 1898–1899). Of the greatest service are the Massachusetts Historical Society *Collections* (63 vols., in seven series), and *Proceedings* (37 vols., in two series). Additional serial publications are: *New England Historical and Genealogical Register* (227 numbers in 62 vols., 1847–1903); American Antiquarian Society *Collections* (7 vols., 1820–1885), and *Proceedings* (15 vols., in two series, 1880–1903); *Essex Antiquarian* (7 vols., 1877–1903); Essex Institute *Collections* (39 vols., 1859–1902). A partial list of printed town records may be found in Channing and Hart, *Guide*, 110, 111.

MAINE AND NEW HAMPSHIRE

The history of these colonies during the period under discussion is included in the history of Massachusetts Bay. J. Belknap, *History of New Hampshire* (3 vols. I., 1784, II., 1792, III., 1792), and W. D. Williamson, *History of Maine* (2 vols., 1829), are the standard authorities. Valuable collections are: *New Hampshire Provincial and State Papers* (29 vols., 1867–1896); J. S. Jenness, *Transcripts of Original Documents in the English Archives Relating to the Early History of the State of New Hampshire* (1876); New Hampshire Historical Society *Collections* (10 vols., 1824–1893). Documents for the history of Maine may be found in *York Deeds*, 1642–1726 (11 vols., 1887–1896); and Maine Historical Society *Collections*, 2d series, III.–VIII (1875–1902).

CONNECTICUT

The best history of Connecticut is Benjamin Trumbull, *History of Connecticut* (2 vols., 1797, 1818; new ed., indexed,

1898), which carries the subject to 1794: it says nothing of social or economic life; G. H. Hollister, *History of Connecticut* (2 vols., 1st ed., 1855; 2d ed., 1857), carries the subject to 1857, but is of little value for the period in question. Alexander Johnston, *Connecticut*, in American Commonwealth Series (1887, new ed., 1904), is delightful, but is influenced by an untenable theory regarding the relation between town and state. For sources see *The Colonial Records of Connecticut* (15 vols., 1850–1890); Connecticut Historical Society *Collections* (9 vols., 1860–1903), and *Annual Reports* (1890–1903), containing valuable lists and historical notes. Other publications are, The Acorn Club of Connecticut *Publications* (9 vols., 1899–1904); *The Connecticut Quarterly*, merged in *The Connecticut Magazine* (7 vols., 1895–1903): full of local color. Boundary questions are ably discussed in C. W. Bowen, *Boundary Disputes of Connecticut* (1882).

NEW HAVEN.—E. E. Atwater, *History of the Colony of New Haven* (1881, new ed., 1901), is full and complete, and contains many documents. C. H. Levermore, *Republic of New Haven* (1886), is especially valuable for the period after 1664. The documentary material is chiefly printed in *Records of the Colony of New Haven*, 1638–1665 (2 vols., 1857–1858), and in New Haven Historical Society *Papers* (6 vols., 1862–1900).

RHODE ISLAND

S. G. Arnold, *History of the State of Rhode Island and Providence Plantations*, 1636–1700 (2 vols., 1859–1860; new ed., 1894), though written in rather a heavy style, is an admirable work, scholarly and complete. J. B. Richman, *Rhode Island, its Making and Meaning* [to 1683] (2 vols., 1902), is equally scholarly, and more philosophically presented. The public records of the colony have been printed in the imperfect *Records of the Colony of Rhode Island and Providence Plantations*, 1636–1792 (10 vols., 1856–1865). The Rhode Island Historical Society has issued *Collections*

(9 vols., 1827–1897, to be continued); *Proceedings* (23 nos., 1872–1902, to be continued), and *Publications* (8 vols., 1893–1901, discontinued). Roger Williams' letters, a collection of rare interest and value, appear in Narragansett Club *Publications*, 1st series, No. 4, vol. VI. (6 vols., 1866–1874).

NEW AMSTERDAM AND NEW YORK

The literature and material for the colonial history of New York are very extensive. William Smith, *History of New York* (London, 1757, and later editions; reprinted in New York Historical Society *Collections*, 2 vols., 1829–1830), is a work deservedly famous. For the period before 1689 it has been entirely superseded by E. B. O'Callaghan's *History of New Netherland* (2 vols., 2d ed., 1855), and J. R. Brodhead's *History of the State of New York* (2 vols., rev. ed., 1872). Both these standard works are accurate, detailed, and well supplied with references. Among the works of secondary importance are James Grant Wilson, *The Memorial History of the City of New York* (4 vols., 1892, vol. I., covering seventeenth century); John Fiske, *Dutch and Quaker Colonies in America* (2 vols., 1899); E. A. Roberts, *New York*, in the American Commonwealth Series; and Martha J. Lamb, *History of the City of New York* (2 vols., 1877).

Documentary materials on New York are voluminous. Of first rank are: *Documentary History of the State of New York* (4 vols., 1849–1851; quarto ed., 4 vols., 1850–1851); *Documents Relative to the Colonial History of New York* (14 vols. and general index, 1853–1861); J. Pearson, *Early Records of the City and County of Albany* (1869) (entirely documentary); Joel Munsell, *Annals of Albany* (10 vols., 1850–1859; revised reprint of vols. 1–4, 1869 – 1871), and continued in *Collections on the History of Albany* (3 vols., 1865); *The Records of New Amsterdam*, 1653–1674 (7 vols., 1897), contains the minutes of the court of burgomasters and schepens during the Dutch period.   The Dutch colonial laws are printed in *Laws and Ordinances of New Netherland,* 1638–1674; the "Duke's Laws," in the *Collections* of the New York Historical Society, 1st series, I., 307 – 347; in *Laws of the Province of Pennsylvania* (ed. Linn), 3 – 77; and in *Laws of Colonial New York,* I., 6 – 100.   Later English laws are printed in *Laws of Colonial New York* (5 vols., 1894).

Valuable materials are found in the New York Historical Society *Collections,* 1st series, 5 vols., 3d series or *Publication Fund Series,* 27 vols.; and in the Long Island Historical Society *Memoirs* (vol. I., 1867).   Other documents and reprints in *Historical Magazine, Magazine of American History,* and *American Historical Review.*

For Long Island the standard account is B. F. Thompson, *History of Long Island* (2d ed., 2 vols., 1843), which incorporates bodily the work by Silas Wood, entitled, *Sketch of the First Settlement of Long Island* (1828).   The documentary history of the region can be found in *Documents Relative to the Colonial History of New York,* vol. XIV., and in the town records.

NEW JERSEY

Samuel Smith, *History of the Colony of New Jersey* (1765, reprinted 1877), besides the text, includes letters and documents, some of which cannot be obtained elsewhere. W. A. Whitehead, *East Jersey under the Proprietary Governments,* 1846 (*Collections* of the New Jersey Historical Society, I., 2d ed., enlarged, 1875), with a valuable appendix of documents.   In J. Whitehead, *A Civil and Judicial History of New Jersey,* is an admirable introductory chapter on the constitutional history of colony and state.

Documentary materials for New Jersey history are to be found in *Documents Relating to the Colonial History of the State of New Jersey* (22 vols., 1880–1902): commonly cited as New Jersey *Archives.*   A good account of con-

temporary pamphlet material written to promote emigration, in Winsor, *Narrative and Critical History*, III. 499.

The best and ablest account of the Society of Friends in
America from the historical point of view is that of James
Bowden, *History of Friends in America* (2 vols., 1851–1854,
new ed., 1861), which furnishes an admirable and fair-minded
survey of the Quaker settlements.   The journals of George
Fox and William Edmundson, each issued in many editions,
give graphic pictures of the condition of the Quakers in
America in 1671 and 1672.   The following special essays
may be noted: Henry Ferguson, *Essays in American
History* (1894); Caroline Hazard, *The Narragansett Friends
Meeting* (1899); A. C. Applegarth, *The Quakers in Pennsylvania* (*Johns Hopkins University Studies*, X., nos. 8, 9);
H. R. McIlwaine, *Struggle of Protestant Dissenters for
Religious Toleration in Virginia* (*ibid.*, XII., no. 4).   There
is no satisfactory life of William Penn: Thomas Clarkson,
Memoirs of William Penn (2 vols., 1813; new ed., 1849), is
still valuable, though one-sided and incomplete.   S. M.
Janney, *Life of Penn* (1852), is the best and most trustworthy, though the author is interested in the religious
rather than in the political side of Penn's career.   W. H.
Dixon, *William Penn* (1851, new eds., 1856, 1872), is in-
terestingly written, but idealizes the Stuarts, and frequently
makes statements not borne out by the evidence.

The oldest history of the colony is Robert Proud, *History
of Pennsylvania in North America, 1681 – 1742*, with an
appendix of documents (2 vols., 1797–1798); it is still a
very useful and important work.   T. F. Gordon, *History of
Pennsylvania to 1776* (1829), is an accurate but lifeless
treatise, with little in it to attract the reader.   W. H. Egle,
Illustrated History of the Commonwealth of Pennsylvania
(1880), is a co-operative undertaking chiefly of local interest.   Sidney D. Fisher, *The Making of Pennsylvania*
(1896), is strictly a popular work.   W. R. Shepherd's

scholarly *History of Proprietary Government in Pennsylvania* (*Columbia University Studies*, VI., 1896), is written in a hard and often confused style, appealing only to students. Special works of importance are Isaac Sharpless, *History of Quaker Government in Pennsylvania* (2 vols., 1898–1899): a very able interpretation of the history of the colony from the Quaker point of view. Glenn, *Merion in the Welsh Tract;* J. J. Levick, *John ap Thomas and his Friends* (*Pa. Magazine*, IV.); S. W. Pennypacker, *Settlement of Germantown* (1899), and A. C. Myers, *Immigration of the Irish Quakers into Pennsylvania, 1682–1750* (1902), are important contributions to the subject.

The documentary material for the early history of Pennsylvania is scattered. There is no complete collection of Penn's letters. Valuable materials appear in Samuel Hazard, *Annals*, 1609–1682 (1850); Samuel Hazard, *Register of Pennsylvania* (16 vols., 1828–1834); J. F. Watson, *Annals of Philadelphia* (1830). The Historical Society of Pennsylvania has published *Memoirs* (14 vols., 1826–1895); and the valuable *Magazine of History and Biography* (27 vols., 1877 – 1903). The acts and proceedings of the Pennsylvania council and assembly can be found in the following: *Colonial Records*, 1683–1736 (3 vols., 1838–1840; reprinted with different pagination, and continued to 1790 in 16 vols., 1852); *Pennsylvania Archives*, 1st series, I.; *Votes of Assembly, 1662–1776* (6 vols., 1752–1776); *Charters and Laws of the Province of Pennsylvania* (1879); particularly *The Statutes at Large of Pennsylvania*, vols. II.–VII. (1899, ed. Hildeburn).

DELAWARE

The materials for the history of Delaware are scanty, and no satisfactory history of the colony has been written. Benjamin Ferris, *A History of the Original Settlements on the Delaware* (1846), closes with 1682; Francis Vincent, *History of Delaware* (1870–1871), ends at 1664. J. T. Scharf, *History of Delaware* (2 vols., 1888), is similar in mode of treatment to his history of Maryland and equally poor. The Historical Society of Delaware has issued a series of *Papers* (37 numbers, 1879–1903), chiefly of a biographical character. *Documents Relative to the Colonial History of New York*, XII., includes papers on the Dutch and Swedish settlements on the Delaware.

VIRGINIA

The best general authorities on Virginia are J. A. Doyle, *English Colonies in America*, I., chap. vii.; Charles Campbell, *History of the Colony and Ancient Dominion of Virginia* (1847); and John Fiske, *Old Virginia and her Neighbors* (1897). No one of these works is entirely satisfactory. Of the older writers, J. D. Burk, *History of Virginia* (2 vols., 1805), is the best, giving many details not found elsewhere and printing valuable appendices. Robert Beverly, *History of Virginia* (1722); Hartwell, Blair, and Chilton, *An Account of the Present State and Government of Virginia* (1727), and Hugh Jones, *Present State of Virginia* (1724, Sabin reprint, octavo, no. 5), have almost the value of original documents. The greatest and the essential collection of original material for Virginia's history is W. W. Hening, *Statutes at Large*, 1619–1792 (13 vols., 1823). Next in importance is the *Calendar of Virginia State Papers*, still in process of publication. Many documents of the first importance are printed in the *Virginia Magazine of History and Biography* (9 vols., 1893–1903), and in the William and Mary College *Quarterly* (11 vols., 1892–1903). Occasional documents may be found in the *Historical Magazine and Notes and Queries* (3d series, 23 vols., 1857–1875). John Thurloe, *State Papers* (7 vols., 1742), contain material for Virginia's history from 1650 to 1660; while the *Calendars of State Papers, Colonial*, is a mine of information throughout. Peter Force, *Tracts*, I., contains reprints of some able pamphlets. For Bacon's rebellion we have the *Calendars*, IV., V., and five contemporary accounts of the movement: (1) *The Beginning, Progress, and Conclusion of Bacon's Rebellion in Virginia*, by *T. M.* (probably Thomas Mathews, a member of the assembly in 1676); (2) Mrs. Ann Cotton of Q Creek,

An Account of our Late Troubles in Virginia (the briefest
and most reliable of all); (3) *A Narrative of the Indian
and Civil Wars in Virginia* (Massachusetts Historical Society, *Collections*, 2d series, I., 27–80)—all three reprinted
in Force's *Tracts*, and in *American Colonial Tracts;* (4)
The Report of the Commissioners to the King; (5) *A Review, Breviary, and Conclusion drawn from the foregoing
Narrative, being a Summary Account of the late Rebellion in
Virginia*, together the best extant account; both in *Calendars of State Papers, Colonial*, 1677–1680, nos. 437–439, but
nowhere printed in full.

MARYLAND

J. A. Doyle's treatment of Maryland's history is one of
the least satisfactory in his work; and on the revolution
of 1689 it is distinctly misleading. J. V. L. McMahon,
Historical View of the Government of Maryland (1831),
considering the inadequacy of the material then available,
is a remarkable book. J. L. Bozman, *History of Maryland*, to 1658 (2 vols., 1837), is a classic, full, accurate, and
impartial though diffuse. James McSherry, *History of
Maryland* (1849), is merely a readable compilation.
William Hand Browne, *Maryland, the History of a
Palatinate* (1884), and *George and Cecilius Calvert* (1890),
are based upon full knowledge of the subject, but are not always written with an unbiased pen; the elaborate J. T. Scharf,
History of Maryland (3 vols., 1879), is in many respects
what a history should not be: it contains valuable material,
crudely organized, badly arranged, and unreadable.   The
admirable scientific study by N. D. Mereness, *Maryland as a
Proprietary Colony* (1901), is a series of essays analyzing
the government and organization of the colony.

Maryland possesses a splendid mass of documentary
material for the writing of her history. *The Archives of
Maryland* (23 vols., 1883–1903), published by the Maryland Historical Society, is composed of the acts of assembly (to 1699), journals of council (to 1779), court records,

Governor Sharp's correspondence, and many documents
from the Public Record Office, London. The Maryland
Historical Society has issued *Fund Publications* (37 vols.,
1867–1901), and over sixty occasional papers and reports.
Thomas Bacon's edition of the *Laws of Maryland* (1765) contains the titles of laws not otherwise known.

Bozman is the chief guide for the period to 1658, and after
1650 may be supplemented by documents in John Thurloe,
State Papers, the *Calendars*, and the *Archives*. Among rare
pamphlets are: Lord Baltimore, *Case Concerning the Province
of Maryland* (1653); *Virginia and Maryland*, *or Lord Baltimore's Case uncased and answered* (1655); Leonard Strong,
*Babylon's Fall in Maryland, a fair warning to Lord Balti-
more* (1655), upholds the Puritan cause; compare John Langford in *A Just and Clere Refutation of "Babylon's Fall"*
(1655). Two admirable monographs have been written: F.
E. Sharp, *Causes of the Revolution of 1689 in Maryland*
(*Johns Hopkins University Studies*, XIV. nos. 11, 12), is
rather unfair to the proprietary; B. C. Steiner, *The Protestant
Revolution in Maryland* (American Historical Association,
Report, 1897, 281–353), minimizes the revolutionary spirit.

The controversy between Lord Baltimore and William
Penn has never been fairly written. For the Maryland
side of the case: W. H. Browne, *Maryland;* Archer, *Dis-
memberment of Maryland* (*Fund Publications*, no. 30), with
an undignified show of temper; more temperately, but still
not impartially, N. D. Mereness, *Maryland as a Proprietary
Colony*, 29–33. For the Pennsylvania side, W. B. Scaife, in
Pennsylvania Magazine, IX., 241–271, *Pennsylvania Magazine*, VI., 412–434; W. R. Shepherd, *Proprietary Government in Pennsylvania*, 117–146 (confused).

THE CAROLINAS

For the early history of South Carolina, W. J. Rivers,
Sketch of the History of South Carolina to 1719 (1856), has
long been the standard authority, and has not by any means
been superseded by a longer and more elaborate volume,

Edward McCrady, *South Carolina under the Proprietary Government* (1897).   Little use can be made of the older histories, Alexander Hewatt, *Historical Account of the Rise and Progress of South Carolina and Georgia* (3 vols., 1779), and David Ramsay, *History of South Carolina* (2 vols., 1809, 2d ed., 1858).   In a series called *Year-Book, City of Charleston* (4 vols., 1883–1886), Mayor Courtenay began a new era in the historiography of the state by printing a number of exceedingly valuable contemporary relations.   The *Records of North Carolina* (16 vols., 1886–1902) is a collection of rare value and importance for both Carolinas.   The South Carolina Historical Society *Collections*, V., contains *The Shaftesbury Papers* (1897).   A comparison of the originals, thus published, with the abstracts in the *Calendars* shows how inadequate often are the *Calendars* for historical purposes.

On North Carolina the best work is F. L. Hawks, *History of North Carolina* (2 vols., 1857–1858), although it is marred by prejudice.   In the *Johns Hopkins University Studies* are three monographs of importance: S. C. Hughson, *Carolina Pirates and Colonial Commerce* (XII., nos. 2 to 7); E. L. Whitney, *Government of the Colony of South Carolina* (XIII., nos. 1 and 2); and J. S. Bassett, *Constitutional Beginnings of North Carolina* (XII., no. 3).

ISLAND COLONIES

For the island colonies, so important in their connection with the early history of the Carolinas, see R. H. Schomburgk, *History of Barbadoes* (1848); J. H. Lefroy, *Memorials of the Bermudas*, 1511–1687 (2 vols., 1877–1879), and N. D. Davis, *The Cavaliers and Roundheads of Barbadoes, 1650–1652* (1887).

INDEX

355

END OF VOL. V.